Praise for *Integrated Advocacy*

"There are a handful of lawyers who have had tremendous influence over my life and career, and Bill Barton is one of those wonderful humans. I have always learned so much from spending time with him. In our profession, there is no one I have ever met who turns on the flow of wisdom and advice like Bill. So, whenever I get to spend time with him, I try to be a sponge and soak it all in. The truth though, is that I can't. I try to receive all the gifts of wisdom Bill has to give, but there just isn't enough time or bandwidth. Important gifts of wisdom spill over and get lost. Not anymore though! This wonderful book makes me smile because so much of Bill's wisdom has been written down. This book is a precious gift. Thank you, my dear friend, so many of us love you so much. This book is spectacular!"

—Nicholas Rowley, has won over $1 billion in settlements and verdicts for injured plaintiffs and coauthor of *Trial by Human*

"Lawyers are notoriously bad business people. They can tell a story, charm a jury, and write a killer brief, but when it comes to financial records… well, many went to law school because they were bad at math. Bill Barton's book, *Integrated Advocacy*, is the solution for those who are struggling with the business side of the practice of law. His chapters on 'Running a Law Business' (with financial nuts and bolts) and 'Evaluating Cases' will begin to make or save you money the day after you read them. Based on years in the business, Bill's insights into the work we do, finding and being your authentic self, and how to become a success both inside and outside the courtroom are invaluable for new lawyers and those who have been doing this for years."

—Randi McGinn, New Mexico trial lawyer and first woman president of the Inner Circle of Advocates

"Bill Barton has played many roles in my career: father figure, mentor, friend, and occasional therapist. I'm certain that there are hundreds of Oregon lawyers who share the same experience. I was honored to attend the inaugural Barton Boot Camp in 2005. It was there that I learned the incredible amount of time and energy Bill dedicates to studying, improving, and teaching every aspect of trial advocacy and what I call the holistic practice of law. This book is a continuation of Bill's decades-long passion and commitment to improving and teaching trial advocacy, not just for the betterment of trial lawyers and their clients, but also for the families and loved ones who support all of us in our journey as trial lawyers. I consider it a must-read."

—John Coletti, awarded Oregon Trial Lawyers Association's Distinguished Trial Lawyer of the Year and member of the Inner Circle of Advocates

"This book has been written by an acknowledged trial master with years of successful trial experience to back it up. Barton shares his trial wisdom in this book with clear and understandable advice proven by his own professional successes. His advice is practical and within every trial lawyer's ability to adopt and apply for more successful trial practice."

—Paul Luvera, past president of the Inner Circle of Advocates and Washington State Trial Lawyers Association, member of the American Board of Trial Advocates, and a fellow of the American College of Trial Lawyers, the International Academy of Trial Lawyers, and the International Barristers Society

"On the pages of this book are the recorded thoughts of a brilliant and innovative trial lawyer who has achieved justice for his clients, in and out of the courtroom, for more than fifty-one years. The book offers a treasury of advice and insight into pre-trial and trial practice, borne of Bill's vast experience, wisdom, and dedication to the improvement of his craft and the legal profession. However, and perhaps of equal importance, the advice and wisdom set out in the book is infused with Bill's overriding commitment to humanistic values. The trial practice and life circumstances of every lawyer, from beginner to courtroom veteran, will benefit from reading this book and doing so regularly."

—Hon. Paul J. De Muniz (ret.), former Oregon Supreme Court Chief Justice and Distinguished Jurist in Residence at Willamette University College of Law

"In the history of legal giants, Bill Barton holds profoundly unique wisdom and insight. Reading *Integrated Advocacy*, I can hear Bill's voice crack as he digs deep for the meaning he so eloquently expresses. Bill pursues creative excellence and provides legal savvy in his exploration of legal and trial thoughts. His teachings cannot be overstated both in his epic and intense boot camp and his writings. With dedication to our profession and the students of the profession, Bill's most recent book passes on generational wisdom and ancestral knowledge that must be preserved. His first masterpiece, *Recovering for Psychological Injuries*, was the first legal self-help book I read, and *Integrated Advocacy* could easily be the last."

—Eric Fong, Public Justice board member and Trial Lawyers college instructor

"As a new plaintiff's lawyer, this book is essential to mastering the intricacies of effective trial advocacy, personal authenticity, framing damages, storytelling, and various aspects of courtroom work. The inclusion of chapters on criminal defense, plaintiffs' personal injury, legal foundations, and cross-examination gives a holistic approach to trial practice. Overall, this book is a must-read, well-rounded guide for new and seasoned trial lawyers."

—Emily Templeton, attorney at OlsenDaines, Oregon Attorney for the Underdog, Barton Boot Camp attendee

"While many legal texts teach you techniques on how to be a more skillful lawyer, and this book does, it also reminds you to listen to your better angels and not lose yourself along the way. Bill Barton's book is practical and aspirational, filled with valuable insights on advocacy, the business of law, and personal growth. Wisdom for both the practice of law and the practitioner."

—Ron K. Cheng, Attorney at Cheng Law LLC, Barton Boot Camp attendee

INTEGRATED ADVOCACY

Getting Better, Faster, While Building a Satisfying & Sustainable Law Practice

By William A. Barton

TRIAL GUIDES™

Trial Guides, LLC, Portland, Oregon 97210
Copyright © 2024 by William A. Barton.
All rights reserved.

TRIAL GUIDES and RULES OF THE ROAD are trademarks of Trial Guides, LLC.

ISBN: 978-1-951962-61-6

These materials, or any parts or portions thereof, may not be reproduced in any form, written or mechanical, or be programmed into any electronic storage or retrieval system, without the express written permission of Trial Guides, LLC, unless such copying is expressly permitted by federal copyright law. Please direct inquiries to:

Trial Guides, LLC
Attn: Permissions
2350 NW York Street
Portland, OR 97210
(800) 309-6845
www.trialguides.com

Developmental Editor: Tina Ricks
Production Editor: Travis Kremer
Assistant Editor: Amanda Fink
Copy Editor: Patricia Esposito
Cover Designer: Alexandra Starkovich
Original Interior Template Design by Laura Lind Design

Printed and bound in the United States of America.
Printed on acid-free paper.

*To JoAnn, my wife;
my children and grandchildren;
my law partner and son, Brent;
all of my Boot Campers; OTLA;
and all of the youthful,
energetic, and diverse members of
the profession I love: thank you.*

CONTENTS

PUBLISHER'S NOTE xix
FOREWORD xxi
    By Rick Friedman xxi
    By Howard Nations xxv

INTRODUCTION xxix
    What Is Integrated Advocacy (IA)? xxx
    Why This Book? xxxi
    About Myself xxxiii
    Additional Ways Integrated Advocacy Will Help You xxxvii
    Conclusion xxxvii

1. WHAT INTEGRATED ADVOCACY OFFERS YOU 1
    The IA Advantage 1
    Conclusion 7

2. BEING A JURY TRIAL LAWYER 9
    The Challenges of a Courtroom Career 9
    My Own Journey 11
    What Are Your Deepest Values? 13
        Parenting Insights 14
    Try to Learn to Love This Work 15
        The Honorable Oliver Wendell Holmes, Jr. 17
        To Be a Better Lawyer, Become a Better Person 20
        Learn to Nourish Yourself 21
        Learn to Fall in Love with Your Client & Case 22
        Embracing the Long View 23
        Have Compassion for Yourself 23
        What Does Your "Best" Really Mean? 24
        Control Your Emotions or They'll Control You 25
        Identify & Reduce Your Self-Marginalizing Behaviors 28
        Identify Emotional Fatigue 29
        Learn to Delegate 30
        Be Careful of Your Pride & Arrogance 31
        Trust the Jury System 31
        Work to Win Gracefully 32
    Conclusion: Am I a Success? 33

3. THOUGHTS ON LOSING & BEST PRACTICES AFTER A LOSS..........35
Effort versus Results 38
Losing Means a Lot of Different Things 40
Do a Trial Premortem..........41
Confront Your Fears..........41
No, You're Not the Client..........42
Another Perspective..........43
It's Not about Me or Even My Clients 44
The Long View Perspective 45
I Feel Like I Should Suffer 46
Run Directly to & through Your Pain 47
Anger Can Be Helpful..........48
There's a Process to Grieving 49
Grieve with Your Client 51
Compartmentalizing..........51
Healing from Losses..........52
We're Team Captains & Cheerleaders 52
Informed Consent Letters 53
What Athletics Can Teach Us 54
    Performance Enhancement Experts..........56
Insights from Philosophy, Science & Wisdom Traditions 57
Questions to Ask after a Loss 59
Create a Box of Losses..........62
Sharing with Others..........63
Conclusion 63

4. WHAT MOTIVATES YOU? 65
It's Never Too Late 69
We Are All Connected 70
Conclusion 70

5. CONSTRUCTING YOUR LIFE STORY 71
Narrative Psychology..........74
Awakening the Hero(ine) Within..........76
    The Departure 77
    The Initiation 77
    The Return..........77
Writing Your Obituary 80
Conclusion 81

6. DIFFERENT TYPES OF COURTROOM WORK 83
Finding the Right Fit for You... 84
Life in Big Firms.. 85
Experience in a Solo Practice 86
Specialties in Trial Work—Asking for Help 87
    Professional Lawyer Groups... 88
Public Sector Compared to Private Sector 90
Differences between Insurance Defense & Plaintiffs' Work........................91
Working at Personal Injury Defense Firms................................. 93
District Attorney & Public Defenders 93
Gaining Jury Trial Experience 94
    A Few Comments on Prosecuting.. 95
On Becoming a Judge... 96
Conclusion 98

7. DIFFERENCES BETWEEN CRIMINAL DEFENSE & PLAINTIFFS' PERSONAL INJURY......................99
Criminal Trials 99
Cross-Examination... 100
The Business Side of Trial Work... 103
The Challenges of Doing Criminal Defense 104
Conclusion 109

8. HEURISTICS & BIASES............................ 111
Lawyers Think (& Judges Instruct) Deductively, Yet Jurors Think Inductively 112
    Instructions 113
What Jurors Believe: Their (Prejudices) Outcome-Determinative Values 114
How Jurors Think: Information Processing Behaviors........................ 120
Counterfactual Reasoning: Applying Biasing Errors to the Issue of Causation....... 123
Conclusion 127

9. (PRE)TRIAL CHECKLIST 129
Trial Notebook 130
(Pre)Trial Idea List...131
Trial Strategy 134
    Trial Frames, Stories & Themes... 135
    Jury Instructions 135
    Liability... 136
    Investigation 137
    Focus Groups.. 138
    Your Opponent.. 139
    Pretrial Motions *In Limine* 140

Learn Your Judge's Jury Selection Habits 141
Learn Your Judge's Trial & Procedure Preferences 142
Jury Selection 143
Your Opening Statement 145
Direct Exam 146
Defense Motion(s) after You Have Rested 148
Cross-Examination 149
Jury Instructions 151
Closing 151

10. LEGAL FOUNDATIONS & MAGIC WORDS 155
Motions in Civil Cases 156
Questions for Your Experts in Personal Injury Cases 157
   Lump-Sum Method 160
   Confirm All Agreements in Writing 161
Foundation Liability Questions in Professional Negligence Cases 163
   Practice Comment 166
High versus Low Tech 167
   Technology Can Fail 169
   You're More Important Than Technology 170
Conclusion 171

11. DIFFERENT TYPES OF CROSS-EXAMINATION 173
Start with Knowing Your Judge 174
   A Note about Anger 175
Alternative Cross-Examination Styles 175
   No Questions, Your Honor 176
   Style 1: Constructive Cross-Examination 177
   Style 2: Younger's Yes/No Ten Commandments 178
   Style 3: Storytelling Cross-Examination 184
   Style 4: Self-Impeachment for Obvious Partisanship 189
   Style 5: "Self-Accrediting" Cross-Examination 191
Use What Works for You 193
   My Approach 193
   Further Reading 194
Conclusion 194

12. FRAMING YOUR DAMAGES ... 195

- Quantitative Analysis for Damages ... 196
  - Horizontal Axis ... 197
  - Vertical Axis ... 197
  - Traditional Law-School Model ... 199
- The Alternative: Qualitative Thinking ... 200
- Applying Qualitative versus Quantitative Thinking ... 202
  - Unappealing Plaintiff with Limited Losses ... 202
  - Think Qualitatively about Disabilities ... 204
  - Disability versus Impairment ... 205
  - Explain the *As Is* Rule ... 205
  - Find Lay Witnesses ... 206
  - Vary Arguments for Each Jury ... 206
- Qualitative Thinking & Variations on Damages Arguments ... 208
  - Liability Provokes Damages ... 208
  - Damages Provoke Liability ... 209
  - A Fragile Plaintiff Can Help Explain Causation ... 209
  - Ground Your Case Themes in Desirable Community Values ... 210
- Effective Damages Proof & Arguments ... 212
  - Anchoring ... 213
  - The Law/Instructions ... 214
- Setting Your Damages Theme during Jury Selection ... 215
- Your Confidence ... 216
- My Favorite Plaintiffs' Damages Arguments ... 218
- Arguments against Businesses ... 219
- Breach of Contract Arguments ... 221
- Conclusion ... 222

13. MEDIATION FROM THE PLAINTIFF'S PERSPECTIVE ... 223

- Mediation versus Trial ... 223
- The Psychology of the Mediation Participants ... 225
- Have the Right Mindset for Negotiations ... 227
- How to Respond to the Other Side's Arguments ... 228
- Thoughts on Mediation ... 230
  - After Mediation ... 231
- Why Mediation? ... 231
  - Structural Aspects of Mediation ... 233
  - When to Choose Mediation ... 233
- Strategies for Negotiating ... 235
- Common Mistakes ... 239
- Conclusion ... 240

14. ON PERSONAL AUTHENTICITY 241
Speaking from the Heart 241
How to Argue a Case with Authority 242
Learning How to Speak "Heart Talk" 243
    Heart Talk with Free Association 244
    Speaking from the Heart 245
    Common Questions & Concerns about Heart Talk 245
Conclusion 248

15. THE CRAFT OF STORYTELLING 249
Storytelling Is an Art Form 249
Adapting Storytelling for the Courtroom 250
Elements of an Effective Trial Story 251
    Where to Begin Your Trial Story 251
    How to Dramatize Your Trial Story 253
    Talk about Injustice 253
    Stories Are about Listeners 254
Developing Trial Stories and Themes 255
    How to Choose Your Trial Story & Themes 256
    Being Effective Requires Credibility 257
    Simplify… 257
What Are Your Rules of the Road? 257
My Storytelling Checklist 258
    Checklist 258
    Exercises 260
Conclusion 260

16. THE UBIQUITOUS PRESENCE OF MONEY 261
Money in Your Firm 262
Financial Goals 262
    Costs Advanced 263
Make a Business Plan—Start with Fixed Expenses 263
    Banking & Credit 265
Steps to Successfully Running Your Practice 265
    Cash Flow 267
Setting Up a Professional Corporation 268
    Sharing Office Space or Partnership 268
Do You Have What It Takes? 269
Conclusion 269

17. RUNNING A LAW BUSINESS 271
Financial Nuts & Bolts. 272
   Hanging Out Your Shingle. 272
   At the Big Firms: Grinders & Finders. 273
   A Note about "Beauty Contests". 273
Doing the Work: IA's 70/30 Rule 276
   Invest in Your Better Cases 276
   Limited Case Inventory Example 277
Deal with the Cases You Hate. 278
Self-Promotion versus Courtroom Results. 279
   Building a Practice 280
   Building a Personal Injury Practice 280
   High-Volume Settlement Practices 281
   Choosing Quality or Quantity 281
   When Law Firms Split Up 282
   Making Law Firms Tick 283
Conclusion 283

18. EVALUATING CASES 285
Learning to Analyze Cases. 285
   Factors to Consider when Evaluating a Case 286
   The Truth about Bad Cases. 288
Prepare a Case Budget 290
Caring versus Capital (Money) 293
Learn When to Say No 295
Be Choosy in the Cases You Accept 295
Types of Liability: Simple & Complex. 297
Fee Agreements & Appeals 297
Building a Practice. 298
Bad Faith Claims 299
Medical Negligence Claims 301
   Settling Malpractice Cases: NPDB & Consent 303
Conclusion 304

19. WHEN & HOW TO REFER YOUR CASES 307
Financing Cases 307
   What about ALF Loans? 308
   Associating with Other Lawyers. 310
   Include Mentoring in Your Association Agreements. 311
   How to Associate Cases & Win 312
   Fees to the Associating Lawyer 314

Do the Math: A Story Problem. 315
    Scenario 1: Don't Refer the Case 315
    Scenario 2: Associate with an Experienced Lawyer 316
Settle or Go to Trial?. 317
Getting Value for Your Claims. 318
Money & Ethics about Settlement 318
A Different Way to Look at Settlement. 320
Conclusion 320

RECOMMENDED READING 321
ABOUT THE AUTHOR 325

This is the true joy in life, the being used for a purpose recognized by yourself as a mighty one; ... the being a force of Nature instead of a feverish, selfish little clod of ailments and grievances, complaining that the world will not devote itself to making you happy.[1]

I am of the opinion that my life belongs to the whole community, and as long as I live, it is my privilege to do for it whatsoever I can. ... It is a sort of splendid torch, which I have got hold of for the moment; and I want to make it burn as brightly as possible before handing it on to future generations.[2]

—George Bernard Shaw

---

1. George Bernard Shaw, *Man and Superman: A Comedy and Philosophy* (1903; repr., New York: Warbler Classics, 2022).

2. Archibald Henderson, *George Bernard Shaw: His Life and Works, a Critical Biography* (Whitefish, MT: Kessinger Publishing, LLC, 2004).

PUBLISHER'S NOTE

This book is intended for practicing attorneys. This book does not offer legal advice and does not take the place of consultation with an attorney or other professional with appropriate expertise and experience.

Attorneys are strongly cautioned to evaluate the information, ideas, and opinions set forth in this book in light of their own research, experience, and judgment; to consult applicable rules, regulations, procedures, cases, and statutes (including those issued after the publication date of this book); and to make independent decisions about whether and how to apply such information, ideas, and opinions to a particular case.

Quotations from cases, pleadings, discovery, and other sources are for illustrative purposes only and may not be suitable for use in litigation in any particular case.

The case examples described in this book are from actual cases, and the names of participants, litigants, witnesses, and counsel have been fictionalized or removed, unless otherwise cited. Any similarities between such fictionalized individuals and entities and real persons are strictly coincidental.

All references to the trademarks of third parties are strictly informational and for purposes of commentary. No sponsorship or endorsement by, or affiliation with, the trademark owners is claimed or implied by the author or publisher of this book. The author and publisher disclaim any liability or responsibility for loss or damage resulting from the use of this book or the information, ideas, or opinions contained in this book.

FOREWORD

By Rick Friedman

You hold in your hands a book written by the wisest trial lawyer I have ever met. Many trial lawyers are financially successful. Bill Barton is one of them. Many trial lawyers have enormous natural talent. Bill Barton is one of them. Few lawyers have tried literally hundreds of cases. Bill is one of them. Even fewer trial lawyers have read extensively about the art and craft of trial work. I know no one who has read more extensively in this area than Bill. There are plenty of thoughtful trial lawyers, Bill included. But wise trial lawyers?

Sad to say, there are not that many wise trial lawyers. There are several reasons for this, but I will mention just two. First, our profession does not reward wisdom. It rewards hard work, preparation, emotional intelligence, quick thinking and response, but not wisdom. Second, as Bill says later in the book,

> Even if you become (financially) "successful," there are new and different challenges. You will find your deepest fears and insecurities are still with you, just in new costumes.

In other words, we often self-destruct before we can attain true wisdom. Self-destruction doesn't necessarily mean you get divorced, go bankrupt, or get disbarred—although all of these are occupational hazards. Self-destruction can be much more mundane. It can simply mean that you stop growing. Lawyers often find a way to be successful—according to whatever definition appeals to them—and then simply perform a "rinse and repeat" cycle indefinitely. There is nothing wrong with this, but it does not give rise to wisdom.

Simply stated, Bill Barton never lost his enthusiasm for what we do, or his curiosity about how to get better. He reads widely and thinks deeply. He carefully observes himself and others operating in the trial environment. And he tries to make sense of it all.

After more than fifty years toiling in the fields of the courtroom, he shares his harvest of insights on topics ranging from how to set up and run a law office to the different styles of cross-examination. You'll find more good advice for trial lawyers in this book than in any other book I can think of.

A rarity among books for trial lawyers, this book seldom advocates for a single solution for a problem. Instead, with clear eyes and an open heart, Bill explores the complex realities of our job. For example, in the chapter on cross-examination, after describing the various styles of cross, Bill concludes with a section titled "Use What Works for You":

Try all of the cross-examination styles. We all fear failure; however, growth demands pushing yourself.

In short, reading this book is like sitting and talking with the perfect mentor: someone who has seen it all, lived it all, and thought long and hard about it all; someone who understands how difficult our jobs are and the complexity and stress of the decisions we have to make; and someone who is trying to help us think through our own approaches to practicing law rather than telling us what to do.

Risk-averse lawyers tend to settle sooner and for less. Settling cases assures fewer appeals, and by settling, they avoid the risk of big losses, which, of course, levels the fiscal peaks and valleys. More aggressive plaintiffs' lawyers seem to tolerate more risk. You see how it's all interrelated and every choice comes with benefits and burdens. Risk-aversion and risk-seeking are both dysfunctional at their extremes; somewhere in the middle is that sweet spot, also known as good judgment.

When Bill does take a firm position, it is usually indisputable. For example:

> [A]t no time should you call a witness a liar. If it's obvious the witness has lied, then you don't need to say so; and if it isn't obvious, then it's too risky. It's just that simple.

But a word of warning: Bill's writing style is so matter-of-fact, and his suggestions and observations so simple and commonsensical at times, that you might breeze right by some of the most powerful advice he has to offer. For example:

> [M]ake it a career goal to target a case load in which you operate *slightly under capacity*. Why? It affords you the ability to jump on a great case when it walks through your door. Plus, it makes your practice less stressful and more enjoyable.

This is life-changing advice. If more trial lawyers followed it, there would be fewer divorces, fewer alcoholics or drug addicts, fewer legal malpractice suits, and thousands of happier lawyers. And there is life-changing advice throughout this book—so read carefully!

In the end, Bill is a problem solver, and this book is an encyclopedia of the types of problems we all face as trial lawyers—and creative solutions to those problems. Here's one of the innumerable original and surprising solutions Bill delivers:

> In some bigger cases, I have hired an ethics lawyer to review my analysis and decision-making. These lawyers have occasionally recommended that I hire and pay for a third lawyer who is both conservative and unquestionably competent to persuasively disagree with me. At my request, this third lawyer then writes my client an opinion letter critiquing my analysis and valuation and setting forth their assessment and conclusions regarding the value of the case.... This process ensures that real informed

consent occurs. I alone pay for the bills of the ethics lawyer and then the third (contrary-opinion) lawyer without passing the costs back to the client. I provide my client with this differing opinion for two reasons. First, it's the moral thing to do. Second, if we should lose the case, or if the jury awards an amount that's less than I had recommended my client settle for, this opinion letter is evidence that I not only met but exceeded the standard of care—I fulfilled my responsibilities to provide my client with real and informed consent.

Reading a book is a one-way conversation, but a conversation nevertheless. You will never have a conversation about practicing law with a wiser lawyer. So read slowly and pay attention. And think! Stay open to what Bill is saying, and prepare to have unexpected insights about your life and your law practice.

Rick Friedman
November, 2023

P.S. Maybe the editor will leave this in and let me publicly thank Bill for being such a huge influence in shaping my own style of advocacy—not to mention my own style of writing books for trial lawyers. It is a delightful gift from the universe when one's hero also becomes a friend.

By Howard Nations

Those of us who choose to labor in the vineyards of justice enjoy the great privilege to stand before a judge and jury and breathe life into the Constitution by advocating for a client's cause.

Being a trial lawyer is very demanding, sometimes to the point of being overwhelming. It is replete with frustration because the wheels of justice turn so slowly and successful completions in litigation always seem to be slightly out of reach. The demands, obligations, and frustrations of trial work all too often adversely affect the attorney's personal and family life. This can easily flow into burnout for experienced trial lawyers.

At the other end of the spectrum are numerous new prospective trial lawyers who are frustrated by the lack of opportunity to get trial experience. With large student loans pending, numerous young lawyers are seeking a successful pathway into trial work.

In authoring this book, Bill Barton draws on his successful career as a trial lawyer, an author, and a prolific speaker on law, psychology, and other subjects that improve the trial bar. Bill speaks with the voice of experience as he has tried more than 500 cases to a jury and delivered more than 500 speeches to lawyer organizations. Bill is equal parts trial lawyer and legal educator, and he excels at both.

This book addresses issues of frustration and burnout, both at work and at home, among experienced lawyers and offers pathways to self-improvement and lessons in trial skills and law practice for the young inexperienced lawyers. He also suggests paths to maximize personal fulfillment, happiness, and success in both family and professional life.

The pathway to being a fulfilled and rejuvenated lawyer is by being a better person. Better citizenship is achieved by creating a powerful moral center by doing the right thing for its own sake. This leads to development of a body of principles and attitudes that guides you in your daily life. We lawyers are leaders. Embrace this role and build on it. A result is that jurors will welcome you as their teacher and guide when they adopt your trial story.

Integrated Advocacy is achieved by becoming a better person and maturing into a better lawyer. Shakespeare said it best. In *Hamlet*, Polonius is giving advice to his son, Laertes, on how to behave at University:

> This above all: to thine own self be true, and it must follow, as the night the day, thou canst not then be false to any man. Aristotle referred to this as ethos. Lincoln called for us to "appeal to our better angels."

To be a better person, integrate this wisdom of the ages into your daily living and it will positively influence your loved ones, home life, and relationships in your professional life.

The second tenet of Integrated Advocacy emphasizes the significance of professionalism as our second nature in court. Our moral compass calls for lawyers to conduct themselves in an ethical manner, which will be respected by judges, jurors, and opposing counsel. The intrinsic moral merits of professionalism generate strategic benefits as it enhances your trustworthiness.

Credibility is the necessary link that must exist between a lawyer and jurors. Being a better person and practicing the best of professionalism will maximize your trustworthiness.

The third tenet of Integrated Advocacy is jury empowerment, which emanates from the jury accepting the lawyer as a leader whom they're willing to follow. Jury empowerment involves helping them to understand they have the power to right a wrong and promote public safety and accountability by supporting your client's claims.

Jurors want to feel that they have done something important that they can look back on with pride, and so it is with your career. Give them and yourself the power to do so.

Bill's depth of experience in trial and teaching is on display in the major portion of the book in which he discusses a wide variety of trial-related subjects such as framing your damages, effective damages proof and arguments, elements of an effective trial story, and the ubiquitous presence of money, among many others. Finally, Bill recommends a variety of books and other source materials which are invaluable to improving your trial and people skills.

In summary, a great trial lawyer with finely honed teaching skills has written an excellent book designed to inspire the reader to become both a better person and a more skillful lawyer.

Howard L. Nations
December, 2023

INTRODUCTION

Each generation (re)discovers the art of jury trial advocacy through the voices of its current teachers and leaders. Popular media, television, movies, and *Grishamesque* books all glamorize our craft. This occurs against a social backdrop of diversity, focus groups, forensic and social psychology, psychodrama, technology, social media, marketing (networking), arbitration, mediation, and the disappearing civil jury trial. The landscape is forever shifting; however, the principles endure. If you doubt it, read Aristotle's *Rhetoric*.

Today's aspiring jury trial lawyers face both a significant challenge and a rare opportunity. The old way of learning by trial and error simply isn't available. With the success of mediation, the number of personal injury cases being tried is shrinking. At the same time, older lawyers with long careers of civil jury trial experience are retiring and leaving openings for the next generation to step in. There's a winning strategy available that will help you to become better, faster. It's called "Integrated Advocacy."

Today's legal market is saturated. The economic law of supply and demand is real. For example, in 1970 the United States had a population of 203,392,031 and 326,000 lawyers. By 1980 the population of the United States had grown to 226,545, 805 and the number of lawyers jumped 76 percent from 1970's number to 574,000. Today there are over 1.3 million lawyers in a population of about 330 million. Add to this the economic reality that many graduates today have student loans of over $125,000 (or more). Average students from average law schools often don't have a lot of options and the desirable public sector jobs are limited in number. These new lawyers have little choice but to hang out their own shingle, and almost all initially struggle to eke out a living.

Jury trials are partial referendums on the parties' and their lawyers' *citizenship*.[1] Effective advocacy is about earning the jury's trust. It's about becoming their guide. Integrated Advocacy (IA) involves the application of your best citizenship to enhance persuasiveness. It's a body of principles, attitudes, and practices that improves you, and thus your effectiveness, in court and life. As plaintiffs' lawyers, we're the only one facing the burden of proof. We must always wear the white hat, or at least the whitest hat, in the courtroom.

What Is Integrated Advocacy (IA)?

IA is three inter-related propositions:

1. If you want to become a better lawyer, then strive to become a better person.
2. Good citizenship and professionalism are embraced not just for their intrinsic merits and morality, but also because it's smart lawyering and will help you win more often. Why? Because it maximizes your credibility. I call this "weaponizing professionalism."
3. IA empowers the jury to fully serve as the conscience of the community. By stopping a bit early, you leave something important for the jury to do with their verdict.[2] You will learn to judge acts, not people. Judging people is the jury's job, and the size of their verdict will reflect their decision.

---

1. I use *citizenship* as a synonym for the Greek "ethos" or character. It's much more than professionalism, which focuses on how you conduct yourself as a lawyer. Citizenship is much deeper and is you at your core.

2. Thank you, Moe Levine. *The Historic Recordings* (Trial Guides, 2009), DVD; *The Lost Recordings, Vols. I and II* (Trial Guides, 2012), DVD; *The Summation* (Trial Guides, 2011), DVD.

Why This Book?

There are many reasons for this book. IA is always practical and strategic. Through it, you learn how to:

1. Best grow from a loss, thereby increasing your odds of winning in the future.
2. Learn how to love this job without it devouring you. Said differently, it's about you running your practice, instead of it running you.
3. Refine your personal answers to our profession's (and life's) biggest questions.
4. Learn how to self-nourish, resulting in improving your physical health and mental well-being.
5. Maximize your ever improving credibility and reputation.

Yes, clinical skills are important. I recommend you read *Trying Your First Case*,[3] *The Elements of Trial*,[4] the two-volume set entitled *Anatomy of a Personal Injury Lawsuit*,[5] and *Trying Cases to Win: In One Volume*.[6] Watch experienced lawyers pick a jury, deliver an opening statement, and present a compelling case in chief. Attend the three-week Spence Camp and their many weekend programs around the country. Don Keenan has an impressive step-by-step program. It was previously known as the "Reptile," but he's renamed it the "Edge."[7] I agree that

---

3. Nash E. Long, ed., *Trying Your First Case: A Practitioner's Guide* (Chicago, IL: ABA Press, 2014).

4. Rick Friedman and Bill Cummings, *The Elements of Trial* (Portland, OR: Trial Guides, 2013).

5. John F. Romano, ed., *Anatomy of a Personal Injury Lawsuit* (Portland, OR: Trial Guides, 2015).

6. Herbert J. Stern and Stephen A. Saltzburg, *Trying Cases to Win: In One Volume* (Chicago, IL: ABA Press, 2013).

7. Don Keenan, *The Keenan Edge 6*, 381.

"[e]xperience is way, way overrated. Hard work and preparation are way, way underrated."[8]

I encourage you to cultivate mentors and positive role models. Watch and listen a lot. Nobody's perfect. Some of my greatest mentors were both gifted and cursed. A strength can also be a weakness. To the alert student, both provide teaching moments.

Commit to identifying and pursuing your evolving better nature; Lincoln referred to this as our "better angels." Take the long view of self-interest. I call it your enlightened self-interest. It's a lifelong process of becoming an ever-improving version of yourself. When an opponent goes low, you go high. No exceptions.

IA invites you to enhance and express the best of yourself through your caring, character, and competence. Traditional trial advocacy focuses on gaining skills and techniques. Of course this is important, but it's just part of the story. The view of trial lawyers as gladiators involved in a "fight to the death" can be off-putting and even vulgar, but there is some truth to it. I preach IA and the strategic weaponizing of professionalism. However, IA as an abstraction doesn't fully capture the reality that jury trials are a form of combat. It's certainly not a debate nor an academic exercise. To our clients, the trial might be everything. They have chosen us to represent them, and we have accepted that responsibility. I encourage you to be an effective IA advocate and acknowledge the primal importance of what we do without tacitly suggesting you should do anything that will demean yourself or our profession. Why? Because it's not effective advocacy and doesn't help you win. While you might pursue IA to win more cases, it's most effective when embraced in the larger context of your life's journey.

IA will help you function at optimal levels, both in court and life. I want you to do more than survive—I want you to thrive. Build a practice and life grounded in your values, talents, and interests. I'll try to help you in that effort by identifying and discussing the core tenants of IA that are embedded in wisdom, traditions, religions, philosophy, and popular culture.

---

8. James H. McComas, *Dynamic Cross-Examination: A Whole New Way to Create Opportunities to Win* (Portland, OR: Trial Guides, 2011), 341.

Years ago, I was an unmentored solo practitioner. I had all the same fears, doubts, and questions you have. This book will save you time, money, losses, and heartache (maybe even a divorce or two) by sharing the insights, lessons, and best practices I've learned the hard way.

I draw heavily on the IA training I've offered and refined in the boot camps I've conducted since 2005. It involves two weekends in Portland, Oregon with twenty-one hours of instruction. Most of what I teach is autobiographical and littered with generalizations. I view my life as a personal and professional pilgrimage.

About Myself

My first legal job was in 1972 at an office practice of property, business law, and estates. After seven months, I was given the option of either resigning or being fired. I then moved to Newport, a town on the central Oregon coast with 5,000 people and two stop lights. Two months after my arrival my boss was shot and killed in a murder-suicide. There I was, alone and unmentored. I started out on the criminal side doing court appointments, defending DUIs and misdemeanors. My practice gradually grew to serious felonies, including appointed death penalty cases, and an occasional personal injury claim. I've done criminal defense and plaintiffs' personal injury for over fifty years.[9] Today, I focus on plaintiffs' medical negligence and birth trauma, claims of sexual exploitation, and psychological injuries.

I wasn't born to be a professional, and certainly not a lawyer. I am in my seventies and have invested in multiple bouts of serious therapy. I am the oldest of four children from a modest blue-collar background. Early in my career, I saw myself as an outsider to our profession; I had nightmares into my thirties that I would be discovered as an imposter.

---

9. Oregon civil practice has no interrogatories and no discovery of experts beyond records of the treating doctor and a written report by defense medical experts. Remittitur is barred by Oregon constitution. It's called "trial by ambush," and in a sense, that's correct. You've got to be good on your feet, in real time.

Maybe that's why I remain so grateful to the practice of law and the opportunities it has provided me.

While I've had some good wins, I have also suffered some major losses. Yes, I've learned more from the losses than the wins. They are probably what best qualify me not just as a teacher, but also as an empathetic friend and understanding guide for you. I wouldn't have much to offer without these unwelcome growth opportunities. I hope my verdicts and settlements have improved my clients' lives and the quality of our health care, youth service organizations, product safety, and the accountability of religious groups. We improve our communities by our legal work and the results we achieve for our clients. At this stage of my career, my highest service is to teach and empower you to continue the work I have committed my life to.

We operate at the intensely public intersection of values, rights, and economics. Jury trials are local government at its best. I think of each of us as social and legal architects who impact our communities.

I have long been a student of the Honorable Oliver Wendell Holmes, Jr. (1841–1935), Associate Justice of the United States Supreme Court (1902–1932).[10] I have traveled the country delivering lectures as Justice Holmes

---

10. Today, Justice Holmes has no natural constituency, and his popularity ebbs and flows with the times. *See*, Thomas Healy, *The Great Dissent: How Oliver Wendell Holmes Changed His Mind and Changed the History of Free Speech in America* (New York, NY: Metropolitan Books, 2014); Grant Gilmore, *The Ages of American Law* (New Haven, CT: Yale University Press, 1977); Robert W. Gordon, ed., *The Legacy of Oliver Wendell Holmes, Jr.* (Stanford, CA: Stanford University Press, 1992); Adam Cohen, *Imbeciles: The Supreme Court, American Eugenics, and the Sterilization of Carrie Buck* (New York, NY: Penguin Books, 2017); Stephen Budiansky, *Oliver Wendell Holmes: A Life in War, Law, and Ideas* (New York, NY: W.W. Norton & Company, 2019); Albert W. Alschuler, *Law Without Values: The Life, Work, and Legacy of Justice Holmes* (Chicago, IL: University of Chicago Press, 2002); Frederic R. Kellogg, *Oliver Wendell Holmes, Jr., Legal Theory and Judicial Restraint* (Cambridge, UK: Cambridge University Press, 2011); Susan-Mary Grant, *Oliver Wendell Holmes, Jr. Civil War Soldier, Supreme Court Justice* (New York, NY: Routledge, 2016); Liva Baker, *The Justice from Beacon Hill: The Life and Times of Oliver Wendell Holmes* (New York, NY: Harper-Collins, 1991); Catherine Drinker Bowen, *Yankee From Olympus*, (Boston, MA: Little, Brown and Company, 1972); Sheldon M. Novick, *Honorable Justice: The Life of Oliver Wendell Holmes* (Boston, MA: Little, Brown and Company, 1989); G. Edward White, *Justice Oliver Wendell Holmes: Law and the Inner Self* (New York, NY: Oxford University Press, 1995).

and have done so before members of the US Supreme Court. Justice Holmes wrote *The Common Law* (1881) and is known as the "great dissenter." A powerful result of our work is the social and moral progression of our nation's common law. The United States is one of a few countries with the guaranteed the right to civil jury trials.[11] Justice Holmes's thoughts about the nature and social functions of our work are insightful.

During their first interview, most injured clients say a part of the reason they seek representation isn't just personal redress, but to also try and ensure this doesn't happen to anyone else. I fully acknowledge my fiduciary duties to represent only my clients' interests, however, my state's Rules of Professional Responsibility provides:

Counselor

Rule 2.1 Advisor

In representing a client, a lawyer shall exercise independent professional judgment and render candid advice. In rendering advice, a lawyer may refer not only to law but to other considerations such as moral, economic, social, and political factors, that may be relevant to the client's situation.

This provision allows me to speak in favor of an ultimate resolution that addresses the common law in a manner that best assures what happened to my client won't happen again. For example, by making sure that a

---

11. "Compared to most European countries and the Commonwealth nations (former colonies of the British Empire) the U.S. is currently one of the few that still grants civil jury trials as a right." Nicholas J. Dilley, "Constitutional Amendments Series–Amendment VII–The Right to Jury Trial in Civil Affairs," *The Reagan Library Education Blogs,* www.reagan.blogs.archives.gov/2022/08/18/constitutional-amendments-series-amendment-vii-the-right-to-jury-trial-in-civil-affairs; "Civil juries do not exist elsewhere in the world, even in England." Fred Einbinder, "Mass Torts: Dispute Resolution in France and the United States—the Vioxx and Mediator Cases Compared," *Washington International Law Journal* 29, no 3 (2020): 575; "Juries were never used in civil proceedings in civil law nations and have been abolished in almost all common law jurisdictions except the United States and for libel cases in England." *Id.* at 134 (citing John Henry Merryman and Rogelio Pérez-Perdomo, *The Civil Law Tradition: An Introduction To The Legal Systems Of Europe And Latin America,* 3d ed. (Stanford University Press, 2007), 113).

settlement isn't sealed and hidden from the public, appealing rulings that limit victims' rights, and so on. Of course, it's always the client's decision; but as lawyers, we have input. One victim publicly stepping forth is empowering for others. Think here of the #MeToo movement.

There are trade-offs, pluses and minuses, to any line of work, so in a sense every job is a choice. I think of it as a Faustian bargain. Many trial lawyers have a love–hate relationship with our work. It's maybe 70 percent okay, 10 percent exhilarating, and 20 percent hell. There's no better feeling in a tough case than recovering a substantial verdict for a deserving client. The worst feeling is losing; the more deserving the client, the more painful the loss. Losing is at least twice as bad as winning is good. There's an adrenaline rush to this work that can be intoxicating, even mildly addictive, but it comes at a cost to you and your loved ones.

My primary goal in my work has been to run my job instead of letting it run me. Looking back, I'll admit this has been more an aspiration than a reality. Is it possible to do this demanding work part-time? Not really. Excellence as a jury trial lawyer demands a serious and sustained commitment.

The primary ingredients of our work are serious responsibilities to our clients, which necessarily generates lots of stress. The butterflies in your stomach never go away, you just "teach them to fly in formation."[12] It never gets easier. The more you grow, the bigger the cases and the responsibility–not to mention your opponents are better funded and ever more talented.

Responsibility, stress, and public competition are organic to our work. Sure, hard work is necessary for success. But given the embedded stressors, perspective, and temperament are essential for any semblance of equanimity, not to mention satisfaction and happiness.

---

12. James W. McElhaney, *McElhaney's Trial Notebook*, 4th ed. (Chicago, IL: ABA Press, 2005).

Additional Ways Integrated Advocacy Will Help You

IA will arm you with attitudes, perspectives, and behaviors that will allow you to flourish over the course of your career resulting in a deep satisfaction.

I have long been a student of my craft and carefully studied the careers of those before me. For the last twenty years I've hired retired philosophy professors to teach me. I mention this because it expanded my thinking and the choices available to me in facing life's challenges.

Conclusion

IA won't just improve your courtroom persuasiveness. It combines the professional and personal in a way that improves both. We jury trial lawyers needn't be splintered and fractionalized. The very best of ourselves, personal or professional, emanates from the same deep sources. You don't stop being you when you leave home or walk into the courtroom. IA isn't just for the practicing lawyer; it's for the person practicing law.

I've divided *Integrated Advocacy* into five sections. The first section involves IA and the challenges of combining your career, family, self, and life in the largest sense. The second section overviews different types of trial work and comments on three important differences between criminal defense and plaintiffs' personal injury. The third section is clinical and involves heuristics and biases, checklists, legal foundations, cross-examination, damages arguments, and mediation. The fourth section focuses on the importance of personal authenticity and the craft of storytelling. The last section discusses the challenges of running a profitable personal injury practice.

I'm looking across at you, and maybe even up. I respect you as my legal heirs and peers, and I am confident the future of our profession is in good hands. I feel like a freshman who continues to learn. After all, I've never been this age before! I'm excited about our shared pilgrimage and future. Thank you for considering my thoughts.

1

What Integrated Advocacy Offers You

Law school changes you. It changes the way you think, speak, and can shrink you, making you less of a person. Compare this with Integrated Advocacy (IA) which enlarges you. IA will help by making the moral and strategic markers along your life's journey more obvious. It is an overarching canopy under which your evolving best is given full expression.

The IA Advantage

Excellence as a jury trial lawyer has nothing to do with which side of the table you occupy or the type of cases you try. The highs are incredibly high, and the lows are incredibly low. Losing leads to feelings of inadequacy, guilt, shame, anger, and an urge to externalize by blaming your opponent, the judge, "dumb jurors," and the insurance industry. We're also quick to blame ourselves. What did I do wrong? What should I have done different, what could I have done better? It's all here: responsibility, ego, pride, performance, stress, anxiety, honor, the loftiest of ideals, plus plenty of talented and well-funded opponents. You're only as good as your next trial, and without perspective, values, and healthy choices, it's almost impossible to enjoy—not to mention love—this work.

Juries and judges like IA because it encourages you to embrace everything harmful that's coming into evidence. Jurors like it because it's ABC (accurate, brief, and clear), discourages personalized aggression, treats everyone with respect, and honors the full measure of the jurors' responsibilities which I characterize as *jury empowerment*.[1] Opponents will trust you because they can.[2] Why do you (always) behave in keeping with the best of our profession? Because it enhances your persuasiveness and credibility, and therefore is to your advantage.

You'll welcome IA because it's easier and less stressful than traditional adversarial approaches. Consistently applying IA eliminates the necessity of being an emotional chameleon as you navigate between the competing demands of your personal and professional worlds. Yes, you might still lose, but it won't be for the wrong reasons, meaning you unknowingly self-marginalized and thus forfeited credibility.

With IA, you:

1. **Respond, Never React**

    In the heat of battle, you don't react; you respond. Easy to say, tough to do. When an opponent cuts corners or is underhanded, IA's answer is always the same: you stay centered and take the high road. The jury must never confuse you with your opponent. This isn't to say you don't practice smart defensive lawyering. You do—but that's just the start. You respond in professional ways that reflect the best

---

1. *See* chapter 11, "Different Types of Cross-Examination."
2. I'm grateful for having received the Owen Panner Professionalism Award from the Oregon state bar's litigation section, consisting of both plaintiff and defense attorneys. I've also received the Award of Merit which is my state bar's highest honor.

of you and of our profession. As plaintiffs' lawyers, we must conspicuously be more trustworthy and credible than our opponents. This keeps the focus on your ethos and calculated professionalism, all of which you can control.

2. **Question Your Gut and Moral Intuitions**
This seems almost heretical, but you must learn to question your own judgment, particularly in cross-examination. Don't abandon your instincts, just be willing to assess them in real time and ask how they might betray you. This is a corollary to responding rather than reacting. In particular, I repeatedly ask myself: when might a strength become a liability, or when can you have too much of a good thing, and what would that look like?

3. **Consider Therapy**
We are all reluctant to embark on the painful inner journey of self-exploration; it's called being defensive. And yes, we all have self-destructive habits and thinking errors. IA and therapy will improve your self-awareness and reduce your reactive behaviors. Examples can include overconfidence and assertiveness. You're not a broken record—you have choices.

4. **Embrace Your Conservative Values**
Passionate liberals naturally resist this.[3] I'm not asking you to change your opinions; please don't. Instead, have the discipline to temporarily suspend or bracket them. The better you understand your opponents, their arguments, and the jurors, the more effectively you can advocate. This is one of the benefits of psychodrama and its role reversal.[4] This insightful process will minimize the number and size of your patriotic blind spots. You owe your client this kind of objectivity. Striving to understand your opponent's perspective isn't treason or betrayal; it's a smart act of patriotism.

---

3. Rick Friedman, *Becoming a Trial Lawyer: A Guide for the Lifelong Advocate*, 2nd ed. (Portland, OR: Trial Guides, 2015), 147.

4. Joane Garcia-Colson, Fredilyn Sison, and Mary Peckham, *Trial In Action: The Persuasive Power of Psychodrama* (Portland, OR: Trial Guides, 2010), 77.

5. **Choose Your Cases Wisely**

   Be disciplined in your case selection, even when you are starting out and struggling to pay the rent. The legal market is fiscally blind and socially Darwinian. You are one of over 1.3 million lawyers trying to make a living. IA will assist you in gaining the insight and discipline to know which cases to accept, which to decline, and why. Chapter 12, "Framing Your Damages" offers creative approaches to presenting your case that will turn weaknesses into strengths. An example is strategically employing the previous infirm condition, or *as is* instruction, that emphasizes the fragilities of your client.

6. **Prepare Your Clients to Testify**

   We must accept complete responsibility for preparing our vulnerable clients for the rigors of trial. Our instincts are to protect; it's who we are. We represent our clients during their most vulnerable times. However, it doesn't necessarily follow that we should rush to shield our clients from an aggressive opponent. Rather, we should prepare and empower them to become effective witnesses in the face of this predictable hostility. The more effective a client is in their depositions, the less the defendant will want to face them in court (and of course the converse is equally true). This makes it less likely your client will have to endure the rigors of trial and increases the prospects they will receive full compensation, which also promotes social change.

   This also improves the likelihood the litigation experience will ultimately be cathartic for our injured clients. They come to us as vulnerable victims but, with best practices, you will leave them fully empowered. They will no longer be victims. We're the professionals and guardians. The best form of protection is the confidence that flows from thorough preparation. It's our jobs; it's what we're supposed to be doing.[5]

---

5. I recommend Jesse Wilson's *Witness Preparation: How to Tell the Winning Story* (Portland, OR: Trial Guides, 2022).

IA is always under your control. It's also internally coherent, complete, and correct, but don't take my word for it.[6] Test it for yourself. As you continue in your career and life's journey, you'll be striking an ever-improving composite of who you are. As you internalize IA's insights, they will become embedded as your core values, instincts, and intuitions.

But IA only works when you do the necessary (pretrial) preparation on both (inside) you and (outside) your case. You usually have an idea in advance about what's going to upset you. Visualize what's going to get your goat; now stop and identify your alternatives. You've got choices… what are they? Ask yourself how you can turn an opponent's aggravating, aggressive, and arguably unethical conduct to your advantage. View this as a challenge and a disguised growth opportunity.

Being emotionally prepared is just as important as knowing the facts in your case. It's all one. However, this can't and won't happen without you doing the necessary work, both inside and outside.

IA doesn't offer you short cuts, tricks, or excuses. Being a trial lawyer is demanding, stressful, and exhausting. That ain't going to change, but IA will help. Losing sucks and that also isn't gonna change—nor should it. If you want to excel in any competitive and demanding life undertaking, think of Malcolm Gladwell's 10,000-hour rule.[7] What IA does promise is you'll get better, faster, and yes, be happier in both court and life.

---

6. These "3Cs," meaning coherent, complete, and correct, are propounded by Thomas V. Morris in *Philosophy for Dummies* (New York, NY: Wiley, 1999), as a test to use in assessing any philosophical proposition. Ask yourself: is my position *coherent*, meaning internally consistent, is it *complete* given the universe of admissible facts, and is it *correct*? And here I don't just mean legally correct but, even more important, does it conform to community notions of morality, equity, and fair play? By the way, Dr. Morris is an internationally recognized teacher of philosophy, not just the author of a book for dummies which I found helpful. I have five additional Cs: *credibility, competence, caring,* and the two big Cs you'll later meet—*capital* and *competence.*

7. Malcolm Gladwell, *Outliers: The Story of Success* (New York, NY: Little, Brown and Co., 2008).

Today our profession is much more open about our many mental health challenges, including substance abuse, depression, anxiety, and suicide. Mindfulness, meditation, and therapy are now welcome career companions.

Most trial advocacy teachings begin and end at the courtroom door with the focus on skills, like tools in a toolbox. IA starts with you exactly as you are, as a whole person, right now, where you're at. You'll probably chafe at some of my suggestions; that's good. Test them for yourself. Better yet, modify IA to fit you where you're at right now. In the process, you'll be personalizing and internalizing IA and thus making it authentically yours.

Mediation is consuming the field, resulting in an ever-widening experience gap between generations. Many excellent jury trial lawyers have become judges or mediators, and some of the best trial judges retire early to mediate. Insurance companies ultimately determine which cases go to court by how much they're willing to pay to settle. Obviously, they only try the cases they are confident they will win. That's why health-care defendants win about five out of six of the cases that actually go to trial. This leaves judges and juries with the false impression that plaintiffs' lawsuits are almost always of dubious merit. This then tends to become a self-fulfilling prophecy, making it even more difficult for plaintiffs' lawyers to win cases.

The right to a jury trial is worth no more than the competence of the lawyers and judges involved. It is no exaggeration to say that previous generations have died to protect the fifth, sixth, and seventh Amendments.

We American trial lawyers are educated and socially empowered. We have the tools to improve ourselves, our profession, our nation, and, indeed, the world. Society needs a serious commitment from each of us in order to have a community of highly functioning lawyers. This book is intended to be a catalyst to that end.

Conclusion

IA is about you and your commitment to personal and professional growth. Don't embrace IA just because it flatters our profession; do it because it's good for you as a spouse, parent, partner, person, and, yes, lawyer. That, my friend, is much larger and more important than just your courtroom win–loss record.

Growth involves embracing change, refining your skills and increasing your potential. Resilience is your ability to recover from setback and turn adversity into another (often well-hidden) growth opportunity. Strength emanates from within and, when wedded to values, will become a powerful force in your life.

2

Being a Jury Trial Lawyer

The Challenges of a Courtroom Career

Integrated Advocacy (IA) speaks to the predictable challenges all jury trial lawyers face over the course of their professional lives. Everyone's career starts from different places, criminal prosecuting or defending, big firm or small firm, or hanging out your own shingle. I can identify multiple enduring challenges in a jury trial lawyer's career.[1] We begin with the reality that it's a saturated job market.

For better or worse, you have to start practicing law somewhere. It can take time to find a good landing place. Hanging out your own shingle includes generating paying work (marketing), meeting the monthly overhead, having enough to eat, and repaying your student

---

1. Not everyone experiences all of these challenges or in the order presented, and some will overlap—such as the unending challenges of work and family.

loans. You will take any paying work that walks through your door. In the early years, there are often divorces and job changes. Challenges include having an overwhelming workload, financial problems, stress, a bad fit in the nature of the work or the people involved—you name it. Look for work that's satisfying, not perfect, mind you, but feels like a decent fit for you.

Gaining competence and confidence takes time. To help clinically jump start you, I offer a working pretrial checklist that includes common mistakes attorneys make and offers suggestions about what excellence in those situations looks like. I've also included the table of contents to a trial notebook.

It's challenging to maintain a healthy separation from our work with the ubiquitous presence of cell phones, email, and technology. After the pandemic, with more of us working remotely, it's now called a work–life "blend" rather than a "balance." Something gained, and something lost.

Throughout your career, you'll face the enduring problem of combining work responsibilities with family (in all its many and diverse expressions), it eases a bit once the children are in school, but it continues until they leave home, and sometimes—take a deep breath—it never seems to end.

You can't escape the existential threats and challenges of losing. It's demoralizing, painful, and at its worst, debilitating. The most you can do is struggle to find your best personal answers to its unending presence. It's easy to slide into pessimism and cynicism, which can lead to depression, career burnout, an early exit from the courtroom, and maybe even the practice of law. I've dedicated an entire chapter on losing with suggestions on how to frame and deal with it.

When I talk privately with some of my boot campers, they're concerned about their student loans, marriage or sustained partnerships, whether to have children and if so when and how many, and how they will ever afford the down payment on a home—and yes, even with two working persons in their relationship. The idea of retirement is so far down the road, it's hardly ever mentioned.

Even if you become (financially) "successful," there are new and different challenges. You will find your deepest fears and insecurities are still with you, just in new costumes. It's also guaranteed that you can never get enough of whatever you hunger for. I discuss the challenges of success, its various expressions, knowing the difference between want and need, and offer my recommendations for how to best deal with it.

Either you grow and seek therapy to improve your mental health, self-awareness, and self-mastery as reflected in the choices you make, or you will slide into a life dominated by your insatiable neurotic needs.

My Own Journey

We all know that jury trial work is demanding and stressful, no news there! I've found being a spouse and parent to be almost as challenging, albeit in different ways. Long before I entered the courtroom, I wanted to marry, have a family, and do my best to love and be loved. At times, it felt like I was being drawn and quartered from the competing demands of family and work. I had one foot in both family and work, and I was falling short in both. This is separate from my efforts to run my law business, obtain paying legal work, contribute to professional organizations, get in a daily workout, and yes, occasionally do a little pro bono work. I've had multiple bouts of helpful therapy along the way.

On the personal side, I married in 1974. My wife had a three-year-old daughter, Monique, whom I eagerly adopted. In 1976 we had our second daughter, Almine, and in 1980 we had our third child, a boy we named Brent.

I think of my life as an unending dance; sometimes the music is fast, and other times it's faster. It's an alloy of the demands of work and family, and, beneath it all, something called life. The biggest challenges for me were:

1. Balancing work and family.
2. Learning to love this job without being devoured by it; stated a little differently, "I wanted to run my job, instead of it running me."
3. Coping with losing trials.
4. Paying the bills, that is, the economics of running a profitable law business.

In chapter 5, I invite you to generate both a life and career narrative, and encourage you to view your work as a hero(ine)'s journey. The chapter closes with how to write a private obituary you would like to be worthy of.

I've often had many loud voices in my head, pulling me in opposite directions. In the chapter on losing, I do my best to give full expression to the cacophony of voices that tormented me in successive stages of my career. If you could have peeked inside of my head, you would have thought there was a riot going on, and you would have been correct.

Let's start with the stuff that keeps us up at night. We're all a bundle of inconsistencies, brilliance, stupidity, vanity, insecurities, bravery, cowardice, vision, and blindness. Our drive to succeed or win is often strongly fueled by a desire not to lose or embarrass ourselves. This includes being seen as a failure in the eyes of our clients and significant others, resulting in guilt, shame, and feelings of inadequacy. Yes, we tend to be perfectionists. There's nothing like a little sublimated insecurity! Learning to honestly confront these inner fears, in their many expressions, is difficult and painful for all of us.

What Are Your Deepest Values?

As an oversimplified exercise in identifying your personal values and priorities, take a sheet of paper and draw a large circle that represents your life.[2] Then within this life circle, draw three smaller circles. One for your career, family,[3] and a third for you. You can add additional smaller ones—which will vary from lawyer to lawyer and at different times of your life—such as church, community, pro bono work, hobbies, or what have you. Between the work and family circles, which is the biggest? What is the most important, and is there a difference? Why? Will the circles' sizes and content change over time? Of course.

If you're starting out on your own, it's overwhelming just to meet the monthly overhead. Also, there's a big difference between one, two, or three children and whether they're babies, toddlers, or school age. I'm not asking what's most important on any given day, week, or month. I know when you're in court, trial is always the priority. When you're dashing between the demands of work and family, the first thing that usually goes is your sleep. It's hard trying to double- and triple-task and do any of it well.

My work and family were both very important to me; however, on a long-term forced choice, I put my family first. Maybe it would be more accurate to say I tried to place it first. For a different perspective and choice, see Gerry Spence's "The High Price of Success," where he agrees he chose work over family.[4]

---

2. The work you do here is the first step in constructing your life story and aspirational obituary. We will continue this effort in chapter 5, "Constructing Your Life Story."

3. I appreciate that many of today's lawyers may not be interested in marriage or children. That certainly removes an element I chose to accept. However, family can mean different things today. We can add stepchildren, and yes, aging parents. Times are a'changin, and nothing is static.

4. Gerry Spence, "The High Price of Success," *Be Who You Are* (Portland, OR: Trial Guides, 2014), DVD. This is a wonderful DVD. I admire Gerry for his honesty.

Parenting Insights

I'm going to presumptuously offer a few suggestions on parenting:

1. When my kids were younger and I was in trial, I explained to them that for the time being it had to be about the "quality of my time with them, not the quantity." They seemed to understand, or at least I wanted to believe they did.
2. When I was with my children, I did my best to be 100 percent present and not let my mind wander and start thinking about tomorrow's closing argument. I did my best to not be in two places at the same time. This means I turned my cell phone off, or better yet, not only turned it off, but left it in another room. When I was in trial, I focused on my immediate task at hand—yes, even if my kid was sick at home. Hard to do? Absolutely. Impossible? We all know that all you can do is the best you can do.
3. As often as possible, I tucked my kids into bed at night. This might mean I had to get up at three or four on a Monday morning if I was trying a case out of town.
4. I planned ahead for my kids and my family. I looked around the corners of each day, week, and month. Where could I create opportunities or windows I could set aside just for my family? Maybe it was a special evening every week or two, or a weekend, or a holiday. If you don't plan, then it's not going to happen. That's just how life works—particularly for busy trial lawyers.
5. When school was out, I took my family to the seminars I attended. If school was in session, occasionally I would take one of my three kids on the road with me. We treated it as an adventure, and yes, we did our schoolwork in airports, on airplanes, and on the road. Looking back, the trips were great fun. New York and San Francisco look different through the eyes of a teenager.

Try to Learn to Love This Work

For me, loving this job was easy; my problem was not letting it devour me. During the difficult times, it helped me to remember what initially prompted me to want to be a trial lawyer. Reflect on why you have chosen this difficult, stressful, and demanding job. Let me share my many overlapping motivations:

1. **I am a shepherd.** It is my *raison d'être*. I was parentified when I was ten years old. I'm still a natural "fixer" for everyone around me. I have to fight the urge to become a human life raft. I enjoy helping people. It's in my DNA.
2. **Creativity.** I enjoy the process of generating trial themes, stories, demonstrative exhibits, and organizing the trial proof. I see myself as a legal artist working in the medium of the law.
3. **Challenge.** The work is intense, demands all my abilities, and sometimes more!
4. **Competition.** I like it, no, I love it. Okay, I've admitted I'm an adrenaline junkie.
5. **Shaping public policy.** We're also social architects; our jury verdicts define our communities. We are legal acrobats who publicly perform with no safety nets. Policy is the macro, or large, while helping one client at a time involves the micro, or specific application of policy.
6. **Contributing.** I strive to be a grateful and serious lawyer who gives back to my profession and community. I also think of my parenting efforts to help my three kids grow up as healthy adults as one of my most important responsibilities and contributions.
7. **Camaraderie.** I enjoy the friendship of my trial lawyer allies, and yes, worthy opponents.
8. **Teaching.** I write books (such as *Recovering for Psychological Injuries*) and lecture (over 550 professional presentations) on the art and

science of our craft.⁵ Through my boot camp, I'm privileged to mentor future legal generations. I am old, white, and yesterday; they are young, diverse, and tomorrow. I strive to be a "transgenerational keeper of the meaning,"⁶ aka to pay it forward.

9. **Philanthropy.** I can fund a moral legacy, Yakona.⁷ My wife, JoAnn, and I married later in life, and this nature preserve and learning center is the child we never had. It's a 400-plus-acre unfenced sanctuary dedicated to nature, education, and wildlife (elk, three bears, deer, a cougar, and many bobcat) and is located across the bay from our home in Newport, Oregon (population 10,000). Check out our website, yakonaoregon.org. If you ever visit the central Oregon coast, we provide guided tours. It's kid and family friendly.

10. **This job forces me to grow.** Like a Zen warrior who honors his opponents, I see opposing counsel as my whet stones; they force me to be at my very best. My son and I tried a birth trauma case in which the first table had the best defense lawyer in America, the second table had the best in the Northwest, and in the back was the best in Oregon. I am grateful to each of them. Thank you, they are and were a gift. By the way, we lost. I will appeal, reverse the judgment, and win it next time.

11. **Passion and purpose.** I hope the way I embrace the challenges of my work is a good example for my children, boot campers, and the next generation.

Generate your own list, knowing it will morph as you grow.

---

5. William A. Barton, *Recovering for Psychological Injuries*, 3rd ed. (Portland, OR: Trial Guides and AAJ Press, 2010).

6. George E. Vaillant, *Aging Well: Surprising Guideposts to a Happier Life from the Landmark Study of Adult Development* (New York: Little, Brown Spark, 2008), chapter 5. This chapter is one of my favorites.

7. Yakona, www.yakonaoregon.org.

The Honorable Oliver Wendell Holmes, Jr.

Getting to really know the "great dissenter" from the inside out with the benefit of professional acting coach Tom Capps has been a unique growth opportunity.[8] His passion for life and career inspires me. I also appreciate his deep insights into the law and the important role we lawyers play in it.

The following are quotes from speeches and writings by Justice Holmes on his views of what commends the practice of law. As the overlord of the American common law, he knew the road to justice was always under construction. "…he was at once an artist, expressing the spirit of the common law—and a scientist describing its slow evolution."[9] All the quotes are from the 1880s and 1890s so it speaks in the masculine, but again it's the ideas behind the words.

> *How can the laborious study of a dry and technical system, the greedy watch for clients and practice of shopkeepers' arts, the mannerless conflicts over often sordid interests, make out a life?*[10]

> *Of course, the law is not the place for the artist or the poet. The law is the calling of thinkers.*[11]

> *A man may live greatly in the law as well as elsewhere, that there as well as elsewhere his thought may find its unity in an infinite perspective, that there as well as elsewhere he may wreak himself*

---

8. William Barton and Tom Capps, "What Tom Capps Has Taught Me About Effective Communication," *Litigation Journal* 36, no.1 (2017): 1–4.

9. Sheldon M. Novick, *Honorable Justice: The Life of Oliver Wendell Holmes* (Boston, MA: Little, Brown and Company, 1989), 172.

10. Oliver Wendell Holmes, Jr., *Collected Legal Papers* (New York: Harcourt, Brace and Co., 1921), 29. "The Profession of the Law." From the conclusion of a lecture delivered to undergraduates of Harvard University, February 17, 1886.

11. *Id.*, 29-30.

upon life, may drink the bitter cup of heroism, may wear his heart out after the unattainable.[12]

Your business as thinkers is to make plainer the way from some thing to the whole of things; to show the rational connection between your fact and the frame of the universe.[13]

Do not think I am pointing you to flowery paths and beds of roses—to a place where brilliant results attend your work, which shall be at once easy and new. No result is easy which is worth having.[14]

For I say to you in all sadness of conviction, that to think great thoughts you must be heroes as well as idealists.[15]

He should be passionate, as well as reasonable—that he should be able to not only to explain, but to feel; that the ardors of intellectual pursuit should be relieved by the charms of art, should be succeeded by the joy of life become an end in itself.[16]

Not mathematical formulas having their essence in their form; [but] organic living institutions transplanted from English soil. Their significance is vital not formal: it is to be gathered not simply by taking the words and a dictionary, but by considering their origin and their line of growth.[17]

I have said that the best part of our education is moral.[18]

---

12. *Id.*, 30.
13. *Id.*, 30.
14. *Id.*, 31.
15. *Id.*, 32.
16. *Id.*, 48. "The Use of Law Schools." Oration before the Harvard Law School Association at Cambridge, November 5, 1886.
17. *Gompers v. United States*, 233 U.S. 605. (1914).
18. Oliver Wendell Holmes, Jr., *Collected Legal Papers*, 48. "The Use of Law Schools."

The law is the witness and the external deposit of our moral life. Its history is the history of the moral development of the race.[19]

And so the eternal procession moves on, we in the front for the moment; and, stretching away against the unattainable sky, the black spearheads of the army that has been passing in unbroken line already for near a thousand years.[20]

We all want happiness. And happiness, I am sure from having known many successful men, cannot be won simply by being counsel for great corporations and having an income of fifty thousand dollars. An intellect great enough to win the prize needs other food besides success. The remoter and more general aspects of the law are those which give it universal interest. It is through them that you not only become a great master in your calling, but connect your subject with the universe and catch an echo of the infinite, a glimpse of its unfathomable process, a hint of the universal law.[21]

It is proper to study it as an exercise in the morphology and transformation of human ideas. The study pursued for such ends becomes science in the strictest sense. Who could fail to be interested in the transition through the priest's test of truth, the miracle of the ordeal, and the soldier's, the battle of the duel, to the democratic verdict of the jury.[22]

I doubt if there is any more exalted form of life than that of a great abstract thinker, wrapt in the successful study of problems to which he devotes himself, for an end which is neither unselfish nor selfish in the

---

19. Oliver Wendell Holmes, Jr., *Harvard Law Review* 10, no. 8 (Mar. 25, 1897): 459.

20. Oliver Wendell Holmes, Jr., *Collected Legal Papers* (New York: Harcourt, Brace and Co., 1921), 140. "Learning and Science." Speech at a dinner of the Harvard Law School Association, June 15, 1895.

21. *Id.*, 202. "The Path of the Law." An address given at the dedication of the new hall of the Boston University School of Law, January 8, 1897.

22. *Id.*, 212.

common sense of those words, but is simply to feed the deepest hunger and to use the greatest gifts of his soul.[23]

After all the place for a man who is complete in all his powers is in the fight. The professor, the man of letters, gives up one-half of life that his protected talent may grow and flower in peace. But to make up your mind at your peril upon a living question, for purposes of action, calls upon your whole nature.[24]

A Pulitzer Prize winning book, *The Metaphysical Club*,[25] presents Holmes and his contemporaries' contributions to American values, moral philosophy, pragmatism, and legal realism.

To Be a Better Lawyer, Become a Better Person

A core tenet of IA is that the best way to be a better lawyer is to become a better person. My friend Rick Friedman says it well:

> Here is the hard lesson no one wants to hear: If you are going to be the best trial lawyer you can be, you have to strive to be the best *person* you can be. You have to strive for this inside and outside the courtroom, twenty-four hours a day. It is true that some bad people get good results as trial lawyers; they would get better results if they were better people.[26]

Does tucking my child into bed have anything to do with improving my personhood? Does family time provide me with empathy and understanding in a case involving the wrongful death of a parent or child?

---

23. *Id.*, 224.
24. *Id.*, 224.
25. Louis Menand, *The Metaphysical Club* (New York: Farrar, Straus and Giroux, 2001).
26. Richard Friedman and Bill Cummings, *The Elements of Trial*, (Portland, OR: Trial Guides, 2013), 220.

You know the answer. Study and learn our craft, but along the way, refining your personhood adds to your presence. Why? Because you're speaking *heart talk* from your deepest values, and, yes, you know what it's like to cry yourself to sleep.

Learn to Nourish Yourself

If climbing the mountain is our goal, then it necessarily involves many small steps. Like a wood carver, I try to find pleasure in the many small things I do each day: each stroke of the knife shaving away the wood, each step in the long journey. I also try to take satisfaction in a task well done. I sometimes tell myself that "to do the common things uncommonly well" is virtuous. I think of this as a small but deserved pat on the back.

Suppose you lose a case. Should any amount of honor ever be available or even permissible? If so, when, and what does it look like? Personal honor after a loss sounds kind of like an excuse; however, if I "suit up, show up, and leave it all on the field," then I'm willing to allow myself a dose of honor. I've had losses in tough civil rights cases that I felt okay about. I didn't like the outcome, but I understood the problems and knew the odds going in.

It's the tough cases, the ones that are longshots where I feel the least pressure. Worrying about losing a good case, one I should win, now that's pressure! When the deck is stacked against me is when I'm loosest and at my best. I'm comfortable taking risks, and when my back is against the wall, part of me feels bolder, strangely even relaxed, and at ease.

I choose to be repetitively thankful for the privilege of being a lawyer and the opportunity to help others. I call it an "attitude of gratitude;" and it's how I strive to begin and end my days. Just a few moments of deep thanks helps. It's free, I try to be worth it, and it helps sustain me.

I urge you to thoughtfully self-nourish, both mentally and physically. Think of your body like a machine. It won't last or perform well on caffeine, alcohol, or drugs. Build in an exercise routine. Think about a hobby or interest you can escape to. When I was younger, each winter,

I picked a different aspect of jury trial, work, or a particular advocacy teacher, and dived deep into it. So much for my work-life balance, but this craft is my calling—as is my family!

Learn to Fall in Love with Your Client & Case

With each successive client, case, and trial, I consciously choose to fall in love again and again. How do I do this, sometimes getting my heart broken, and yet keep enthusiastically bouncing back? Maybe it's a little like "the challenge an actor faces when he's played Romeo 384 times before, and for this matinee performance, when he wakes up next to Juliet, he needs to really experience her, again, as dead for the first time, again!"[27]

I work to find some aspect of the case, or my client, that touches me deeply, that resonates with me and allows me to go all in. Not blind love, mind you, but a serious, measured, and deep respect for a carefully selected feature of my client or case. Every client deserves this effort, and if you can't find something you can love, then maybe you haven't looked long enough or hard enough. I dig until I find something, however well-hidden. It's an important part of my job.

If you want to have one love (client), then become an in-house counsel. Each successive client and love affair stands on its own. Sometimes committing to a client or case is easy, such as in sexual exploitation cases. The problem is becoming deeply immersed while maintaining professional boundaries; and if you do lose, then somehow healing quickly enough that you can start another case—tomorrow morning.

Let me give you an example: I had a client named Spencer in a wrongful death case that had to do with a fairly minor impact and soft tissue injury, after which my client took his life. There wasn't much to commend Spencer; he had failed at about everything he'd ever tried. For example, he failed at the military, at being a husband, at being a father, and he wasn't very smart. He'd been fired from multiple jobs:

---

27. Michael Leizerman, *The Zen Lawyer: Winning with Mindfulness* (Portland, OR: Trial Guides, 2018), 68–69.

not for being late or stealing tools or misconduct, it was just that he wasn't good at much. However, he never quit. I loved that he kept trying, coming back to work, one job after another, again and again, and always doing his best. It was an honorable slice of his character.

Embracing the Long View

Part of mental health is gaining the perspective that flows from embracing a long view of life, and yes, history. Sometimes, the only way that I can make sense out of a loss is to step back, way back, and try to see myself as part of a much bigger, longer process, a societal journey called our American common law. We're all just drops of rain in life's storm, part of history's long march towards a more just world. It's an intensely personal, and yet highly public trek. Progress is rarely a straight line. The road to justice is always under construction. I don't win them all, but I try. My enduring consolation is I've had the privilege of being a lawyer, trying to help people, and participating in our wonderful American common law tradition. In the process, I hope the world's a little safer and better place.

Have Compassion for Yourself

A long, variegated view of life provides balance, but it's not as simple as a pill you can take. When I was younger, every case was a world war, and the losses were devastating. I would never be as hard on anybody else as I was on myself. It's a shitty place to be, and my fears of a failure or a loss were often as bad (or maybe even worse) than the actual loss. The unending chatter in my head was deafening. After many years, losses, bouts of therapy, trials, and reflection, I decided that I simply had to do better—or I couldn't keep going—I couldn't survive.

Now, I do my best to be emotionally centered and live mindfully. I know what the sucking gravitational pull of fear is. I've been there, and now I do my best to consciously choose a different path. I want to be the best lawyer I can be, but I also want a life, to be a good spouse and parent, to love and be loved. I know myself; I'm not lazy, and never make excuses, I'm not perfect and have never claimed to be. I always "bring it," and would never cheat or fudge to win. I don't win them all, but I really do try. That's all I've got, and it's the best I can do, so I've come to not just live with this realization, but to embrace it. Later we'll talk about focusing on the process rather than the result, your effort rather than the outcome. This doesn't eliminate the pain of losing, but in the Buddhist tradition it helps reduce the suffering.

When I lose, I mindfully engage in best practices, carefully deconstruct the loss, administer myself a small dose of compassion, and of course always make sure I'm there for my client. I appreciate the confidence they showed in me, and I try to be worth it. But now I also choose to be kind to myself. I refuse to destructively choose to be loyal to my personal martyrdom. I can do better; I must do better, ultimately I have no choice.

What Does Your "Best" Really Mean?

This is another slice of an honest and healthy perspective that leads to some self-compassion. Life forces all of us to make choices and compromises. There are only 168 hours in a week. We've all got to eat and sleep and, after these, anything we don't give to our clients is arguably a subtraction from our best. No, none of us can have it all, and I know it's convenient to say, "I did my best." I want to parse my use of the word "best." I believe my honest best, in reality, should be called my *triaged* best. Our level of commitment to anything is ultimately expressed in each of the minute to minute and hour to hour choices we make. I am a serious, proud lawyer, but I'm also a husband, father, and yes, person.

When thinking about doing my best, I reflect on the rock band the Byrds. In the mid-eighties, while in Bend, Oregon, I saw a sign advertising the Byrds in concert on a Thursday night. They were between shows on their way north from California to the Tacoma Dome. I couldn't believe it. The Byrds! In Bend, Oregon![28] That night there were twenty-six people in the audience. The house was all but empty.

The band came out. The lead singer, Roger McGuinn, began the show by saying, "We're the Byrds, and every night we do a better show than we've ever done before." They rocked, they rolled, and they dripped sweat. It was fantastic.

In a small town with barely two dozen paying customers, they put on a show I'll never forget. They taught me something about what it means to be a true professional, regardless of the size of my case. If I have trouble getting motivated in a smaller case, I think of the Byrds playing for twenty-six customers. I might even pause and play one of their albums. When I'm through, it's easy to remember that I, too, am a professional and in every one of my trials, no matter its size, I do my (triaged) best. This commitment has many headwaters. No matter how big or small the case, to my client it might be the most important thing in their life. I accept this responsibility, but there's more, a lot more. It's also my pride. I'm the attorney of record, my name's on it, and I'm bringing it.

Control Your Emotions or They'll Control You

Our job is to be persuasive, and that begins with caring for my client and being passionate about their case. See David Ball's discussion on premature advocacy when we start expressing our opinions before first building credibility.[29] See also Gerry Spence's discussion on the importance of channeling our anger.[30] That's why our craft is a learned

---

28. In 1980, Bend, Oregon, had a population of about sixty thousand.

29. David Ball, *David Ball on Damages*, 3rd ed. (Portland, OR: Trial Guides, 2012), chapter 5, "Premature Advocacy," 111, "Inability to control one's advocacy urge long enough to avoid a disappointing outcome."

30. Gerry Spence, *Win Your Case: How to Present, Persuade, and Prevail—Every Place, Every Time* (New York, NY: St. Martin's Press, 2005), chapter 6, "The Dangerous Power of Anger," 61–65.

one. When it comes to expressing emotions in jury trials, like spices—season lightly. I think of Contac cold medicine with its time-released capsules. Jury trials demand you navigate a cluster of paradoxes and dualisms. Here are a few of the more obvious:

1. If you want the jury to listen to you in closing, then you first must listen to them during jury selection. It's a kind of social contract.
2. Of course you should show you care for your client, but don't be over the top. This occurs if it appears to the jurors that you're trying to play on their emotions, or maybe you're so patriotic that you have lost your objectivity and, thus, your credibility.
3. Don't be ashamed of your compassion; show it, just be measured and circumspect. Practice in front of a mirror or video. You will be impressed with the poise and emotional self-control that comes from watching yourself. Think of this as emotional "cross-training." It's okay to pause, close your eyes, draw a deep breath, and then slowly continue.
4. You must emotionally be all in, yet a part of you must remain detached and objective. You are responsible for maintaining professional boundaries. You owe it not just to yourself, but even more to your client.
5. Our instincts are to protect our clients, but we do that best not by "shielding" them, but instead by preparing them for the rigors of trial. Then they're no longer victims.
6. You must be real and authentic, but you can't express your personal opinions; it's legally unethical.
7. You must vigorously represent your client, yet paradoxically it's ineffective to make the case about the plaintiff. Being effective starts with the counterintuitive reality that you should make the case about the defendant and their choices. Heuristics, including the plaintiff's comparative fault, whether formally pled or not, include defensive attribution (the jurors saying to themselves, "I would never have …") and counterfactual reasoning ("If only the plaintiff hadn't …").
8. The commandment to be yourself is only partially true. Give voice just to your best, what Lincoln called our "better angels."

9. The harder you argue the more jurors resist; it's called the paradox of persuasion. Don't tell the jurors what to think. Instead share, use non-directive analogies and stories, all of which invite the juries in.
10. You want to energetically represent your client, but be cautious of "premature advocacy," meaning arguing too early, before you've earned credibility.
11. You want to be clear yet also allow the jurors to discover your final point or ultimate conclusion on their own. Why? Because then it is their idea and they will defend it later during jury deliberations. This is a fine line.
12. If you really want to be heard, don't raise your voice. Instead, lower it. Maintain eye contact and speak slowly while closing the distance between you and the jurors. Linger in the pauses; the silence can be deafening!
13. Don't treat kind in kind. View an opponent's bad manners as an (unwelcome) opportunity. The worse they get, the better you should become. If it's unethical then invite the judge's attention, just be measured and specific.
14. Less is more: be *accurate*, *brief*, and *clear* (ABC). Don't waste anyone's time. It's always quality over quantity.
15. If you're doing your job well, you shouldn't receive many complaints. Why? Because when you're at your best the merits of your case should be so obvious that observers will believe any law student could have won it!

Here are techniques for tempering my enthusiasm for my clients and cases:

1. I emphasize step four of David Ball's opening statement formula, where he anticipates and undermines the opponents' best facts and arguments.[31] This forces me to surgically analyze the biggest problems with my case (meaning my opponent's strengths) and the viability of my best responses.

---

31. David Ball, *David Ball on Damages*, 145–148. S*ee also* Keith Mitnik's *Don't Eat the Bruises*.

2. The next step is to focus group my case, remembering that I'm supposed to lose the first effort because that's when I seek to learn about my problems. Later focus groups are where I test my potential responses.
3. Write a thoughtful and strongly worded informed consent letter to your client, discussing all the problems and downsides of turning down a settlement and/or going to trial. Don't confuse patriotism with legal effectiveness. There are two sides to every lawsuit; otherwise, there wouldn't be a trial.
4. Use psychodrama with its role reversal to help you develop a better understanding of your opponent's perspectives.

You're not going to be very happy or last very long in this job if you're an undisciplined emotional hemophiliac. Remember earlier, I discussed the aspects of our work that are stressful. Even as I write this, a big part of me resists any discussion of detachment. Why? Because it feels good to be all in. It means I care and yes, I'm alive! I get it. However, even though part of me feels disloyal for doing this, I force myself to step back and impose emotional boundaries. I read about Gerry Spence's admitted complete and total identification with his clients and wonder if I'm less of a lawyer because I choose to temper my enthusiasm. I know the level of commitment I would want from my lawyer if I was a client, it's 100 percent-plus. Clients feed off our patriotism. It's what they want to see and hear! However, we're the professional, not the client.

Identify & Reduce Your Self-Marginalizing Behaviors

Whatever your personal weaknesses, this job will find them, guaranteed. If you're unhappy at home, it's easy to escape to the demands of work. Responsibilities are always there, like a siren, beckoning and calling. This can conveniently be interpreted as an honorable discharge allowing us to duck our familial responsibilities—without too much guilt.

My enduring hope, as a person and lawyer, is not to repeat the same mistake twice, albeit in a different form. The difficulty is identifying our destructive habits and resulting behaviors in all their permutations. We tend to misinterpret enduring problems by viewing each of their splintered expressions as something new and different. We need to see both the forest and the trees.

It's easy to see the warts on others, rather than ourselves. It's called denial and rationalizing, particularly when scrutinizing the qualities we view as strengths. Pause, take a big step back, and reflect upon your habits. How can something good be better? Ask others. Continue to refine and reframe the question, keeping a bull's-eye on how you may be coauthoring your own problems. Continue to ask yourself if you can have too much of a good thing, and if so, what it might look like.

Here's where keeping a personal journal and therapy helps. We all naturally grade ourselves on a preferential curve. Share with your spouse or partner. Talk a little and listen a lot.

Identify Emotional Fatigue

Let's start with the reality of career burnout. Yes, we must learn to walk a mile in our clients' shoes; however, the cumulative effect upon us can be devastating.[32] This is another aspect of loving our work, yet somehow not being consumed by it. We suffer a secondary wounding as a result of vicariously experiencing our clients' traumas. On direct exam, we encourage our clients to speak in first person and testify as if the event is happening now. We have front row seats to the reliving of incest, child rape, abuse, violence, and death. In addition to secondary trauma, mental health professionals have identified compassion fatigue as something we also suffer from.[33]

---

32. Hallie Neuman Love. "Lawyers Are at Risk for Secondary Traumatic Stress," *Bar Bulletin* 56, no. 7 (February 15, 2017): 8-10.

33. *See* "Compassion Fatigue," ABA Commission on Lawyer Assistance Programs, https://www.americanbar.org/groups/lawyer_assistance/resources/compassion_fatigue.html.

To help minimize compassion fatigue, reflect upon the distinction between compassion and empathy. Compassion is a concern for the suffering of others and taking some steps to alleviate it. Empathy, on the other hand, is stepping into the shoes of another and truly understanding their plight. It's important to remind yourself that while you care—no—love your client, you are not your client. You need to be able to have both compassion and empathy.

Maintaining a separate identity allows you to function at a higher level while minimizing your own trauma. This is central to our self-care responsibilities.[34] I know being able to share from the inside out with my wife and son, who is my law partner, eases my load.

Learn to Delegate

Delegation is an acquired skill and is rarely available when you're starting out. You almost certainly have more time than money. Consider hiring law students for legal research projects or indexing depositions. It's win-win. The clerks are learning and you're creating time for yourself. Delegating actually creates time. When you assign work, what you do with the time you create for yourself is an important choice. Adding to the size of your firm through associates and paralegals can create time, but most of us continue to work just as hard; after all, now you have to generate more paying work to fund the additions, not to mention the increased administrative responsibilities.

I've never aspired to be big, only good. If I were a clockmaker, I'd have no interest in manufacturing one hundred clocks. Instead, I'd want to build one beautiful cuckoo clock that, on every hour and half hour, would have a small exotic bird exit its beautiful house and chime the correct number of cuckoos, in exactly the right note. I want to be a legal craftsman. Success will allow you to focus on what you enjoy most and delegate what you like least. I've outsourced lots of work during

---

34. Jeena Cho, "A Distressing Business," *ABA Journal* 104, no. 6 (2018): 28–29, https://search.informit.org/doi/10.3316/agispt.20190605011680.

my career, paid well, and received excellent services. I've never believed I could afford a bargain; they are too expensive!

I've met a few immensely talented trial lawyers who appear to be constitutionally incapable of delegating. Maybe it's because they are perfectionists, too cheap, or so smart they think no one can equal the quality of their work. I'm not that smart, but delegation is key to me running my practice, instead of it running me. My clients deserve excellent representation. However, it doesn't have to be only from me, even though I'm responsible for it.

Be Careful of Your Pride & Arrogance

Be cautious about the emotional arrogance that can creep in if we gradually become pious, condescending, morally sanctimonious, or too confident. In what ways, in your practice and life, are you too sure of your own importance? Do you always have to be right, and how does that impact your personal and professional relationships? The problem is not a strong ego—we have to have one to do our jobs—the problem is a big ego. I strive to project a measured optimism. After all, if I don't believe in my case, then why should the jurors? Yes, I might be wrong, but I'm not in doubt, at least not publicly.

Trust the Jury System

If you want the jury to trust you, then you've got to trust them. Seriously, we're totally vulnerable. When we hand our case and client over to twelve jurors, at the end of the day, we may find ourselves rejected—again. How lousy does that feel? I sometimes mutter to myself that it's better to have loved and lost than to have never loved at all. To me, this vulnerability is part of the necessary "buy-in." The alternative is the work of a sterile, impoverished technician. One who has never lived.

Work to Win Gracefully

Win or lose, IA insists on professionalism—and yes, there are also best practices when winning. I served on my state's nominating committee for the American College of Trial Lawyers. We heard lots of complaints about rejected nominees for being bad losers, however, it gave me a lot to think about when I heard a litany of complaints about a fellow plaintiffs' lawyer being a bad winner.

Now, if I win, I don't bad-mouth my opponent, and to the extent possible, I speak their praises. Why? Because it doesn't say much for my success if they were so bad. Besides, gloating after a favorable verdict distracts me from working on the inevitable defense motions for a new trial, motion JNOV (judgment notwithstanding the verdict), hearings on appeal bonds, and whatever else clever opponents who are paid by the hour can dream up.

I also make an assumption most of my fellow plaintiffs' lawyers reject. It's that if I win, I presume (I'm sure often incorrectly) that the opposing lawyer emotionally suffers as much as I would if I'd lost. I further accept that my opponents are as passionate about their clients and trials as I am about mine. All clients, no matter which side of the table they are on, deserve this. Why do I make this (probably false) assumption? Because it helps me to be a gracious winner.

When I lose a major case, I force myself to buy my opponent a gift of seafood from Newport. I am the only one I know who so conspicuously honors their opponents. Is it easy? I hope not! Maybe you're like some of my uber talented friends and need to be opposite the devil in order to be at the top of your game, or perhaps you view my purchase of gifts as an obsequious sign of weakness. I speak only for myself, but it's an idea for you to consider. Personally, I submit it's the height of professionalism.

A significant portion of my case inventory involves referrals from prior opposing counsel. I take this as a compliment, and of course, it's an effect of IA, not a cause. I (try to) do the right thing, including professionally treating them better than they may deserve (buying them seafood) for the right reason—because it reflects the best of my ever evolving self.

Conclusion: Am I a Success?

Now that I've written about navigating the work-life balance, full disclosure requires I reveal that the eighteen-year marriage with my children's mother ended in divorce. There are no guarantees in court or life. Philosopher Cornel West says, "I am a prisoner of hope,"[35] as am I. So, am I a success or failure? It's almost certainly some of both.

---

35. Sewell Chan, "Cornel West Says U.S. Democracy Is in Crisis," *The Harvard Crimson* (June 8, 1995), www.thecrimson.com/article/1995/6/8/cornel-west-says-us-democracy-is.

3

Thoughts on Losing & Best Practices after a Loss

I've struggled with how to present my thoughts on the difficult topic of losing in our work. I've rewritten this chapter many times, trying to fully capture the emotional realities of our jobs. My thoughts are necessarily autobiographical, so you'll find a lot of first person. I can't help it. This is my professional and life journey, not just from the outside in, but even more from the inside out. I suspect the only thing unusual in my journey is the number of cases I've tried, my willingness to supplement the advice of my mentors with insights from psychology, philosophy, and various wisdom traditions, and the extent of my honesty.

I hope to offer you suggestions on how to maintain your enthusiasm and commitment to growth, all while getting hammered by your opponent. This chapter unfolds like my career, with many lessons building on those before. In order to sustain your passion while enjoying your work, you'll need to be prepared for many on-the-job self-repairs in real time. As they say, it's difficult to drain the swamp when you're up to your ass in alligators. Applying best practices when you lose not only reduces the risk of future losses, but also helps keep the emotional wake of a present loss to more manageable levels.

Our profession and culture worship success. We all aspire to be winners, and in a saturated legal profession with its demands of self-promotion and marketing, we must forever present ourselves to the world in the most positive light. Social media guarantees we're all victims of the "cancer of comparison."[1]

My role models all told me losing a case made them feel like a part of them died, and the fear of a future loss motivated them to work even harder today to avoid the pain of a loss tomorrow. I get it. This was my starting point. I've come to more fully appreciate that I will not die, even though a part of me feels that way. The pain of losing is roughly proportionate to my emotional vulnerability; however, as my career has lengthened, I've come to better appreciate that I am not my client. I've also come to appreciate that perfection is a seductive myth that just messes with my head.

This is a long chapter dedicated to losing—strange! But it's certainly been one of my two greatest inner struggles, the other being money. If you want to learn where I'm at today, you can go straight to the conclusion of this chapter. I don't claim to have your answer, just mine, but I suspect our paths will be similar enough that there is real value in retracing my steps. Note, I didn't say mimicking them; just stepping back and asking if you can see any of yourself in my journey.

Losses are daggers to my heart, self-esteem, and ego. I accepted their cases, signed the complaints, developed the proof, and delivered the arguments. Their cases were and still are an extension of me. I was emotionally "all in." I believed in my clients and cases then, and I still do—I should have won! The losses feel like a damning referendum on my competence, judgment, and, indeed, my very self. Jury trials are very public high-wire acts—with no emotional safety nets.

---

1. Rick Friedman, *Becoming a Trial Lawyer: A Guide for the Lifelong Advocate*, 2nd ed. (Portland OR: Trial Guides, 2015).

Viewing losses as unwelcome growth opportunities, while difficult, is a lot smarter than whining and looking for causes outside yourself. You'll do a better job in screening and analyzing future cases, as well as trying the ones you accept. Why? Because you will have learned from your prior mistakes. This is good for you, your future clients, the profession, and society. The system will be working better because you are operating more effectively. The more you win, the less your opponents will want to see you in court again. Success builds on success; it's an ascending helix.

As famous trial lawyer Edward Bennett Williams said, "The lawyer who never loses a case is a myth made for television."[2] Perfection is a fiction; there's no such thing as an exactly straight line. I give myself permission to do my triaged best and know that, as a practical matter, that's really all I have to offer or sell.

During my first ten years, I defended many DUIs, one-day criminal misdemeanors, and domestic relations. I had lots of practice losing. I remember a couple of child custody fights in divorces that really hurt. After five years I got ulcers.[3] I then shifted to plaintiffs' personal injury contingency fee work where the competition was better, the trials were longer, and when I lost, not only did I not get paid for my time and effort, but I also was out all my hard-earned costs advanced (it felt like throwing good money after bad), and even if I won, there were often lengthy appeals. My *Goddard* bad faith decision involved seven appeals and took twenty-one years.[4]

In this chapter, I chronicle my convoluted path. I share this poem because it communicates the idea that the insights and perspective I'm offering today are the result of my fifty-plus year professional journey:

---

2. Evan Thomas, *The Man to See* (New York, NY: Simon & Schuster, 1992), a biography of famous Washington trial lawyer Edward Bennett Williams.

3. I would have never, ever dreamed that I would or could have ulcers. My father's mantra was "We don't get ulcers, we give them." Well, maybe not!

4. *Goddard ex rel. Estate of Goddard v. Farmers Ins. Co. of Oregon*, 173 Or. App. 633, 22 P.3d 1224 (2001); *Goddard v. Farmers Ins. Co. of Oregon*, 202 Or. App. 79, 120 P.3d 1260 (2005); *Goddard v. Farmers Ins. Co. of Oregon*, 203 Or. App. 683, 126 P.3d 682 (2006); *Goddard v. Farmers Ins. Co. of Oregon*, 344 Or. 232, 179 P.3d 645 (2008).

> For age is an opportunity no less
> than youth itself, though in another dress
> and as the evening twilight fades away
> the sky is filled with stars, invisible by day[5]

When I was younger with a volume practice, there were a couple of times I would have a jury out deliberating in one courtroom, and down the hallway in another courtroom, I'd be picking a jury in a second trial. We would take a break in the second trial to receive the verdict in the first. Not much time to emotionally convalesce.

Pick and choose from my thoughts and offerings, and then test for yourself to find what works for you at this particular stage of your career. My suggestions aren't intended to be critical of anyone, particularly my many mentors. To each their own. A chapter on losing seems a natural sequence to the prior chapter on the embedded challenges of our work, and the difficulties balancing it with family, self, and life.

I have many inconsistent voices within me, and sometimes they're all shouting at once. I force myself to pause, slow way down, breathe slowly, and mindfully impose an inner stillness. This is all part of my learning to respond rather than react.

Effort versus Results

Let me start with my gestalt of life. To over-simplify, there are two big variables: *effort* and *results*.[6] These two components can generate four combinations:

---

5. Henry Wadsworth Longfellow, "Morituri Salutamas: Poem for the Fiftieth Anniversary Class of 1825 in Bowdoin College," 1875, https://www.poetryfoundation.org/poems/44639/morituri-salutamus-poem-for-the-fiftieth-anniversary-of-the-class-of-1825-in-bowdoin-college.

6. I have previously mentioned this core idea of effort and results in my previous book, *Recovering for Psychological Injuries* (Portland, OR: Trial Guides, 2010).

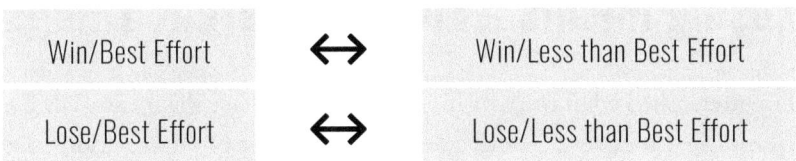

Obviously, the preferred combination is doing your best and winning; however, everyone knows we can give it our best and still lose. Or we can give less than our best, get lucky, and win. It's easy when we win, deserved or not. It's the losses that cause the ache. That's a huge reason to work hard and always try your level best. It doesn't make the pain of losing go away, but it does make it more tolerable. I respect the process, and frankly, if I don't occasionally lose, I wonder if I'm playing it too safe and am turning down deserving cases just because they might be risky or difficult. That ain't me.

To see how you view failure, think of yourself in the following ways:

1. Who you think you are,
2. Who others think you are,
3. Who you want others to think you are, and finally,
4. The real you.

The first three exist; the last doesn't, it's purely an abstraction.

Most of us have difficulty reconciling who we want to be, with who we think we really are. We want to be great, but suspect that we're not, and maybe even doubt that we deserve to be. Part of us feels scared, little, and impotent; yet we want others to see us as confident, successful, and powerful. We try desperately to reduce the difference between who we want to be and who we think we are. Sound familiar? These gaps are the stuff of insecurities and therapy. The bigger the differences, the more the insecurity.

Losing Means a Lot of Different Things

I'm often asked what my win-loss record is, or what's the most trials I've won or lost in a row. I don't keep track for a lot of good reasons. Let me explain. There are many outcomes where there's no obvious answer, such as when a client is convicted in a criminal case of a lesser included offense, but it was a major victory given their exposure. In the civil arena, maybe the insurance company offered X and the jury awarded X plus 15 percent, which covered the increase in the attorney's fee plus the costs advanced necessitated by going to trial, but is that really a win? I have tried no-offer cases, lost, and felt okay about it.

Small verdicts are obviously more tolerable when accompanied by a substantial attorney's fee award. So, what if I received a big verdict, but the insurance company appealed, and my client died during the appeal? That doesn't feel like much of a win to me. What good is a seven-figure verdict with no insurance coverage? What if you receive a nominal verdict, but create new law? A hung jury is usually a victory in a criminal case. And what about those who oppose the death penalty on principle and give it their best to the bitter end, and then their client dies of natural causes in custody?

In spite of my commitment to do my best for each client, I know there's a big difference between a misdemeanor conviction and a felony, going to prison or not, or a verdict that fully funds a life care plan for a severely injured client and one that doesn't. As I look ahead at my trial calendar, I know that not all outcomes will be equally consequential to all my clients, even though my ethical duties to each client are the same, and even though to each client, their trial may be the most important thing in their life.

Let me confess to one string of losses I later went back and counted. When I was out of law school a couple of years, there was an interval during which I lost fourteen misdemeanors in a row. This was when our local jury panels lasted for three months. No one won during that panel. Ouch!

Do a Trial Premortem

Consider shifting the time you put into autopsies of losses up earlier into your pretrial preparation. While working on a case, ask yourself, "Why might I lose?" and then ask, "How can I avoid or minimize these anticipated problems?" or, alternatively, "How can I make something good even better?" Of course, we should be doing this anyway; however, thinking about this early as a structural element forces me to prepare sooner and better, and thereby hopefully lose less.

Confront Your Fears

I try to honestly identify my fears, separate and label them, confront them, and then carefully consider my best responses. These are some of the common fears and problems we trial lawyers face:

1. I'm broke and can't afford to fully fund the experts in my next lawsuit, and I sure as hell can't pay my bills if I lose it.
2. I love my client, and I want to win the case for them—and yes, for me. They trust me and are counting on me. Now I'm scared I'm going to lose their case. Losing a good case is the worst.
3. I'm opposite a seriously talented opponent, I am just getting started and don't want to embarrass myself, let my client down, or get my ass kicked.
4. It's obvious the judge doesn't like me or my case.
5. I'm in federal court where I've never tried a case, and I just learned that my assigned judge does all the jury selection for me.

Fully giving voice to your fears doesn't make them go away, however, it does invite you to carefully plan how you can best deal with them, and the underlying problems that give rise to them. Responses might include using a focus group to identify and refine your strengths, weaknesses, trial story, and themes. Consider calling the mediator and asking for additional feedback. Or you might ask for advice from lawyers you admire, or maybe associate an experienced lawyer to help with capitalizing and trying the case. Consider alternative financing or a traditional banking institution to obtain a line of credit.

No, You're Not the Client

I offer a quote from Gregory Cusimano's article, "Becoming the Best We Can Be" (1996), published in the May 2021 edition of *Trial*:

> During those early years of being a trial lawyer, it was difficult not to measure my value by the number of cases I won on behalf of my clients.... In the process of maturing as an individual and as a lawyer, I have learned that my commitment to becoming a good trial lawyer is really the same as my commitment to achieving personal growth....
>
> Our growth as individuals becomes synonymous with our growth as lawyers because our values and behavior—what we think, feel, and do—must be congruent. If they are not, we will become anxious and frustrated.... As we work on becoming the best we can be, we lose the necessity of justifying our existence by the number of symbolic dragons we slay in the arena of the courtroom....
>
> Our work provides a tremendous challenge and satisfaction for each of us. We must learn to seek balance and harmony in all aspects of our lives.[7]

Well said.

---

7. Gregory Cusimano, "Becoming the Best We Can Be" (1996), https://alabamatort-law.com/becoming-the-best-we-can-be-1996.

Another Perspective

There are other aspects of losing that are real for me but I haven't heard others giving them voice. I didn't get to my present emotional place until after maybe thirty years and 250 to 300 jury trials. Therefore, much of what follows is probably a function of my survival instincts driven by experience.

There's a real part of me that scoffs at my worries and fears about losing. I'm not scared (or at least not very much)! I don't make excuses. Losing a well-tried case is no sin; shit happens.

Sure, going to court is stressful, but a part of me enjoys it. Besides, if this job was easy, anybody could do it. Bring it on! I've already admitted to being an adrenaline junkie. I always try to accept a case with the expectation, nay the hope, that I will actually get to try it—seriously. I know that 80 to 90 percent settle, and that's also true for our office. It's because we're eager to try our cases that we settle as many as anybody else and always receive good money when we do.

You don't need to bluster or shout. I also guarantee that, if we do try the case, we'll spend and do whatever it takes to present the case to its maximum potential. Of course, back when I did court appointments, I couldn't pick and choose my clients or cases, but to me the principle is the same. My name's on the pleadings, and I'm going to bring it—every time. That's just the way it is, and for me, the way it has to be. Whether I like my client, case, judge, or opponent, this attitude allows me to live with the ever-present reality that I might lose this case, and the next case, and then the next, and so on. I do my best to be a hardy, durable, and honorable soldier.

There are many advantages to embracing this positive, can-do, all-in attitude. Everything might be going to hell, and yes, that happens, but I'm going to continue to be as prepared and optimistic, even while a big part of me is scared to death. I'll play the hand I'm dealt as skillfully and energetically as I can; it's my job.

Optimism and pessimism are infectious and self-fulfilling, so, while much of this chapter discusses the pain and anguish I feel when I lose, the biggest part of me expects me to heal quickly if I lose. Otherwise, this loss can become a disguised prologue for the next, and I can't let that happen. I focus on what I can control, which starts with my attitude, and I'm fully responsible for that!

Have you ever seen a cornered mother bear protecting her cub? I don't care what the odds are, I promise she's snarling and showing her teeth. She will die for her offspring. Well, that's exactly how I feel. I am protecting my client, and I also know a by-product of this is that I'm maintaining my professional reputation. I may get my ass kicked, but somebody's going to have to administer it. That's just the way it has to be.

Cases come and go, but our reputations endure. Am I afraid? Yes, but my survival instincts kick in. All of a sudden, this small creature (me) is giving everything it has and yes, a part of me is ready to die if that's what it takes. I know this is sounds histrionic; however, it's my story, and I'm sticking with it!

Maybe my career has been a delusional soap opera with me as the hero. I'm sure this is partly true, and I think it is also true for some of my immensely successful friends. I get knocked down, pick myself up, brush myself off, and climb back in the ring. What doesn't kill me makes me stronger. I know this sounds like trite locker room bullshit, but it's true for me.

It's Not about Me or Even My Clients

When negotiating, I frequently remind myself it's never about me, it's only about my clients and their interests. They're the principal, and I'm the agent; however, in a larger sense, each one of my clients is the beneficiary of my reputation as a tough negotiator. I explain this during the first interview before a client ever hires me. Later, if they're ever not comfortable with my advice, then I happily will refer them to another lawyer. It hasn't happened yet, but it might… I know, in spite of my admitted pride (let's call it ego), the jury's verdict isn't supposed to be about me, and, in the largest sense, not even about my client. Morally, ethically, and philosophically, it's supposed to be about something much bigger: justice. None of us should believe in a system that isn't merit based. This means that juries should resolve legal disputes based on the facts and law rather than the emotions, sincerity, mindset, or competencies of the opposing lawyers, or which client is the most sympathetic or likeable. Justitia, the Roman goddess of justice, was blindfolded for a reason.

The Long View Perspective

Sometimes, the only way that I can make sense out of painful losses is to step back, way back, and try to see myself as part of a much bigger process, a societal journey. We're all just drops of rain in life's storm, part of a long march toward a safer, better, and more just world. It's an intensely personal and yet public trek. Our profession is involved in improving the hearts, social fabric, and laws of our communities.

I think of the first thirteen verdicts arising from Ford Explorer rollovers, which all went for the defense. Then the fourteenth resulted in a plaintiff's verdict for $23 million in noneconomic damages and $55 million in punitive damages.[8] In an early Boy Scouts child abuse case, I turned down a $1 million settlement offer with $263,000 in out-of-pocket trial expenses. The jury deliberated for six days and returned a defense verdict. I was broke, and heartbroken. Now the Boy Scouts are in bankruptcy and are facing eighty-two thousand pending claims. The common law is a shared journey for all of us, both individually and collectively. It's never a straight line. We win some, and we lose some, but we always suit up and show up. My enduring consolation is that

---

8. Ted Frank, "Rollover Economics: Arbitrary and Capricious Product Liability Regimes," *American Enterprise Institute for Public Policy Research* (January 2007): 1–2.

I've had the privilege of being a lawyer, I've done my best to help people, and in the process tried to make the world a safer and better place.

Now, back to losing…

I Feel Like I Should Suffer

When I lose, of course it's first about my clients, but it's also partially about me, about my feelings of inadequacy, guilt, and shame. My clients trusted me. I feel like I've let them down and somehow even betrayed them. It feels right and natural for me to hurt—and to hurt a lot. In a strange way, my misery feels good; it's kind of a tonic of atonement.

I have a powerful pushback when I find myself trying to emotionally insulate myself from the full pain of my losses. Why? Because a big part of me feels I should suffer, that I deserve it no matter how mighty my effort. After all, I'm responsible. It's as if, by fully embracing all of my pain, it somehow eases my guilt and shame, and maybe even my client's pain. The problem is: when and how do I let go of the misery? Martyrdom is a thorny crown, and sometimes it seems to fit better and last longer than others. There have been a couple of losses when the crown fit so tightly, I couldn't get it off for months, years, and even decades.

My clients don't have the luxury of my mind games; they're living with the full consequences of the loss. They are the ones facing destitution or prison. It was my job to protect them, to have their back, to support and advocate for them, and to do so with care, passion, commitment, and, yes, love. So, who am I now to cut and run, to compartmentalize my emotions? It feels kind of good to feel so bad, like being trapped in a downward emotional whirlpool. I don't deserve to be out, at least not until I've suffered enough, and sometimes that means a lot. There's the feeling that no matter how large or heroic my effort, at the end of the day it wasn't enough; and that's entirely on me. Like my role models all preached, maybe if I'd been even more frightened of a possible loss, then I would have worked harder and we wouldn't be in this mess. When I deconstruct my pain, it's a cacophony of many deafening voices. Some are recent, while others are almost certainly echoes of my earliest fears. It's a synthesis where one experience blends with another.

Run Directly to & through Your Pain

So, now what do I do? When I lose, I do my very best to run straight into and through my pain. I don't permit myself to run away from it. Any other approach invites me to minimize my feelings. So, what's wrong with ignoring the pain? It simply reappears in another form, such as somatic complaints, ulcers, sleepless nights, self-medicated substance abuse, angina, and even heart attacks. Now I try to actually visualize the pain passing right through me. This means it doesn't stay inside and corrode my guts. So, yes, I do try to taste and feel it, and then, with a concerted effort, I do my very best to exhale and let it go. Despite how conflicted I may feel, I know that at some point it's not good for me to keep beating myself up. Am I a masochist? Maybe. As I said earlier, I've come to more fully understand that because of my guilt I'm destructively choosing to be loyal to my suffering and personal martyrdom. Now, I slow down, close my eyes, take a long and deep breath, and then slowly let it out. I get very sad and angry, I feel all of it. Sometimes I cry. I can see the hurt passing through me, and after a while I slowly begin to feel a little better.

Anger Can Be Helpful

Strangely enough, losing isn't necessarily all bad. If we can get beyond our egos' reactions, we can learn a lot from the experience. It's human nature to protect our idealized self-images by looking for external causes for our losses. Losing is an effect, so I begin the painful process of doing my best to deconstruct the experience, and in the process identify and address the causes.

There's a good reason I keep the focus (locus of control) on myself. It encourages me to believe I can do better next time. Any other perspective paints me, and thus my clients, as powerless, and if that's true, then we really are victims! I categorically refuse to be a victim. If I have no power, then I really am helpless. When I feel helpless, then I end up feeling angry and sorry for myself, and that's a total waste of my time. Maybe this is a mild variation of the bargaining stage of the grieving process, which I discuss next; however, keeping the focus on me and trying to do better seems to provide some hope for the future, and a bit of peace within the carnage.

Paradoxically, anger can be a friend. At a deep and primitive level, it's designed to keep us alive. Pain always lurks just beneath the surface of anger. The more anger you feel, the more the pain, and vice versa.[9] Some of this pain probably goes back a long way, probably to early childhood. Anger is primitive and natural. It provides us with an emotional shield and bridge that, with insight, can help us not just survive, but grow.

I think of myself as mentally choosing to suspend my emotions, meaning I mentally put them over to the side, with the understanding I'll come back to them later. I compartmentalize them. This is similar to when Spence "talks" to his anger. The only difference between *anger* and

---

9. Gerry Spence, *Win Your Case: How to Present, Persuade, Prevail—Every Place, Every Time* (New York, NY: St. Martin's Press, 2005), chapter 6, "The Dangerous Power of Anger," 60–65.

danger is one letter.[10] It's an approach that works for me. In other words, I don't deny my feelings. I work to channel them, to harness and control them, instead of them controlling me. I try to *respond*, and not *react*.

There's a Process to Grieving

When we lose something we value, such as a case, our health, or a loved one, we all naturally grieve. And then at some future point, we pick up the pieces and stumble on. With reflection, you'll discern a pattern. Let's review some of the known and predictable steps of our generic grieving process:[11]

1. Anger (It's the fault of the jury, judge, opposing lawyer, insurance company, tort reform, rigged system, and, yes, myself.)
2. Bargaining (I promise, I'll try even harder and do better next time.)
3. Depression (This is so bad; I'm a lousy lawyer; and the sky is falling.)
4. Emotional resolution or acceptance[12] (Okay, it's time for me to pick myself up and move on.)

These aren't exact stops on a horizontal pain line, and we often rearrange the order, repeat, or blend the steps. They are, however, aspects of an arching emotional framework that can help us better understand and address our feelings.

---

10. *Gerry Spence, Win Your Case,* 61.

11. Elizabeth Kübler-Ross, "Five Stages of Grief," Grief.com, https://grief.com/the-five-stages-of-grief/. I didn't mention the first stage, which is stunned shock, denial, and disbelief. Sometimes when the foreperson or clerk reads an adverse verdict, I'm so stunned I need to forcibly remember to request that the jury be polled.

12. Kübler-Ross, "Five Stages of Grief." These stages are generated from her study of death and how we process it. I offer her thoughts as an arching template. She also discusses the stages of denial and disbelief, which I have not included. These help ground me and offer perspective when I lose, and I do.

For me, guilt becomes the inevitable companion in the second, or bargaining, stage. I end up playing the "if only" game by incessantly searching for and finding some fault with my legal services that explains why I lost and, thus, "failed." It's easy to get stuck in a vicious cycle of blame and self-criticism, vacillating between anger, guilt, and pain. A part of me doubts I'm worthy of forgiving myself. I can hear a small voice whispering in my ear, "Put that thorny crown (of martyrdom) back on, you must suffer some more, a lot more!"

Complaining about district attorneys who overcharge, dishonest police officers, an underhanded opponent, a biased judge, or the way insurance companies have stacked the deck with tort reform propaganda doesn't do much good for me or my clients. These problems are embedded aspects of my job, and many of them are the very reasons why our clients need us. I view all the external structural and ambient problems like a firefighter who complains about too much smoke to put out the fire.[13] Instead, I now choose to internalize attribution and refuse to blame anyone else for my loss. Don't get me wrong—lots of external factors may have contributed to the outcome, not to mention just plain bad luck; but for now, my question is: What could I have done to anticipate and blunt these external factors and have minimized their impact?

After some time of (hopefully) intelligent deconstruction and a little self-abuse, I now choose to let it go and enter stage 4 of grief: "the emotional resolution" or "acceptance." The question is always how much self-punishment is enough? For me, at this stage of my career, it's about two long days.[14] At my mid-career, it was about four or five long days. In the beginning, it was more, much more, and sometimes never seemed to end. I actually got ulcers.

---

13. Rick Friedman, *Becoming a Trial Lawyer: A Guide for the Lifelong Advocate*, 2nd ed. (Portland, OR: Trial Guides, 2015), 214.

14. Paul Luvera and Lita Barnett Luvera, *Luvera on Advocacy* (Portland, OR: Trial Guides, 2020), 84. "My personal rule is that I rejoice for my victories only twenty-four hours and limit remorse for losing to forty-eight hours." Paul is one of my heroes and practiced until he was eighty years old.

Grieve with Your Client

Paradoxically, losses can bring me and my clients even closer. My client had someone in their corner who believed in them and fought hard for them. Our ship may have gone down, but it didn't go down alone. It's part of our shared journey.

Compartmentalizing

Is my behavior just a minimizing intellectualization, meaning I'm choosing to wall it off inside of me? Is this good or bad, healthy or unhealthy? I think it's simply adaptive and can be positive when combined with best practices. With time, I get better at simultaneously holding three inconsistent feelings:

1. My pain
2. My resolve to grow
3. Giving myself permission to let go of my pain, and to move on

    I listen empathetically to some of America's finest lawyers when they talk about the depth of their enduring anguish and pain after a loss. When I was younger with ulcers, I totally agreed. Now, I promise myself to leave it all on the field, grieve for two days, deconstruct, apply best practices, and then move on, better and stronger, to my next client and case. Am I less a lawyer or person than my fellow lawyers who continue to suffer and berate themselves? Maybe, maybe not. Again, I ask, can you have too much of a good thing (pain, guilt, and anguish), and if so, what might that look like? All I can know is my answer, for today.

Healing from Losses

It's a challenge being all-in, losing, and then somehow expecting to move on to my next client, case, and trial with enthusiasm. What am I, an automaton? Absolutely not. It helps to think of me reenergizing myself like the phoenix from Greek mythology—a bird that dies and then repeatedly rises to live again and again. To draw on examples from nature, the sun rises anew each morning, spring naturally follows winter, and, yes, dawn follows the night.

We're Team Captains & Cheerleaders

We're always being watched, always under a microscope. Clients and jurors can smell our fear and, conversely, our confidence. We're responsible for our clients, our trial team, and, of course, ourselves. Our attitudes are contagious. I separate internal messaging with my client and trial team from external messaging with the jury, opposing counsel, and judge. During the first interview with a prospective client, I carefully explain reality—the distinction between my effort and results. I can't sell a win;[15] I can only offer my best. When messaging opposing counsel (the external), I fully acknowledge the challenges and warts in my case, and then put my best foot forward while projecting a measured optimism. All trial lawyers work at the intersection of risk, fear, and responsibility. I may be wrong, but (to the external world), I'm not in doubt. I'm measured, circumspect, and never raise my voice. Volume doesn't improve the quality of what I have to say. Whether or not something is true doesn't depend on whether it's whispered or shouted—and often, less is more.

Put yourself in the position of a patient before brain surgery. What attributes would you want your doctor to possess? How about

---
15. Mind you, on a contingency fee, it's a separate matter that we don't get paid if we lose.

competence, confidence, and a heavy dose of compassion? Sounds like our jobs. It's not just smart, it's also good business. Why? Because when you go down swinging, your clients are less likely to blame you.

Informed Consent Letters

A big part of my internal messaging to my clients is grounded on informed consent letters. I know of no lawyer who talks about the content or importance of informed consent letters. They ethically serve as brakes on my optimism by forcing me to identify and assess all the bad things that might go wrong in a naked, cold-blooded letter that thoroughly discusses the procedures, alternatives, and risks. Why do we write these letters? First, we write them so our clients can truly make an informed decision. Second, we write these CYA (cover your ass) letters in case we lose. The standard of care demands it. We obviously don't need them if we win. We know the rules. We're agents; the clients are the principals. We provide clients with our recommendations, and then, after being fully informed of all the risks, they make the final call, all of which is confirmed in writing. We have a legal and fiduciary duty to provide our clients with everything they need to know to make an informed decision, including the pluses and minuses, the good and bad. I compare it to a doctor providing presurgical informed consent.

I make sure my letters err on the long side when discussing the risks and problems. It's easy when it's a low-offer case. It's quite another when, even if the offer is inadequate, it will make a big improvement in your client's life.

What Athletics Can Teach Us

Athletics offers wonderful age-appropriate insights into healthy competition and constructive losing. Beginning in Little League, athletics taught me to practice hard, give it my best, and then live with the outcome. I played high school sports, Division III college basketball and, later, 3-on-3 basketball nationally into my late forties. I enjoyed the camaraderie, competition, and sweat.

I was the manager of our college track team. Carefully watch 400- and 800-meter runners; increased distances demand they find a way to intelligently pace themselves, easing back just a little during the middle of the race. Then, coming into the final stretch, they give it everything they have left in a final burst. If you're always sprinting, you're not going to win many cases, and you're going to exhaust yourself early. You must learn to pace yourself.

Since 2010, I've served as the life coach of the Portland State University (PSU) men's basketball team. We are a mid-conference Division I team in the Big Sky Conference. I have a contract issued by the PSU Athletics Director. I am answerable to the head coach and am subject to all the National Collegiate Athletic Association (NCAA) rules. I am involved in every aspect of the program, and trial schedule permitting, travel with the team.

I see talented high school recruits struggle as college freshmen. However, the good ones show up early, stay late, and work hard. After a year or two of getting their butts kicked, they start growing up right before my eyes. I think it's similar to being a trial lawyer. The good ones keep getting up when they're knocked down, again and again. Improvement is never a straight line. They'll struggle, improve, and plateau. The one constant is their effort.

Field goal kickers in football must have short memories and cleanup (home run) hitters batting fourth in baseball often lead their teams in strikeouts. You may have lost your last case, but tomorrow's client certainly doesn't want you looking over your shoulder, depressed about yesterday! That was then, this is now. In basketball, good shooters may miss ten shots in a row, but I promise you they are positive the next one is going to swish. That's why they're great shooters! Obviously skill is a big part of their success, but it's not enough; they all have an unnaturally high level of confidence. Some players want to take the last shot, and some don't. Michael Jordan said, "I've missed more than nine thousand shots in my career. I've lost almost three hundred games. Twenty-six times I've been trusted to take the game-winning shot and missed. I've failed over and over and over again in my life. And that is why I succeed."[16]

Baseball player Reggie Jackson said, "I don't mind getting beaten, but I hate to lose."[17] I would respectfully suggest that, even if I lose, a big part of me feels I'm never beaten. Why? Because I always bring it and do the best I can. If I leave it all on the field or in the courtroom, then I can live with the final score. I may lose, but nobody's going to beat me.

My favorite athlete is now-retired Megan Rapinoe. She was interviewed after she missed a key goal and the American women's team was eliminated from the 2023 Women's World Cup competition:

> Honestly, something that has made me so successful in penalty kicks for so long is the acceptance and the realization that I will miss them. I miss them in training regularly. I've been lucky not to miss a lot in actual competition, but eventually, that can happen. But I love taking them. I would take them all the time. I would take that one again. I would pick me to take them.
>
> For a long time, I have thought about missing one in a really big moment. What are you going to do? The only other thing

---

16. This line was written by Jamie Barrett and spoken by Michael Jordan in "Failure," a Nike TV commercial (1997). https://www.shmoop.com/quotes/failed-why-i-succeed.html.

17. Sepia Magazine (March 1977), https://www.baseball-almanac.com/quotes/quo-jackr.shtml.

you could do is to not take one. I'm not going to do that. I would rather step up and be in that moment.[18]

Performance Enhancement Experts

Let's step outside our profession and consider the advice of experts who make their living helping elite performers in many mediums of human effort, from Olympic athletes to leadership, business management, law, and life. I offer their thoughts on how to achieve a passionate life committed to excellence, with a full awareness of its benefits and burdens. The authors of *The Passion Paradox* recommend living mindfully with a high level of self-awareness:

> Mindfully living with a passion can be the key to a life well lived. … Only by understanding the pitfalls of obsessive and fear-driven passion… does passion gain the potential to be productive. An equal challenge is… actively adopting the mastery mind-set: maintaining drive from within; focusing on the process over results; not worrying about being the best but worrying about being the best at getting better; embracing acute failure for chronic gains; practicing patience; and paying full attention to our pursuits. … "Balance" is more often than not an illusion…. Instead of striving for balance, then, the passionate person should strive to be self-aware. … Self-awareness ensures that you control your passion rather than your passion controlling you.[19]

In sports, there's only one national champion. Everyone else's season ends on a loss. Smart coaches invite their players to stay in the pain of a loss long enough that they're motivated during the off-season to improve, and avoid the bad taste next year. That's exactly what my legal

---

18. Franklin Foer, "Megan Rapinoe Answers the Critics," *The Atlantic*, August 22, 2023.
19. Brad Stulberg and Steve Magness, *The Passion Paradox* (Emmaus, PA: Rodale Books, 2019), 162–164.

mentors were talking about when they said lingering in today's pain helps motivate them to work even harder to avoid future losses.

Insights from Philosophy, Science & Wisdom Traditions

For the last twenty years I've hired philosophy professors to teach me. Why do I share this? Because many of the tenets of philosophies, religions, wisdom traditions, and psychology offer powerful IA insights into learning, well-being, happiness, and life.[20]

Consider Buddhism's second noble truth, the wisdom truth; that is, the benefits of attaching to our *efforts* without grasping or clinging to the *results*. It's what we mean when we do the best we can while mindfully not attaching to the outcome. Why not attach to the outcome? Because it's out of our control. The Buddha says uncertainty and change in life are inevitable and obviously cause pain; however, attaching to conditions we cannot control results in unnecessary suffering.[21] Pain is inevitable; self-inflicted suffering is optional and is on us. On a similar note, we all would be wiser if we followed the Serenity Prayer: "God, grant me the serenity to accept the things I cannot change, the courage to change the things I can, and the wisdom to know the difference."[22]

Classic stoicism agrees and is much misunderstood. It has little to do with keeping a stiff upper lip or "stoically" enduring. Stoicism was founded in Athens by Zeno of Citium in early third century BCE and

---

20. My favorite teacher-philosopher is the now-deceased Dr. Robert Smith. He was a Fulbright Scholar, receiving his PhD in world religions, thus, my exposure to Buddhism. Robert was my dear friend and mentor.

21. See my friend Michael Leizerman of Toledo, Ohio. He is an active practicing Buddhist. I recommend his book, *The Zen Lawyer: Winning with Mindfulness*.

22. Attributed to Reinhold Niebuhr.

became a popular western discipline. It's based on the idea that the cause of most of our problems is our perception of things rather than the things themselves. It emphasizes self-mastery, perseverance, and wisdom. It grew to be popular in Rome during the second century. Stoics included Seneca (4 BCE–CE 65), a playwright and Roman power broker; Epictetus, a former enslaved person, exile, and teacher; and my favorite stoic, Marcus Aurelius, a powerful Roman emperor (CE 161–180) who chose to sleep on the floor to keep himself humble. He wrote *Meditations*, a series of private reflections that helped him stay centered. Vice Admiral James B. Stockdale studied stoicism. As the senior officer in a North Vietnam prison camp, he applied the tenets of stoicism to endure five years of confinement and torture. You think you've got problems. He was awarded the Medal of Honor.

When I write my list of fears, I sometimes place the names of Marcus Aurelius in the top left-hand corner and James B. Stockdale in the right. Perspective is important. We can only control ourselves. The verdict isn't ours, it's the jury's, as it should be. A second plank of stoicism is to view adversity as an opportunity to improve and show our character.

"Maintaining this in our consciousness can bring tremendous clarity about how we want to live, how we want to do our work, how we want to make our mark, and how we want to be remembered."[23] Think here of your obituary. This is akin to viewing problems as "unwelcome opportunities," to see what we're really made of.

Cognitive behavior therapy (CBT), and its predecessor, rational emotive behavior therapy (REBT), are both contemporary applications of Stoicism.[24]

Rarely are religion, philosophy, and psychology in such unanimous agreement, and contrary to much of the advice my mentors gave me. Over identification with the client leads to a psychological life and death situation when we/they lose. It's all very understandable and has

---

23. Len Niehoff, "The Stoic Litigator: Ancient Advice on Finding Happiness in Our Work," *Litigation* 49, no. 1 (Fall 2022): 19.

24. Donald Robertson, *The Philosophy of Cognitive-Behavioural Therapy: Stoic Philosophy as Rational and Cognitive Psychology*, 2nd ed. (Routledge, 2020).

some value, but at quite an expense to everyone, starting with the lawyer and their family. Your choice.

In Ralph Waldo Emerson's essay "Compensation," he explains that a virtuous act is its own reward, that there is an instantaneous "gain in character" that results when you choose to conduct yourself in a quality manner. Your efforts, and their preceding thoughts, are the evolving refinement of your personhood. Character is habit engraved.[25] This is the essence of Greek virtue ethics. The accent is always on your growth, that is, the process of refining and edifying your personhood or "nature."[26]

American pragmatism[27] emphasizes the "cash value" of our choices, and its concept of fallibilism is that we must be willing to assume the possibility that we might be wrong. Mind you, you needn't admit you're wrong, but you must assume just the very small possibility that you might be. I have a distrust of "the comfort of certitude," in myself and others, particularly given our powerful emotional need to be sure (of ourselves).

Questions to Ask after a Loss

Military strategists study battles, analyzing the conflict from multiple perspectives, including the terrain, munitions, supply lines, troop deployment, training, support, tactics, and leadership. It's akin to what we should be doing after all our trials, win or lose. There's always cause and effect.

Let me offer a healthy example of deconstruction:

---

25. Plutarch wrote that "Character is simply habit long continued." Plutarch was a Greek Middle Platonist philosopher. He also was an historian, biographer, essayist, and priest. He became a Roman citizen.
26. *See* Will Durant, *The Story of Philosophy: The Lives and Opinions of the World's Greatest Philosophers* (New York: Pocket Books, 1991), and Ralph Waldo Emerson, "Compensation."
27. Charles Sanders Peirce and William James are the founders of American pragmatism.

1. What were the probable or potential causes of the loss? Ask yourself; ask others. Start by accepting that you might be defensive and not tough enough on yourself.
2. Did you conduct pretrial focus groups to identify the case's problems and explore and test your best responses? There are always three stories: the plaintiff's, the defendant's, and the jury's. You want to tell the jury's story—but in the plaintiff's voice. Did you fully anticipate, appreciate, and blunt the defendant's story? Remember that the purpose of the initial focus group is to identify all your problems. Then in follow-up sessions, you test your responses.
3. Was your investigation early enough and thorough enough?
4. Were your case themes and story anchored in the key words and phrases of the court's instructions?
5. With the benefit of hindsight would you conduct your jury selection differently? How? Why? Did you collect the information necessary to thoughtfully exercise your preemptory challenges? Did you develop your trial themes? Did you anticipate, preempt, and reframe your problem areas?
6. Did you strategically anticipate and then own the defense's best facts or, as Keith Mitnik says, to "put them in context"?[28] Did you affirmatively work to generate credibility?
7. Did you research your trial judge? Did you watch them select a jury in an earlier case? What was their threshold for challenges for cause? Were they gatekeepers (when it came to evidence)? Should you have filed any (FRE 401-403) pretrial motions? How might such motions have made a difference? Did you request continuing objections so that you didn't have to keep objecting in front of the jury?
8. Was it because of the facts? In what particulars? Did any one or two things preordain the outcome? Why? With the benefit of hindsight, what could or should you have done differently? Did you listen to, and learn from, your focus group?

---

28. Keith Mitnik, *Don't Eat the Bruises: How to Foil Their Plans to Spoil Your Case* (Portland, OR: Trial Guides, 2015), chapter 13.

9. Should you have hired more or better experts? Were your experts fully prepared? Could they have been better teachers and communicators? Be specific. If they were good, how could they have been better?
10. How about technology and computer assistance? Did your demonstrative exhibits "sing"?
11. Would jury notebooks have helped?
12. How about the (written) instructions? Did you prepare special instructions and consider a separate set for each juror? Did you personalize them?
13. Were your emotions too early, too much, or maybe too late?
14. How about your opponent? Did they surprise you in any way? If so, what could and should you have done differently?
15. Once it's appropriate, consider talking with the trial judge and your opponent. Do they have any suggestions or constructive feedback?

We naturally filter information to fortify our preexisting views; it's a heuristic called the *confirmation bias*. We tend to limit discussions of our cases to loyal friends who see it our way; yet if we were smart, we'd be doing the opposite. Don't be defensive and allow your insecurities to stunt your growth. Opponents and critics can be powerful information sources for real growth. Earlier in this chapter, I discussed the benefit of pretrial *mortems* on why you might lose. Rather than waiting until after you lost, you can start this process by carefully reviewing this list before trial.

Create a Box of Losses

You may want to buy a small wooden box as a symbolic mini-crypt for you to "bury" your losses in. Solemnly place a copy of the verdict in your box of losses, perhaps with your client's photo and a copy of a memorable exhibit. This isn't a joke. When I do this with respect and solemnity, it helps me bracket the experience and move on. If this sounds a little like a funeral, in a sense, it is. I bury my dead, beat the drums slowly, and then move out. This occurs soon after my two days of grieving has passed.

I keep my box of losses in my office on the back of my desk. I respectfully and privately burn the box's contents every five to seven years. This is part of my larger philosophy of not letting my losses define me, but instead refine me.

There are currently three losses in my crypt. The first is a birth injury case. The mother and baby's photos are attached to the defense verdict. We received $3 million in a settlement from the pediatrician but lost against the ob-gyn. The second is a no-offer social host liability claim. We won a big verdict against the minimally insured drunk driver but lost against the social host who had a homeowner's insurance policy. The third is another birth trauma case in which the jury found the defendants negligent, but found there was no causation. This crypt is my personal way to honor these clients, and to show continuing respect for them. I consider this crypt entirely separate from my rule requiring that I heal in forty-eight hours. In an odd way, this helps make my prompt healing more doable.

As I reflect upon my losses over my career, I can't help but remember the cases I'm sure I would win if I tried them today. Here's my response: Top surgeons are doctors of last resort who routinely perform high-risk surgeries. This means they are going to leave some of their patients dead on the operating table. It's a tough, gut-wrenching part of the job. They didn't start out doing the most challenging surgeries; they've spent a career perfecting their skills. They are committed to always improving and doing their best. Their competence grew, just as mine does, and yours will too. I never said to forget the past, but I do say we should learn from it.

Sharing with Others

Maybe it's a best friend, loved one, spouse, partner, or parent—it always lightens the load when we can speak our pain and get it out. Sharing with someone whom you can be vulnerable with is a gift, a safe harbor in the storms of life. Like a little boy, I know they care about me and won't hurt me. Don't forget to return the favor. We're all connected.

Conclusion

If you don't somehow come to grips with the reality that your next case might be your next loss, then you're doomed to the life of a martyr. It's a choice.

I started out doing what all my mentors unanimously told me: identifying with my clients such that a loss was almost a death. After twenty years I couldn't keep it up.

My reading in psychology and philosophy clearly advised me to do my best and attach to my efforts, but not the results, because I could only control myself, not the outcome. My problem in applying this advice was and is: I'm all too human. The idea is great, and easy to say, however, it was too aseptic for me. I'm not a robot. So how did I resolve this dilemma, and where am I at now? Somewhere in the middle. I love every client and a part of me can't help attaching to the result, I care so much. However, if I over attach to the outcome (and lose), it prevents me from being 100 percent present for my next client and case, which I have an equally undivided loyalty to. As I mentioned earlier, a couple of times I had a jury out in one case, and was down the hall picking a jury in another. Plus, every moment I spent unnecessarily suffering was time I could, and should, be spending with my family.

Like most things in life, it's a choice and a balancing act. As the Greeks and Buddhists both say, it's the middle way.

This highly personal middle way also offers systemic benefits because it allows committed lawyers to care, while also providing a path to healing. Not an easy path, but a shorter and clearer one.

For the lawyers who choose not to find their middle way, there is one more depressed, cynical, and wounded lawyer who is less available tomorrow to represent those in need with gusto and enthusiasm.

I've come to believe it's ultimately a matter of choice, perspective, and personal discipline. We all struggle with losing, it's part of the job. The balance you strike goes a long way to determining if you can love this work—without it devouring you. It's a choice.

4

What Motivates You?

There are plenty of culturally embedded stories of what American success looks like. Where's your life heading? What would you like it to be, and how do you want it to end? Giving voice to your deepest values with specific goals expressed in a life map will lengthen your stride.

We all seek lives of meaning, purpose, fulfillment, and satisfaction. Sharing our evolving life story and dreams with trusted others can be affirming. Invite loved ones to contribute, or even coauthor, your life story; after all, today's dreams are tomorrow's possibilities. The career we have chosen allows us to participate in the saga of the ever-evolving American common law.

Are some dreams better for us than others, and if so, what are their qualities? IA says yes and endorses the self-determination theory (SDT).[1] SDT is a macro theory of human motivation and

---

1. Edward L. Deci et al., "Self-Determination Theory in Work Organizations: The State of Science," *Annual Review of Organizational Psychology and Organizational Behavior* 4, (January 11, 2017):19-43, https://doi.org/10.1146/annurev-orgpsych-032516-113108.

personality that emphasizes people's inherent growth tendencies and innate psychological needs.

Are there uncertainties and risks in planning your life? Of course. There will always be challenges, setbacks, changes, and failures—it's guaranteed. I'm not talking about failing to play the hand of cards you're dealt. We're all born to a certain gene pool, ZIP code, family, and culture. Psychologists call this your *facticity*. Instead, I'm focusing on the attitude and effort you sustain in furtherance of the large life-defining choices you elect to make. This demands self-awareness, honesty, planning, energy, enthusiasm, and a serious proactive commitment.

Let's consider our work as jury trial lawyers. There's 168 hours in a week. It's the same for all of us. We trade our time and apply our talents in a stressful and demanding job. This occurs against a backdrop of media and popular culture that often glamorizes and caricatures our work. We all know that very little of our time is actually spent in front of a jury. All of this is in addition to the economics of running a law practice and making a living. We live in a world of marketing professionals who sell themselves to help us market ourselves. You must self-promote, and it's not much fun. No wonder government employment can be so attractive; win or lose, you get a check every month, you don't have to advertise or run a business, and you can have some semblance of a life.

There is a study named "What Makes Lawyers Happy? Transcending the Anecdotes with Data from 6,200 Lawyers."[2] The clear findings are that inner psychological needs or intrinsic motivations are the strongest predictors of lawyer happiness and satisfaction. The group with the lowest incomes and grades in law school, public service lawyers, had the strongest self-direction and purpose, and were happier than those with the highest grades, income, and prestigious positions. The bottom line is it's about you choosing work that is interesting and personally meaningful to you. Increased well-being promotes health, energy, optimism,

---

2. Lawrence S. Krieger and Kennon M. Sheldon, "What Makes Lawyers Happy? Transcending the Anecdotes with Data from 6,200 Lawyers," *The George Washington University Law Review* 83 (February 20, 2014). FSU College of Law, Public Law Research Paper No. 667, http://dx.doi.org/10.2139/ssrn.2398989.

creativity, altruism, and work performance. We're all a mix of intrinsic and extrinsic motivations, and our temperaments and interests.

The study's findings call into question the American Dream paradigm that the rewards of money or status are the foundations of a happy life. The legal profession socializes us to value external criteria. Think about it: we strive for high undergrad GPAs and LSAT scores, then we attend the best law schools that will admit us. We then compete for class standing, law review, and after graduation and passing the bar, it continues in practices that emphasize money, achievement, recognition, status, and the usual trappings of success. It's obvious that the content and tangible results of the American dream are external, like a house, car, fancy vacations, trophy partners, high-achieving kids, toys, stuff, and so on.[3]

No profession is more publicly peer reviewed than ours, with groups like Super Lawyers, Best Lawyers, by invitation-only groups, American Board of Trial Advocates, The American College, International Society of Barristers, International Academy of Trial Lawyers, and so on. Ubiquitous lawyer advertising, social media, and websites all assure it's an ultra-competitive market. Participation in this electronic shouting match is an unfortunate necessity for all of us, even though the process arguably demeans each of us individually and our profession collectively.

There is an interesting study cited in the book *Gross National Happiness* by Arthur C. Brooks that involved faculty, staff, and students at Harvard University in which participants were asked to choose between earning $50,000 per year while everyone else earned $25,000, or earning $100,000 per year while others made $200,000.[4] The researchers stipulated that prices of goods and services would be the same in both cases, so a higher salary really meant being able to own a nicer home, buy a nicer car, or do whatever else they wanted with the extra

---

3. Robert Emmons, "Personal Goals, Life, Meaning, and Virtue: Wellsprings of a Positive Life," *Flourishing: Positive Psychology and the Life Well-Lived*, eds. Corey L. M. Keyes and Jonathan Haidt (Washington, DC: American Psychological Association, 2002), 105-128.

4. Sara J. Solnick, David Hemenway, "Is more always better?: A Survey on Positional Concerns," *Journal of Economic Behavior & Organization* 37, no. 3,(1998): 373–383

money. But those material gains mattered little to the 56 percent who chose the first option, forgoing $50,000 per year in order to maintain a position of *relative* affluence.

I suspect the 56 percent who valued relative affluence are today's successful, but not very happy lawyers. As an insecure neurotic, I can vouch that it's an emotional hole that can never be filled. Think about it, it's never enough—it can't be, that's why it's neurotic! However, playing this external game isn't necessarily inconsistent with maintaining a parallel set of inner values that nourish us and ultimately, are the best source of happiness and well-being. So, while you're doing the necessary marketing, you also know that life's deepest answers are found within, not without.

In spite of our socialization favoring the extrinsic, we attorneys really aren't much different from anyone else. We desire and need a sense of self-determination, relationships, supportive mentoring, altruistic values, and a focus on self-understanding and growth. This mindset is empowering and promotes a healthy sense of personal responsibility for outcomes; so that if we lose, we have the sense that we can improve and do better. Secondary results from the study found personal life choices such as marriage, relationships, children, vacations, and exercise were all supportive of happiness.

Big firms are eager to hire top law school graduates and pay them well; it's called the golden handcuffs. A 2013 study tells us big firm associates were the second most unhappy job in America,[5] and it didn't get much better. Junior partners, associates who have generated sufficient billable hours long enough to move up the firm ladder into the junior partnership ranks, weren't much happier. Why? Because once you make it that far, you're too invested to leave. The good news is this study is dated, and the big firms are getting the message that today's graduates want more than just a paycheck; they want a life.

---

5. Jacquelyn Smith, "The Happiest and Unhappiest Job in America," *Forbes*, March 22, 2013, https://www.forbes.com/sites/jacquelynsmith/2013/03/22/the-happiest-and-unhappiest-jobs-in-america.

Many of my aging peers are critical of today's younger lawyers as being more European in their aspirations, meaning their jobs aren't as important to them. Today's beginning lawyers aren't as motivated by money and the trappings of success that my generation was. Today's gen X, Y, and Z face an uncertain future. Many may never enjoy the level of affluence their parents did, and to most, retirement is just a far-off abstraction. It takes two working parents to support a family, and the American dream of home ownership seems a distant possibility to many. They want a meaningful (non-work) life, a family, to love and be loved, and yes, to have and enjoy vacations. Many of today's young lawyers were raised in families where they rarely saw much of their two working parents, and now they're committed to providing their children with something more.

I applaud this shift in values. It's not just healthier for the lawyer-person, but I also suggest that knocking 10 percent off the billable hours and investing it in your personal life and loved ones will make you at least a 10 percent better lawyer, not to mention a happier person. It should be obvious IA's canopy starts with the best of you, the authentic true-blue inside of you, and then builds outward and up, grounded in your personal values.

It's Never Too Late

I conclude with the reality that one can be overweight yet dying of malnutrition. In other words, you can get a paycheck but remain unfulfilled. Some enjoy success, and a high standard of living, while working in unsatisfying careers. When they get into their mid-forties and fifties, they often have an existential crisis. They have successfully climbed the vocational ladder only to realize they placed their ladder up against the wrong wall.

You have choices, you always did. Ask yourself how you can incrementally inject meaning and generative behavior into your present work and life. Take baby steps. As a thought experiment, assume that you must change jobs or retire in three years. What might a reset button look like? Are there adjacent careers you could explore that might be more to your liking?

We Are All Connected

It's good news that even though we operate in a competitive marketplace, we are all part of closely knit legal communities. The common law connects us all at the hip. AAJ and their state affiliates provide important opportunities for each of us at every stage of our careers to participate, learn, grow, share, and bond. Friends, peer groups, and mentors foster a sense of connection and belonging.

Conclusion

It's the same aspects of our work that generate incredible highs when we win; and devastating lows when we lose. No wonder so many have a love-hate relationship with our work.

5

Constructing Your Life Story

I run a twice-a-year boot camp for trial lawyers, and each year I ask my boot campers to write three things: their own brief life story, hero(ine)'s journey,[1] and a private obituary they can aspire to be worthy of. We'll discuss them in order.

This exercise isn't natural or easy. Most want to retreat to the clinical, "show me how to (do something) in court. I don't have time for this psychobabble. There's work to be done and bills to be paid." I understand, I really do, however, we get so wrapped up in the business of lawyering that we forget why we chose this profession and the importance of our specialty as jury trial lawyers within it. I think of this as (understandably) getting lost in the weeds.

Reflecting on Joseph Campbell's monomyth reveals how our work can provide us with the opportunity for a more fully realized life. You already know that our work as jury trial lawyers who help injured clients promotes community interests in safety, deterrence,

---

1. Joseph Campbell, *The Hero with A Thousand Faces,* 3rd ed. (Novato, CA: New World Library, 2012). Originally published in 1949 by Pantheon Books.

and public accountability. Our work nicely tracks the hero's return in Campbell's monomyth. This observation doesn't minimize the many challenges every aspiring trial lawyer, or prospective hero(ine), must face and overcome.

Build your life story upon the best of you. Start with narrative psychology as expressed in *The Redemptive Self* by Dan McAdams, then supplement your story with the benefits of framing your career and life as a hero(ine)'s journey.[2] Both self-narratives and heroic stories are matters of personal invention, reinvention, and perspective. It's about how you choose to use your gifts and create a life of meaning that reflects your core values—you being the best of you.

Bill Moyer's six-part interview in 1988 with Campbell was seen on public television by 30 million viewers. Campbell died in 1987 shortly before it was released. He's best known for his advice that we should "follow our bliss." Campbell's story of the hero has spawned a number of articles on storytelling tracking off the monomyth formula.[3] This model became culturally embedded when film director George Lucas created *Star Wars* and the journey of Luke Skywalker based upon the

---

2. Dan McAdams, *The Redemptive Self: Stories Americans Live By*, revised and expanded edition (Oxford University Press, 2013). The book is a cookbook of how to write your life story. For a quick introduction to McAdams' teaching, *see*, "American Identity: The Redemptive Self," *The General Psychologist* 43, no.1 (Spring, 2008): 20.

3. The Bible until Campbell's seventeen-step hero (1949) was Aristotle's *Poetics* (circa 350 BC) and his five parts of tragic storytelling:
   1. Beginning; prosperity of hero/protagonist
   2. Hamartia; miscalculation, tragic flaw, hubris (pride)
   3. Peripeteia; reversal of fortune
   4. Anagnorisis; recognition, realization, or identification
   5. Nemesis; downfall or retribution of hero/protagonist, "just desserts"

Hollywood screenwriters have followed Campbell's formula for decades. In 1985, Christopher Vogler reduced the hero's journey to twelve steps, and in the late 1990s, director and screenwriter Dan Harmon generated a fascinating eight-step story circle. You can read Vogler's 1985 memo "A Practical Guide to Joseph Cambell's The Hero with a Thousand Faces" at: https://www.thinking-differently.com/creativity/wp-content/uploads/2014/01/The-Heros-Journey.pdf. Read more about Harmon's circle at: https://boords.com/blog/storytelling-101-the-dan-harmon-story-circle.

monomyth.[4] As Campbell reviewed history, he observed that the hero's journey was almost universally masculine, however that's not true for today—and certainly not for tomorrow. I am mindful that we are applying Campbell's 1949 monomyth to today's law school graduates, of which more than half are women. I offer Campbell's formula in gender neutral terms. For this reason, hereafter whenever the term hero is used, I substitute hero(ine).

There's a lot that's attractive about viewing our lives and careers as heroic journeys. Myths involve knights, honor, magic, elixirs, sacrifice, service, and usually good triumphing over bad. Let's remember, however, that the primary purpose of myths, movies, and books is to entertain, while our personal stories are tools to help us grow. The trial stories in our clients' cases are designed to help us win by keeping the focus on the defendant and their misconduct, and only then presenting the plaintiff in a positive light.

In my boot camps, we sit in a small group and share the early drafts of our brief personal narratives and heroic journeys. These can be two separate stories, or combined as one. If it feels like a form of group therapy, you're right. It reminds me of the psychodrama sessions in the three-week Spence Ranch I attended in 2007.

Meaning in life is tied to the stories we tell about ourselves. Many recall the sacrifices of a parent, grandparent, elder, coach, or someone who inspired them—such as a teacher who first said they should be a lawyer. Then they add a few of the biggest challenges they've overcome that made them stronger. Many are the oldest child or the first high school or college graduate in their family. As we share, patterns emerge. Why wouldn't they? We're all aspiring jury trial lawyers who enjoy helping others and are trying to get better. The current iterations (initiation and return) of our hero(ine)'s journeys are often similar. However, our life stories and how we got here can vary dramatically.[5]

---

4. Other movies include *The Lion King*, *Lord of the Rings*, and *The Matrix*.

5. Dan McAdams, "A Psychologist Without a Country, or Living Two Lives in the Same Story," in G. Yancy and S. Hadley, eds., *Narrative identities: Psychologists engaged in self-construction* (London: Jessica Kingsley, 2005), 114.

Perspective is important. When you're thinking about our work and struggles as jury trial lawyers, reflect on the story of the three workers who were hauling bricks from one side of a lot to the other. When they were asked what they were doing, the first said he was moving bricks from one side of the lot to the other, the second said he was building a wall, the third said he was building a temple to his god. Each was correct, but only one had perspective and meaning.[6]

Narrative Psychology

Generative life stories are very American and common to adults who share high levels of optimism and mental health. Dan McAdams and *The Redemptive Self* offers an inventory of powerful life stories. How broadly does a story of service and redemption apply to the general population of 330 million Americans? Maybe not much, although aspects of it certainly resonate with many. However, a generative story of redemption becomes much more likely when we narrow our focus to the 1.3 million plus lawyers, then specifically to trial lawyers, and then again down to the subset of trial lawyers who gravitate to public service on either side of the counsel table in criminal justice, plaintiffs' personal injury work, civil rights, and employment law. Most of us who choose these specialties are passionate about our work and helping others. We find ourselves by losing ourselves in something bigger than us.[7] Sound familiar?

Your life story and hero(ine)'s journey are less objective tellings of the past than a platform to be used in the creation of your evolving self. We embody and live out our personal narratives, drawing upon them to guide us, interpret our experiences, and explain ourselves to both ourselves and the world. As we age, we continue to work on our scripts,

---

6. James W. McElhaney, *McElhaney's Trial Notebook*, 4th ed. (Chicago, IL: ABA Press, 2005), 7.

7. Viktor Frankl called it Logotherapy, meaning he emphasized the centrality of personal meaning to a satisfying life.

unconsciously editing and tweaking, sometimes even radically revising and rewriting them. We collectively pass on valued traditions and create new ones; examples include religious conversions, twelve-step programs, epiphanies, mentoring, selfless acts of public service, and rags-to-riches sagas. We can enact second, third, and even more acts. We search for and find ethical foundations upon which to construct a life of meaning. As life's arrow arcs, many things may change, but our core moral settings tend to endure.

The redemptive self is a story that supports and reinforces some of the most well-meaning efforts of caring, productive, and principled adults to make a positive difference in the world. This evolving narrative provides our lives with coherence and purpose. The stories link our reconstructed past, our experienced present, and our hopes for the future. The redemptive self is resilient, but can also fall prey to arrogance and self-righteousness. An optimistic spirit is a powerful asset during life's tragedies; however, it doesn't eliminate the pain.

Let me share my brief personal narrative, it's about two hundred words. I was born into a lower socio-economic world. Fortunately for me, along the way I had some teachers and coaches who saw something in me. With their guidance, I managed to escape my beginnings and learned the law. I became a jury trial lawyer, a job I never could have dreamed of in my youth.

I now have dual citizenship. What do I mean by this? If we were on the Titanic, even though I'm now privileged to dine under chandeliers with the captain, I was born far below deck. Now I talk law to the judge, but I can also share real and honest feelings with ordinary people, meaning the jurors. I live with a foot in both worlds and think of myself as bilingual. I'm looking across, and sometimes even up, at ordinary folks. Why? Because I've never forgotten my upbringing and roots, where real people suffer and, yes, cry themselves to sleep.

That's my story. You're free to steal or plagiarize any part of it, I did.[8]

---

8. Dan McAdams, "American Identity: The Redemptive Self" and "A Psychologist Without a Country or Living Two Lives in the Same Story." McAdams says he vocationally has "dual citizenship," I added "bilingual." I also considered describing myself

Awakening the Hero(ine) Within

Now let's shift to Joseph Campbell's *Hero with A Thousand Faces* and its progeny. When I was in college, you couldn't be a liberal arts major and not be introduced to Campbell's work. It's multidisciplinary, spanning philosophy, psychology, religion, anthropology, and literature. Ultimately, the journey is really about each of us confronting our inner fears and demons and the "trials" of our work, and how we can grow to serve our communities and become our own best and heroic selves in the process:

> The monomyth is characterized by 'separation—initiation—[and] return.' That is, the 'hero ventures forth from the world of common day into a region of supernatural wonder: fabulous forces are there encountered and a decisive victory is won: the hero comes back from this mysterious adventure with the power to bestow boons on his fellow man.'
>
> This journey is symbolic; it is a psychological or spiritual journey—an inward trek on which the traveller learns about himself and his relationship to the world. It is a journey on which the traveller discovers, or frees, some unknown part of himself, a journey on which the traveller comes to terms with (accepts) his place in the order of things.[9]

The three stages and seventeen steps of the Hero(ine)'s Journey are:

---

as "amphibious." All these adjectives are variations on the idea of the hero(ine)'s final stages, wherein they are the master of "two worlds."

9. Thomas C. Galligan Jr., "The Monomyth Goes to Law School," *St. John's Law Review* 66, no.1 (1992): 129–130.

The Departure

1. The Call to Adventure
2. Refusal of the Call
3. Supernatural Aid
4. The Crossing of the First Threshold
5. The Belly of the Whale

The Initiation

6. The Road of Trials
7. The Meeting with the Goddess
8. Woman as the Temptress
9. Atonement with the Father
10. Apotheosis
11. The Ultimate Boon

The Return

12. Refusal of the Return
13. The Magic Flight
14. Rescue from Without
15. The Crossing of the Return Threshold
16. Master of the Two Worlds
17. Freedom to Live

Campbell celebrated self-reliant individualism. We should be mindful that we are constructing our personal journey and story within the cultural backdrop of American notions of exceptionalism and its emphasis on each of us pursuing our dreams. McAdams repeatedly emphasizes the uniqueness of our American "pay it forward" narratives.[10]

There's a wonderful 2023 article that synthesizes Campbell's monomyth.[11] The authors reduce Campbell's seventeen steps to seven gender-neutral chapters: protagonist, shift, quest, allies, challenge, transformation, and legacy. The article's title says it all, "Seeing Your Life Story as a Hero's Journey Increases Meaning in Life." It's easy to find ourselves in this simplified contemporary illustration. It's a circle within a circle. The outer one tracks Campbell's largest ideas with a woman protagonist, magicians, dragons, and the heroine's final transformation with her legacy of "we, not me." This article is supported by multiple studies which confirm that a hero(ine)'s journey increases people's experience of life's meaning. Reflect upon the circle within a circle. What might your inner circle look like?

Here are some possible hero(ine)'s journey parallels for today's jury trial lawyers. Your narrative and life story can start anywhere. Because we're all lawyers, at some point our departure probably includes undergrad where we earned good grades, took the LSAT, and were accepted to a law school. We entered into a new world and crossed perhaps our first threshold: three years of law school, where we were taught how to "think like a lawyer," and literally learned a foreign language—legalese. We were also introduced to moot court, clerking, and maybe our legal mentors. Then we also took and passed a bar exam.

When we start practicing law, we cross another threshold and descend deep into the belly of the whale, (and yes, our future literally includes many challenging trials). Our legal work is adversarial, demanding, stressful, public, and every trial is the equivalent of entering a cave in which you either slay the dragon or it slays you. We're only trial away from our next loss. In contingency fee cases, you only eat what you kill; so, if you don't win, then you don't eat. We struggle to

---

10. McAdams, "American Identity: The Redemptive Self."
11. Benjamin A. Rogers et al., "Seeing Your Life Story as a Hero's Journey Increases Meaning in Life," *Journal of Personality and Social Psychology* 125, no. 4 (2023). DOI: https://doi.org/10.1037/pspa0000341.

gain confidence, competence, and pay the bills. All the while, we're haunted on the inside by our fears and emotional insecurities. This job tests every measure of one's resources. You enter "the dark night of the soul" many times. If you survive these multiple tests, then you'll have a chance to ultimately emerge transformed and empowered.

The fifth step of the initiation stage is the apotheosis. Here the hero(ine)'s "boon" is your acquired professional confidence, competence, and success; however that's not enough. Under Campbell's formula, the hero(ine) must now apply their legal talents (primarily) in favor of their tribe. Our "return" includes stepping into an even larger expression of ourselves—less Ego with a capital E. Campbell's delving into the psychic "deaths" and "rebirths" in our paths of self-realization are powerful insights in our life-long journey of personal growth and discovery. In the hero(ine)'s final chapter, they are concurrently the master of two worlds, i.e. their inner demons (ego), and the outer world, i.e. our jury trials.

Awakening the Hero Within by Carol Pearson is a very readable inner map of the hero(ine)'s journey.[12] It's a self-help book exploring how Jungian archetypes can assist you in navigating your journey. Pearson discusses gender without limiting choices and offers examples of non-traditional paths. Approach the book with curiosity and open-mindedness. *The Heroine with 1,001 Faces* is another post Campbell work that elevates the role of women in mythology and today's practice of law.[13]

Patriotically making our trial stories too much about our clients violates the basics of social psychology by inviting counter factual reasoning ("yes, but…," and "if only…") and defensive attribution (the jurors' unconscious desire to believe what happened to the plaintiff can't and won't happen to them). Keep the focus of judgment on the

---

12. Carol Pearson, *Awakening the Hero Within* (New York: HarperCollins, 1991). *See also* Pearson's *The Hero Within: Six Archetypes We Live By* (New York: HarperCollins, 2015).

13. Maria Tatar, *The Heroine with 1,001 Faces* (New York: Liveright Publishing Corporation, 2021).

defendant and their bad choices. With this big caveat, aspects of the hero(ine)'s journey can often map onto our clients and their families.

Unexpected injuries upend their lives, overwhelming them emotionally, medically, and financially. We play important roles in their journeys as legal guides and guardians (think here of Campbell's mentors—guides for the hero). Our client's legal challenges are the reason for our professional journeys, and as you know, the jury's verdict is the final chapter of our client's story.

Ultimately, our personal challenge as hero(ine)s is to enjoy and build upon our professional successes without letting it go to our heads. This demands perspective, humility, and a dose of legal modesty. Bon Voyage!

Writing Your Obituary

Newspaper obituaries are formulaic biographies: where you were born and raised, education, family, professional accomplishments, positive glimpses of personality, a comment on favorite hobbies or avocations, family, and survivors. Think of your life story and hero(ine)'s journey as preludes to an intimate and private obituary that reveals who you aspire to become. It's got nothing to do with the world's applause, it's an inner glimpse of your best character and efforts. David Brooks develops this in *The Road to Character*.[14] A cryptic example might be: "I want to be the most effective jury lawyer and the best version of myself I can become. I want to be self-aware and acknowledge the presence and size of my ego, yet mindfully learn to harness it to help and serve others."

Take the time to visit a cemetery and reflect on your life story, hero(ine)'s journey, and private obituary. Imagine you have been dead for twenty years. Notice the flowers on the more recent graves, almost certainly left by family. Now look for graves that are a hundred years old, there's no flowers unless they were a veteran and it's Memorial Day weekend. Perspective is the benefit of a cemetery visit while considering

---

14. David Brooks, *The Road to Character* (New York: Random House, 2016).

your private obituary. The role any one of us plays in the evolution of the American Common Law is both big and small. We help one client at a time, but our future ripple or butterfly effect can be impactful. We expand our horizons when we lift our gaze from a specific client's case to our larger communities (Campbell called it our tribe) and the common law. Oliver Wendell Holmes counseled that we lawyers should view ourselves collectively rather than individually.

We all aspire to lives of meaning, purpose, fulfilment, and significance. That's what generative narratives and the hero(ine)'s journey are about.

Conclusion

You aspire to grow to your full legal potential as quickly as possible. This isn't about me or you; it's about us. The best of all of us is necessary for the continual vitality of our profession and civil justice system. Keep your eyes on the horizon.

Much love…

6

Different Types of Courtroom Work

In the next chapter, I will focus on comparing defense of the criminally accused (criminal defense) and plaintiffs' personal injury work. I've included this chapter for law students and beginning lawyers who are searching for an area of the law they would be most comfortable in. I will discuss different varieties of jury trial work and invite you to ask yourself if the work's a good fit for you. Should you work for the government or in the private sector? What's it like in a district attorney (DA) or public defender's office? How about insurance defense work? How are big firms different from small ones? What about going out on your own and hanging your own shingle? Finding what's right for you isn't easy. It depends on your deepest values, temperament, personality, risk tolerance, work ethic, and talents.

Finding the Right Fit for You

Certain personality types are more suited for certain kinds of trial work than others. The work shapes the lawyer, and, yes, the lawyer also shapes the work. While most big-firm commercial litigators were excellent law students, this isn't true for many doing criminal defense (CD) or in plaintiffs' personal injury (PI). This has powerful implications for the lawyers who self-select to the different lines of work.

I've canvassed the professional literature for work-based personality tests and opinions from within the vocational community as to good fits. The Myers-Briggs test tells us most lawyers are deductive introverts, meaning they prefer to work privately toward careful conclusions. Common sense tells me lawyers who enjoy the public nature of jury trials tend to be extroverts. Products liability (engineering) and medical negligence (medicine) are by their nature complicated; my smart friends revel in the technical aspects. Storytelling is a natural fit for extroverted intuitive thinkers. Stories integrate; they bring everything together. It's difficult to deny our emotional and intellectual predispositions. If you liked debate, public speaking, student government, and people, then you'll probably find jury trial work a good fit. Moot court mimics appellate work much more than trial practice classes resemble the courtroom.

There are studies suggesting lawyers are aggressive and competitive. No news there, but what's interesting is the cause. It isn't because the practice of law demands these traits or that law school and the practice of law teaches us to act this way; it's more that those who self-select to the law were already so inclined.[1] Of course, we're vocationally encouraged and rewarded for being assertive, but this is more reinforced than causal. The public stereotypes of trial lawyers are as follows:

> Self-confident, dominant, argumentative, aggressive, combative, cunning, highly intelligent, ingenious, required or permitted

---

1. Susan Swaim Daicoff, *Lawyer, Know Thyself: A Psychological Analysis of Personality Strengths and Weaknesses* (Washington, DC: American Psychological Association, 2004).

to use drama for effect, committed above all else to prevail for their clients and causes, involved in work, well dressed, driven towards competence, ambitious, competitive, and interested in social issues.[2]

Sound like TV? I'm not sure if art mimics life or life mimics art. It's probably both.

Life in Big Firms

Let me return to my earlier comments on big-firm partners. From my observation, the smarter the lawyer, the more they are inclined to view the world through the lens of a high IQ. This means they intellectualize and analyze everything because they can, and they're good at it; however, in the process, they often squeeze the humanity out of their cases. It's not the big-firm culture to be people-oriented or storytellers. Cases tend to be viewed as fact situations and legal issues rather than competing narratives.

When big-firm lawyers discuss their cases, it's usually in aseptic terms, much like a law school exam. Listen to them—instead of talking about real people, they talk about complex legal theories and sound like they're arguing a pretrial motion for summary judgment. The bigger the firm, the higher the hourly billing rates, and the bigger the words. Compare this with how we plaintiffs' lawyers describe our cases and the injured people we represent. We sound more like a country-and-western song: "Somebody done somebody wrong." At least that's how I see it.

Big firms look for book-smart associates whom they can train and clone. In any firm, the senior partners personify what success looks like for that firm. Are they smart? Probably plenty. Are they people-savvy with a high emotional quotient (EQ)? Some are, and some are not. However, I guarantee every partner is 100 percent sure they're the real deal, and by their firm's definition, they are; otherwise, they wouldn't have made it to

---

2. Daicoff, *Lawyer, Know Thyself.*

the top of that particular pyramid. Law firms tend to be closed systems that define, and then replicate, what success is and looks like.

If you excel in big-firm culture, then you'll probably enjoy a long, successful, and profitable career. But the longer you stay as an associate on the firm's partnership track, the harder it is to leave. With every passing year, you become increasingly invested. Every choice, including the "non" choice of staying, comes with mixed benefits and burdens.[3] Of course, I'm generalizing, and obviously not all big firms are the same, but the billable-hour model and the specifics of a firm's culture tend to promote similarities.

Experience in a Solo Practice

When starting out, you'll take any work that pays and some that doesn't. This includes divorces, deeds, estates, wills, real estate, bankruptcies, personal injury, and any criminal defense work you can sign up. Here's where you'll almost certainly get the chance to do some unintended pro bono work. I suggest you get paid up front in cash when someone charged with writing a bad check wants to hire you to defend them. We both know you've got to keep the lights on and meet the monthly overhead.

Learn by watching, learn by doing, learn any way you can. Some lawyers are seen forever sitting on the dock, waiting for their ship to sail in. More energetic and proactive lawyers have been seen swimming out to sea searching for their ship, yes, maybe even in the dark! Ask an experienced lawyer to help you evaluate your first few personal injury cases. You'll be pleased at how many good lawyers are happy to help, and no, it's

---

3. Gregory R. Mowe, "40 Years (Almost) in the Wrong Profession," *Litigation Journal* 31, no. 3, (Fall 2012), 1–3. I came across an insightful article written by my American College friend Greg Mowe. After forty years in the courtroom, he dryly shared his views on our profession, challenges in the courtroom, and who plaintiffs' lawyers really are. It's a delightful read.

not to get your case as a referral. This is a profession. Many senior lawyers welcome the opportunity to return the favors they received when they were starting out. We're all part of a big wheel, the cycle of life.

Specialties in Trial Work— Asking for Help

In a legal world of increasing specialization, it's an open question whether any lawyer should handle a serious case if their practice area isn't in that specialty. It's dangerous to presume too many competencies. Ask for some help or consider associating an experienced lawyer who will invest in you, meaning teach you. In this section, I discuss how to associate an experienced lawyer to assist in your case and how it can be a win-win for both your client and you.

Even though we're called personal injury, or PI, lawyers, there are many areas of specialization in the noncommercial plaintiffs' world. A client's injuries can be nonphysical (such as in post-traumatic stress disorder), physical, or both. Automobile collision cases are the staple of many practices. Medical negligence and products liability are challenging specialty areas. Other areas include employment discrimination, civil rights, maritime longshoremen's actions, and railroad worker injuries. "Comp," or workers' compensation work, and Social Security disability cases are all administrative rather than judicial, meaning they're held before hearing officers rather than juries. Many lawyers and firms with longtime union associations do volume workers' comp, railroad, Federal Employers' Liability Act (FELA), and longshoremen (Jones Act) work. There's also mass tort and class action work, consumer protection law, creditor–debtor, elder law (nursing home cases), employee benefits, employment and labor, environmental, immigration, questions of insurance coverage (involving declaratory judgment actions), and professional liability (lawyers, architects, and so on).

There's almost no overlap between PI work and business matters. In commercial law, it's typical for firms to do both plaintiffs' and defense work, since their clients are business entities, which both sue and are sued. Whoever wins the race to the courthouse and files first is the plaintiff. There's rarely insurance coverage in business disputes, so each party selects and pays for its own lawyers. High-end commercial lawyers are known as "bet the company" lawyers. Business work is usually hourly, and the billing rates are significantly higher than defense work for insurance carriers, aka general casualty work.

Plaintiffs' lawyers advertise that they specialize in "catastrophic" injuries. Remember that *catastrophic* involves the extent of the damages, while *specialization* involves a particular area of liability or fault, such as medical negligence. All plaintiffs' lawyers want to attract big cases with serious injuries that have insurance coverage, and thus the potential for collecting large damages awards.

Professional Lawyer Groups

Professional groups can help you identify lawyers or firms to associate. Best Lawyers divides the practice into more than 130 specialty areas.[4] Super Lawyers is another resource with over seventy practice areas.[5] Some groups, such as the American College of Trial Lawyers, the American Board of Trial Advocates, the International Society of Barristers, and the International Academy of Trial Lawyers are by invitation only and are highly selective in their membership. A few lawyers get in because of their political resumes more than their trial skills, and some very effective plaintiffs' lawyers are rejected for what I consider to be political and popularity reasons. Invitations to some prestigious groups can be dominated by defense lawyers who maintain a narrow view of professionalism, which a few talented plaintiffs' lawyers don't

---

4. Best Lawyers, https://www.bestlawyers.com/. You can find a complete list of specialty areas and more information on Best Lawyers.

5. Super Lawyers, https://www.superlawyers.com.

always conform to. We can be client-centered, politically active, ideologically driven, and outspoken, and occasionally, we don't play well with others. These by-invitation professional groups don't include all the competent lawyers. I estimate that they're about 90 percent inclusive, with a 10 percent margin of error, split equally between those who shouldn't be in and those who should. This error rate exists for two reasons: First, political prominence and popularity often equal status, which, in turn, mean inclusion. Second, there's a lag between one's reputation and one's competence. Trial lawyers are good about three years before the word gets out, and bad an equal amount of time before their diminishing reputation reflects their dwindling skills. This means that it takes time for the new ones to become recognized and for the old ones to be spotted hanging on too long. There's lots of reasons why we tend to work in smaller firms—I call them totem cultures—built around one or two talented (senior) lawyers. Most of which has to do with personalities, or maybe the lack thereof.

Some plaintiffs' groups, such as AAJ, which I'm proud to belong to, and its various state affiliates, such as Oregon Trial Lawyers Association, which was my professional birthing ground, provide excellent CLE, camaraderie, and real opportunities to become actively involved in our craft and profession.

There's no exact formula when looking for firms to refer to. I've used all of the above. Once I've narrowed the choice down to a couple names, then I go to the lawyers' websites for more information. One thing I don't want is my case to be on somebody's back burner. I don't mind older lawyers in a corner office, but I want to know some younger, talented, and energetic lawyer is keeping my lawsuit moving.

Public Sector Compared to Private Sector

Working in the public sector provides job security, financial stability, and good benefits. You receive a regular paycheck and don't have the never-ending stress of monthly overhead. Working in a public defender's (PD) or district attorney's (DA) office quickly provides you with criminal trial experience, that is, on-the-job courtroom training paid for by the public. Beginning deputy DAs might try up to twenty misdemeanor jury trials a year. Many involve driving under the influence of intoxicants (DUI). You will gain experience handling expert witnesses because the police are trained in matters of scientific proof, such as breath testing equipment and the horizontal gaze nystagmus test.[6] The accused often retain skilled defense counsel who specialize in DUIs. You'll quickly become familiar with trial procedures and basics.

After a time that varies with the size of the office, you'll progress to handling felony cases, perhaps in a specialty unit, such as drugs or sex crimes. The number of trials will drop as you move from misdemeanors to felonies because the cases are more lengthy, serious, and complex. Smaller offices allow you to prosecute felony cases as soon as you're ready, maybe even sooner. In the larger offices, the felony sections are populated by skilled senior lawyers, meaning you must wait in line.

The downside of the DA and PD offices is that they're often sink-or-swim work environments. You're overworked without much mentoring and little or no time to prepare. While you'll quickly try a lot of cases, your professional growth soon plateaus. Here's where a good mentor helps. It's easy to pick up bad habits, which are hard to shake later. You'll tend to repeat the same errors over and over, albeit in new and different forms, and, what's worse, you won't even know it. Everybody makes mistakes; the trick is not to keep repeating the same ones in different forms.

---

6. Intoxylizer and horizontal gaze nystagmus tests are common field sobriety tests for driving under the influence.

Some PDs, DAs, and personal injury lawyers suffer a kind of compassion fatigue from the long hours and emotional nature of our work. *Compassion fatigue* is the physical, emotional, and psychological effect of continuous exposure to other people's trauma.[7] Symptoms include anxiety, insistent thoughts, burnout, and a cynical worldview. A study from the Wisconsin State Public Defender's office showed elevated depression with a negative impact on work, recreation, and home life.[8] All participants, including judges, jurors, lawyers, and witnesses, become emotionally involved in gut-wrenching trials. No one escapes unscathed. As I often say, this work isn't for the faint of heart. You must be emotionally available and thus vulnerable, yet concurrently be able to maintain boundaries and compartmentalize. This takes emotional discipline, maturity, and perspective. Think of it as walking a tightrope. You must focus on the next step, yet not look down. You must be 100 percent in the moment emotionally, yet retain your objectivity. Easy to say, tough to do.

Differences between Insurance Defense & Plaintiffs' Work

Insurance companies are longtime players in our civil justice system. They hire only the best (defense) attorneys, particularly in specialty areas such as medical negligence, products liability, and admiralty. Their go-to lawyers are experienced, talented, and effective; they have many trials booked far into the future. Because of the high volume of cases the insurance carriers assign to them, they try far more big cases than their peers on the plaintiffs' side. This means the big-dollar cases are always well defended—after all, they're processed by insurance

---

7. "Compassion Fatigue," American Bar Association, n.d., https://www.americanbar.org/groups/lawyer_assistance/resources/compassion_fatigue.
8. Dianne Molvig, "The Toll of Trauma," *Wisconsin Lawyer* 84, no. 12 (December 1, 2011).

carriers who carefully select the lawyers to defend their insureds' and, thus, the companies' assets.

Defense lawyers happily accept all the cases insurance companies assign to them. The carriers pay their retained defense counsel by the hour and fund all litigation costs. In contrast, plaintiffs' lawyers work on a contingency fee, and they advance or front all the expenses necessary to prepare and try their cases. A *contingency fee* is exactly what the name implies—getting paid is contingent, or dependent, on us collecting money for our clients. This explains why we must be selective in the cases we accept. If we lose, we not only don't get paid for our time but also lose all the money we've advanced to prepare and try the case. Therefore, bad case selection means a lot more than just no compensation for the time we invested in the lawsuit; we also lose all the money we fronted as costs advanced, which is our profit from past cases. So, more than just a loss for our clients; it's also a loss for us, of both our time and our money.

My judge friends tell me that in most personal injury cases, the defense is better represented than the plaintiff because the quality of the plaintiffs' counsel varies so widely. The quality is consistent on the defense because insurance companies hire only proven performers. However, in the high-end cases, the playing field levels because the referral system tends to assure that the bigger, complex, and more expensive cases are handled by well-capitalized, experienced, and talented plaintiffs' lawyers. These lawyers bring time, energy, money, experience, and expertise to the cases they accept. Plus, the many structural advantages plaintiffs have are fully utilized in high-end cases, such as when and where to file, prompt investigation, and early access to an inventory of skilled expert witnesses. It even includes the order defendants are named in the case caption, which dictates the sequence the parties present their case-in-chief and conduct cross-examination.

Working at Personal Injury Defense Firms

The top defense firms are selective when hiring. Most look for good writers who were strong academic performers in law school. There's excellent mentoring; however, because insurance carriers are the paying clients, there are additional layers of accountability. This means you not only have to please the firm's partners but also the claims representatives from the insurance companies that hire your firm and pay your bills. You often have to work there for three to five years before you're assigned your own cases; they'll be smaller when you start out. You'll be surrounded by talented lawyers who will gradually break you in as a second chair. You'll have far fewer trials than if you begin in the public sector as a prosecutor or public defender, but you'll be gaining valuable experience specific to PI defense work, particularly in pretrial motions and depositions. You'll learn medicine by immersion. You're either good, or you're soon shown the door. Insurance companies hate writing checks for plaintiffs' verdicts. Experienced defense lawyers handling big cases generally don't lose, because the carriers are smart enough to settle the cases they'll probably lose. That's why doctors and hospitals win about five out of six cases that are actually tried.

District Attorney & Public Defenders

Rick Friedman suggests you spend a couple of years in a DA's office learning how to build a case, then move over to the PD's office and learn how to defend and break a case down.[9] Good advice, plus it provides you with multiple perspectives. My only reservation is I'm the

---

9. Rick Friedman, *Becoming a Trial Lawyer* (Portland, OR: Trial Guides, 2008).

only lawyer I've met who makes big distinctions between the clinical skills involved in doing criminal defense versus personal injury.

Political ideologies are at the heart of various specialties. This is not so true in England where barristers are advocates for hire and are trained to advocate both sides of an issue, similar to serving in the Judge Advocate General's (JAG) Corps of the military, where you can criminally prosecute one case while defending another. In America, we have politically charged initiatives, referendums, and legislatures—all public battlegrounds for tort reform, and, occasionally the appointment or election of judges becomes highly politicized. Examples include tort reform efforts for caps or limits on noneconomic damages, modification of common law on joint and several liability rules, and the elimination of punitive damages. These are hot political issues that run in cycles.

Gaining Jury Trial Experience

We've already discussed breaking in on the public side and doing criminal work, be it prosecution or defense. The National Institute for Trial Advocacy (NITA) and AAJ have solid one-week programs that will familiarize you with the basics. Arbitrations don't have a jury, but there's still evidence, testimony, and arguments. Many DA and PD offices have programs where beginning lawyers from the private sector can volunteer for a set time, maybe two to four weeks, with the expectation that they'll be assigned a couple of misdemeanor jury trials. County bar associations have legal aid and pro bono programs that can occasionally lead to trials.

The American Bar Association's litigation section sponsors an audio library of podcasts with practical advice from experienced trial lawyers. The topics range from rainmaking to preparing oral argument to discovery; each one lasts about ten minutes. You can download the podcasts to a mobile device and listen anywhere. [10]

Go watch both civil and criminal trials. Study the jury selection. Does the judge have any special court rules or practices? Must you remain seated at counsel table when questioning witnesses, or are you limited to a podium? There can be big differences between state and federal courts, and from judge to judge. Before trial, I often take my clients and key witnesses to the actual courtroom to give them a feel for the space.

Be on the lookout for a smaller case you can start with. Ask yourself: If I'm going to win, what are the key questions the jury will have to answer in my favor? Alternatively, if I'm going to lose—why, and what are my best responses? Study the pleadings: What are the outcome determinative legal and factual disputes? Review the witnesses' statements. What are your best arguments? Now switch sides. What are your opponent's best and worst arguments? Are there any FRE 401 and 403 pretrial motions you should file to limit the proof? (This is the rule that allows a trial judge to exclude evidence, even though it may be relevant, because it may be too prejudicial, and so on.) Your jitters will lessen once the trial starts. Respect the judge, staff, jury, and, yes, your opposing counsel and parties.

A Few Comments on Prosecuting

DAs often have impressive win-loss records; they represent law and order and can usually plea-bargain the cases they don't want to try. They can quickly get an inflated self-opinion when they win more than their competence justifies. Ex-DAs often have a crisis of confidence when they switch over to doing criminal defense or PI work. They're so used to winning, they're devastated after a few losses. Welcome aboard!

---

10. Go to the ABA website to learn more about this program. "Sound Advice," American Bar Association, https://www.americanbar.org/groups/litigation/resources/sound-advice.

Here's where temperament, grit, and resilience are so important. It's hard to stay positive when you're repeatedly getting your ass kicked.

On Becoming a Judge

I wondered when I was younger if I'd like to be a trial judge. Oregon authorizes the appointment of part-time judges, called judges *pro tem*. You must be recommended by your local bar committee and presiding judge, and then be approved by the Oregon Supreme Court. I've been approved for about thirty years. I quickly realized that being a trial judge demanded a different temperament than mine. It isn't that I wasn't smart enough or couldn't do the work. However, when done well, it takes the patience of Job, and I don't have it. So, my experiment was successful in that I got my answer: it's not my cup of tea. I analogize it to athletes: some players go on to become referees; others get a taste of the competition and know that's where they belong.

With that said, I still serve occasionally as a judge *pro tem*, not because I want to become a judge, but because it helps me become a better trial lawyer. It's good for me to occasionally shed my advocate's mentality and become an impartial decision-maker. When I'm seated between the flags, I work hard to slow down. I carefully listen and try to ask thoughtful questions. I do my best to show respect for everyone. Process is almost as important as being legally correct. However, in my heart I now know I'm a lifelong player, not a zebra or referee. Maybe even more important, serving as a trial judge has provided me with insights into what juries like, don't like, and the why behind their preferences.

Oregon lawyers are prohibited from contacting jurors after a trial. Jurors may contact us, but we can't approach them. After the trial is over, judges can debrief jurors. Also, lawyers appearing before me have often read my books and writings. This provides me with a living laboratory to observe in real time how my teachings are interpreted and applied, and then what the jurors think about the lawyers' delivery of those services. Many years ago, I served for five years on the board of directors of an insurance company, Oregon's Professional Liability Fund (PLF), and spent my last year as the chairperson. It was kind of like a fox in the henhouse! The view on the bus can be entirely different, depending on where you're seated.

Back to a career as a trial judge. The pay and retirement package is decent, it has status and prestige, and the work can be both interesting and boring. I enjoy the necessary analyses in a complicated criminal motion to suppress. You encounter issues of standing and correct procedural order, starting with statutes, then the state constitution, and finally the US constitution. I do my best to make careful findings of fact, and if the law is unclear, then I offer my best analysis and conclusions. It's an intellectual challenge, it's important, and I consider it a privilege.

On the flip side, doing a morning of criminal arraignments is, to me, damned boring. Domestic relations also don't crank my tractor, but like every job, it's a mix. And, again, I know all of them are important to the public, especially to anyone involved.

Appellate judges are the ones who generate the reported decisions law students are so familiar with. Their work involves high-level research and writing. Most appellate judges live solitary, monastic professional lives. Again, not my cup of tea, but it's obviously important.

I'm always happy to see good trial lawyers ascend to the bench. It's easy to issue decisions from on high that don't acknowledge the realities of private practice. Petitions for attorney's fees are an example. The theoretical can be emphasized to the detriment of the practical. It's one of the many reasons I admire Lewis Powell and Thurgood Marshall. They're some of the few Supreme Court justices who were real trial lawyers, and great ones at that.

Administrative law judges, known as ALJs, are governmental employees who serve as hearings officers for agencies such as the department of motor vehicles for alcohol breath tests, social services for denial of benefit applications, and so on. Hearings officers are generally experienced practitioners in their area of hearings. It's an important job and can make for a satisfying career.

Conclusion

No romantic idealizations or public glamorization can change the economic realities or adversarial nature of jury trial work. The courtroom isn't right for everybody. The question is whether it's right for you. I like one advocacy teacher's observation, which I'll paraphrase: In the past thirty years, I've encountered more than a few bright, capable, and hardworking young lawyers who lacked the instincts, the competitive spirit, the mental and verbal agility, and the intestinal fortitude needed to be a successful trial attorney… most were better suited for a different place in the legal profession.

A friend of mine, Rick Martson, past president of the International Society of Barristers, a wonderful trial advocacy teacher and commercial trial lawyer, calls such students "natural hunters." It's a little jingoistic but rings true. The only real way to find out if it's for you is to try it. But understand it takes time to master the craft, so don't quit too early.

7

Differences Between Criminal Defense & Plaintiffs' Personal Injury

Defending the criminally accused and plaintiffs' personal injury require different skill sets. There are good reasons why very few lawyers are accomplished at both, and clinical experience in either has little to do with the other.

Criminal Trials

In criminal trials, you don't learn to put on a compelling case in chief, you never take a discovery deposition, and the cross-examination is uniformly heavy-handed.

Cross-Examination

Cross-exams in civil and criminal cases have important differences, even though the rules of evidence are the same, apart from the constitutional protections that apply in a criminal case. In criminal trials, both sides routinely face structurally embedded targets, which lend themselves to a forceful and destructive cross-examination. Let me explain.

For the prosecutor, these targets are the defendants and their witnesses, who may have tattoos, piercings, and prior criminal convictions. Not to mention, the accused are obviously motivated to save their hide. Conversely, the defense targets police officers, who are professionals trained in the collection, preservation, and presentation of evidence. Cops are fair game if they're fudging, even just a little. These recurring pools of witnesses contribute to a rough-and-tumble environment. Aggressive and destructive cross is the norm.

In civil cases, there are often good and decent citizens on both sides of the dispute, and it's not as visceral when cross-examining nonexperts. Juries will punish you for being heavy-handed if they think you are abusing nice folks, especially when the opposing lawyer is respectful to you and your witnesses. It's hard to shift gears once you've become accustomed to an aggressive style of cross. You'll see a kinder and gentler cross-examination in civil cases, defense medical experts (DME) excepted. It's just as effective, just not so robust.

Decisions about who, when, and how to cross-examine are complicated. It's generally full speed ahead in criminal defense. You must be able to cross-examine on your feet, because you don't have depositions, like you do in civil cases. While I believe the best cross-examiners are in criminal defense, I also believe the top end of the civil bar is more skilled than most of the criminal bar, and elite insurance defense regulars are among the best. They know their medicine and have access to all the best experts.

Plaintiffs often choose to start civil trials by calling the defendant adversely. This can't happen in a criminal case because of the accused's privilege against self-incrimination. Most prosecutors' direct examinations don't involve much more than putting a uniformed police officer on the stand and asking a variation of "Your name, occupation, experience, and training, and then what happened next?" Active pretrial motions to suppress can often lead to plea bargains. Neither criminal prosecution nor defense tends to teach or demand excellence in preparing and presenting direct examinations.

Your job in a criminal defense case is to identify and argue a reasonable doubt. In high-end cases, it's common for the accused to not testify. This is not true in misdemeanor cases. You tear things down on cross-examination, while during jury selection and closing you pound on the big three:

1. The state has the burden of proof.
2. Your client is presumed innocent.
3. No adverse inference can be drawn if the accused doesn't testify, and it can't be commented upon during deliberations.

It's different over on the plaintiff's side. Only occasionally will you see lawyers attempt to gut a witness like you do in criminal trials. In civil cross-examination, the best lawyers bleed a witness to death but do it with a thousand paper cuts. Plaintiffs' lawyers must build their case with great direct examinations as they attempt to overcome the burden of proof. It's always easier to tear something down than to build it up, and if it's fifty-fifty, then in civil the defense always wins because they don't have the burden of proof. Hung juries and mistrials favor the defense both in civil and criminal. Why? Because the plaintiff's side has to front the costs of a second trial and any advantage of surprise is now gone—the defense has already seen their entire playbook. Hung juries in criminal cases are almost always dismissed or plea-bargained.

The cross-examination of hired experts in civil cases can get very robust. They're paid to come into court and offer opinions:

> Q: Doctor, how much were you paid by this defense attorney to testify in this trial?
> Q: You've never treated the plaintiff, have you?
> Q: You only met the plaintiff one time, seven months ago, for fifty minutes, and now you're here to tell the jury about the rest of the plaintiff's life?

You get it. My book, *Recovering for Psychological Injuries,* has a generic list of twenty questions covering the usual areas of inquiry.[1] You can vary them to fit almost any expert.

I went looking for books about the differences between civil and criminal advocacy, and there isn't much. Most standard trial texts emphasize civil work and plaintiffs' personal injury work; they occasionally sprinkle in a few criminal defense examples. The National Institute for Trial Advocacy (NITA) offers both civil and criminal courses. There are separate national colleges for prosecutors and criminal defense practitioners, and active national and state associations for each of the respective civil political camps. State bar associations offer seminars on all aspects of trials, such as jury selection, direct examination, cross-examination, and so on, but almost nothing hands-on where you have to stand and deliver. For that, you're back to the NITA and American Association for Justice (AAJ) regional courses. I'm not sure why there's so little discussion of the different skill sets that are required to excel in each. My comments aren't a devaluation of the criminal bar, just my observations as a trial lawyer who has done both and from when I served as a trial judge.[2] The largest generalizations can I draw are that a good jury selection and strong cross-examination is necessary for criminal defense; and while

---

1. William A. Barton, *Recovering for Psychological Injuries,* 3rd ed. (Portland, OR: Trial Guides, 2010), chapter 20, 334–37.

2. I'm listed in *Best Lawyers in America* for both criminal defense and plaintiffs' personal injury in four areas: Non-White-Collar Criminal Defense, Personal Injury Litigation, Products Liability, and Medical Malpractice Law.

a great direct examination is essential for plaintiffs' work, a powerful cross won't make up for an average case-in-chief.

The Business Side of Trial Work

Let's start with plaintiffs' personal injury. Delays between the original case intake and finally getting paid by a later settlement, verdict, or an appeal are enduring problems. You may have an occasional big payday, but cash flow issues are a serious problem in the meantime. When you file a lawsuit on behalf of an injured person, your clients expect you to win; after all, you accepted their case and signed the complaint. It's difficult for our limited financial resources not to influence our judgment, particularly if cash flow problems tell us we need a fee sooner rather than later, or can't afford to try the case—and lose.

You'll also need to decide whether to do your own appeals or contract them out. Appeals always mean more delays and obstacles to getting paid. All this is a recipe for anxiety, stress, headaches, substance abuse, burnout, and even bankruptcy.

In criminal defense, your case inventory moves more quickly because the criminally accused have constitutional protections to speedy trials; therefore, civil cases are the ones that are delayed when budget cuts hit a state's judicial department. In criminal defense, double jeopardy protections assure that if you win, it's over; not true in civil cases. Big verdicts invite lengthy appeals. Many people can't afford to pay hefty legal fees when they find themselves charged with a serious crime. If your clients can't pay before trial, it's certainly not going to get any better if you lose and they're in jail; conversely, when you win, then they're free and also don't need you anymore. A lot of criminal defense work is done by public defenders because the accused are indigent. An accused may be guilty of at least something, so often lawyers bargain for a guilty plea to a lesser included crime or a recommended sentence by the prosecution.

The Challenges of Doing Criminal Defense

Rules apply when the government accuses a citizen of a crime. Prosecutors are generally thought of as the "good guys" because they represent the public, or "the people," while defense attorneys represent accused drug dealers, pimps, child molesters, terrorists, rapists, and maybe even murderers. I'd like to emphasize the word *accused* because, of course, in our system, everyone's legally presumed innocent. The work of a criminal defense lawyer is an uphill battle; if you compare it to the sport of wrestling, you always start in the down position. There are more losses than wins, and it's easy to get bummed out; plus, it helps to have an anti-authority chip on your shoulder. An important result of criminal defense work is it keeps the government honest.

I'll share two cases that provide glimpses into criminal defense (CD). These experiences challenged my personal and professional ethics and forged many of my present views about what it really means to be a jury trial lawyer. You won't grow if you don't learn from the often unwelcome opportunities life forces upon you. The lessons I learned from these cases are ones I tried to avoid but couldn't. I had no choice. Early in my career, there weren't indigent defense capital murder panels. This meant the presiding judge could order any lawyer to defend an accused. This is how I met John Smith in the early 1980s.

Defending John Smith: I Was a Divided House

I want to start by telling you that John is now deceased. John was accused of first-degree murder. He told me several different versions of what happened, so I knew I couldn't put him on the stand; plus, what he shared with me made me confident he was guilty. Against my strenuous advice, John insisted on taking a polygraph, and further stipulated the results into evidence. Of course, the law has changed since then. He then flunked the "lie detector" or "box," just as I knew he would. I also worried that John would kill again if I successfully defended him, and I knew my job was to gain his acquittal. Privately, a big part of me wanted him convicted so he wouldn't kill someone else. I was truly conflicted on the inside.

It's here I learned how effectively to represent a client when I was morally divided. It's difficult to not allow your personal beliefs to interfere with your advocacy. My competitive nature and professional pride were front and center, all lumped under the canopy of my ego. The prosecutor was a good friend and an immensely talented opponent. It was important to me that, if John was found guilty and executed, that the community could be confident that he had been accorded a vigorous defense, and therefore, the result was according to law. Deep down, I was plagued with questions about whether I could do my job, meaning provide my client with constitutionally adequate assistance of counsel. I wasn't so sure. I filed a motion to withdraw.

In chambers and way off the record, the judge told me, "Your client may be a son of a bitch; furthermore, he may be guilty and ultimately be found so on properly admitted evidence; but for now, for today, for this case, he's presumed innocent and he's your son of a bitch. So, you've got a job to do; now quit whining and go do it."

His later ruling on the record simply read "Motion to Withdraw Denied."

Everyone, including the judge, my client, the jurors, and, yes, the community, expected me to do my best. As the chief judicial officer, the judge told me the county couldn't afford to retry the case. He said he ordered me to represent the accused because he knew I'd do a good job and there wouldn't be any post-conviction relief for inadequate assistance of counsel. Part of me wanted to do an "A" job out of pride; yet another part of me was tempted to do a "C" job with the probability that John would be convicted. Remember, I was personally convinced my client was guilty and, further, that if he was acquitted, he would kill again.

Then a third part of me figured a "B" job would be just fine—let the chips fall where they may. After all, the Bill of Rights, with its Sixth Amendment guarantee of assistance of counsel, only demanded that I do a "C" quality (adequate assistance of counsel) job. At the time, the state paid me just $30 an hour, and I was forced to neglect my paying clients. I knew no one would question my effort; I knew that I could do a "C" job. After all, even Michael Jordan misses an occasional free throw.

After papering the file with lots of informed consent, John followed my advice, and we decided not to submit any lesser included offense instructions. The state wanted the death penalty and also didn't request instructions on any lesser included offenses; so, in other words, both sides rolled the dice. It was all or nothing. John didn't take the stand. At this point, I would like you to pause and reflect on the quality of the job you would do and why. Take some time and remember my strongly held personal opinions. The jury acquitted John.

Within a year, he was arrested and charged with the attempted murder of a young woman at a nearby university. He was convicted and sent to prison. The story doesn't end there. Fellow inmates killed him shortly after he arrived at the state penitentiary. Many of those who were in favor of my doing a "C" job smile and say, "Good. Justice was done." That's a perspective I don't share. In the law, two wrongs don't make a right; therefore, I can't condone John's death at the hands of the inmates.

Despite my strong personal feelings, my defense was successful because I effectively argued that the state had failed to meet its burden of proof; that is, there was a reasonable doubt. One of the lessons this case affirmed for me is that guilty or not, no matter my personal feelings, I was charged with protecting the rights of the accused—my client. We're all part of a larger system of justice. As lawyers, we're duty bound to honor a judge's orders, and further, we must always appear and argue in a representative capacity. The case was about me doing my job within the rules to the best of my ability and, in the process, playing my small but important part in our nation's larger machinery of government and justice. It was not about me or even what I thought; I was not a juror. Like the judge said, my job was to "do my job" within the rules—period.

A few years later, the judge was looking back on the trial. He explained that if he signed an order committing the defendant to a death sentence, society had to know everyone had followed the rules in the process, especially him. He was correct.

But wait. There's one more twist. John also had a Gary Gilmore streak. While protesting his innocence, he also confided that he wanted to die but couldn't bring himself to commit suicide. Of course, I had a number of forensic psychologists and psychiatrists examine John, had preachers visit him, and had therapists counsel him. No one had any doubt that he was legally competent and knew what he wanted, that is, to die. This means even though he denied guilt, he was willing to plead guilty to the first-degree murder charge, but only if the state would guarantee him the death penalty as part of the plea bargain! Of course, the district attorney (DA) was only too happy to oblige; the judge, however, correctly reasoned that the state couldn't be a party to a suicide pact and rejected the guilty plea.

He said the only way he could even consider accepting a plea of guilty was if John clearly and knowingly agreed to a factual basis that supported the charge, and no, John wouldn't do that.

This death wish explains why John took the lie detector test, which he knew he would flunk, and also stipulated to the admissibility of the results before he took the test. He seemed to be trying to sabotage any chance he might have had at an acquittal, and thus assure his death. Had I chosen to provide only a "C" defense for him, I would have unwittingly assisted him in his efforts at a state-orchestrated suicide. He was on a sustained suicide watch during his incarceration.

Defending James Doe: A Map to Bodies

In another capital case, the same judge who previously ordered me to represent John Smith appointed me to represent James Doe. Before trial, James gave me a map with the locations of a number of women he said he'd killed, along with their names and the dates he killed each of them. The women were all listed as missing, and no one had been charged in their disappearances. He authorized me to explain to the DA that I possessed the map and had carefully reviewed it, but further instructed that I couldn't reveal any of its particulars. He instructed me to say that he would take the police to the bodies, but only if the state would waive the death penalty in all of his crimes that were pending, known, and unknown. James explicitly prohibited me from ever showing the DA the map, any copy of it, or indirectly revealing the specifics of it. Of course, every lawyer knows the map was protected by the attorney–client privilege and work-product rules. The state adamantly refused to accept my client's offer.

A big part of me wanted to "accidentally" leave a copy of the map on a corner of the DA's desk so the unknown women's families could have some closure. I returned the map to James, its author and owner, as he had instructed. He then tore it up and flushed it down his jail cell toilet.

Just about this time, my neighbor's daughter was killed in Portland. She was a fine young woman, a few years older than my oldest daughter, Monique. I remember hearing the news on the radio on my way to court. It made me physically sick. I felt I was involuntarily thrust into some surreal horror movie. Good people were being killed by really bad people, and here I was being ordered to "protect" the bad people.[3] One more time, I did my very best to compartmentalize my grief and thoughts in an effort to focus on the task at hand, which by now you know meant me doing an "A" job.

During the second day of jury selection, the Oregon Supreme Court ruled the then-existing death penalty unconstitutional.[4] With the death penalty threat gone, James changed his plea and went off to prison to begin serving multiple concurrent life sentences. James's still alive, and the state has never received any cooperation from him. The attorney–client privilege continues as long as the client lives. This means I can't leak any info on James's map, at least not while he's alive. In truth, it's been so long that I've forgotten any details, so even if he died tomorrow and I wanted to help, I've got nothing to offer.

Conclusion

Ethical principles demand that you provide your clients with competent legal counsel no matter who your client is, what they may be charged with or have done, or what you may feel about it. The

---

3. Law enforcement believes she was a victim of Randy Woodfield, the infamous "I-5 Killer." Woodfield was never charged with her death and now resides in the Oregon State Penitentiary, serving multiple life sentences.

4. *State v. Quinn*, 290 Or 383, 623 p.2d 690 (1981).

principles of IA can guide you through the challenges and ethics of representing all types of clients. The framers of our Bill of Rights wisely acknowledged that some guilty people would walk free in order to assure innocent people aren't convicted. This means, at least to me, that at all times and in all places, we, as lawyers, should do our very best for our clients, our community, and the legal system, and this is true no matter where we sit at counsel table, or in the center as a judge. Nobody said this job was easy.

8

Heuristics & Biases

The idea of thinking "shortcuts" entered the public consciousness with a book called *Thinking, Fast and Slow*, by Daniel Kahneman.[1] The idea is that we all form habits of thought that generally serve us well, called type A, while a slower, analytic, and deliberate way of thinking is called type B. The type A heuristics I discuss in this chapter are common and cause predictable systemic errors in predictions.

Effective trial lawyers navigate between the mandates of the court's instructions and the realities of human behavior. It's necessary to understand not just what people think, but how they think, and how they process information. The more insightful and creative your work becomes, the more interesting and rewarding it will be. Heuristics tend to be thinking "shortcuts," while biases are strongly held personal beliefs that predispose us to act or reason a certain way. This chapter is before the pretrial checklist and mediation materials because you need to understand these concepts to effectively negotiate and present at trial. If

---

1. Daniel Kahneman, *Thinking, Fast and Slow*. (New York: Farrar, Straus and Giroux, 2011).

you expect to walk on water without getting too wet, then you'll need to know where the rocks are located just beneath the surface. Studying heuristics and biases will introduce you to the nuances and psychology of our craft. Untrained instincts won't just fool you, they can betray you.[2]

The application of the law to the facts of the case, when filtered through jurors' commonsense, assures our justice system remains grounded in community values.

Lawyers Think (& Judges Instruct) Deductively, Yet Jurors Think Inductively

We lawyers suffer the disadvantage of being legally trained, which is a burden jurors aren't inflicted with. Legal training teaches us to be logical. Lawyers think in syllogisms. We start with the facts, and then carefully build, from the bottom up, to conclusions supported by those facts. Ordinary folks process information inductively, meaning they think from the top down. They form early opinions, and then later collect facts to support what they already believe. Inductive processing is different from the legal template commanded by the court's instructions. Within these differences exist both challenges and opportunities.

After each of the following standard or uniform civil jury instructions, I bracket the realities of jurors' inductive thinking.

---

2. Three books I recommend are: *Winning Case Preparation: Understanding Jury Bias,* by David Bossart, Gregory Cusimano, Edward Lazarus, and David Wenner (Portland, OR: Trial Guides, 2018); *Judgement Under Uncertainty: Heuristics and Biases,* edited by Daniel Kahneman, Paul Slovic, and Amos Tversky (New York: Cambridge University Press, 1982); and *Luvera on Advocacy* by Paul Luvera and Lita Barnett Luvera (Portland, OR: Trial Guides, 2020), especially page 23 (on the unconscious mind in decision making) and page 30 (on how we are not rational).

Instructions

1. "You will hear the evidence, decide what the facts are, and then apply those facts to the law that I will give you. That is how you will reach your verdict." Stated differently: "Do not attempt to decide the case until you begin your deliberations." [Jurors form early impressions, which they will thereafter defend.]
2. "You must follow the law whether you agree with it or not." [The jurors will do justice, or what they think is fair. At least three aspects of the instructions, (1) commanding jurors to both draw from and rely upon any reasonable inferences, (2) explaining that a verdict can be based solely upon circumstantial evidence, and (3) charging them to apply their considered judgment invites jurors to apply their own notions of commonsense and fair play.]
3. "You must not be influenced by sympathy for, or prejudice against, any party." [This is the heart of jury selection. Despite the best intentions, people's deepest values resist being sanitized from their analyses.]
4. "The jury is not to consider whether any of the parties have insurance, or the ability to pay for any loss." [In determining whether the defendant should bear the loss, they are not to consider the party's ability to pay, hmm…]
5. "Do not determine whether a party was negligent by consideration of subsequent events." [This collides with hindsight bias. An example of this would be an insurance-bad-faith case where the evidence in the later bad-faith trial consists of all the earlier insurance offers in the underlying case and the later final verdict. Subsequent remedial measures can also invoke a species of hindsight bias.]
6. "The amount of money requested by the plaintiff in the complaint should not be considered in arriving at your verdict except that it does fix a maximum amount you can award the plaintiff." [The amount of the prayer is psychologically important. It's known as an anchor or bracket because it's where jurors start their analysis.]

It's my impression that lawyers who try commercial cases are more comfortable with the technical aspects of a trial than they are sharing stories about the people they represent. Without disrespect, many commercial cases are arbitrated or bench trials. As lawyers move further away from juries, the more "book smart" they seem to become. The closer lawyers get to juries, the more "people smart" they must become. These differing orientations color our very perception of "what the problem is." This is called correspondence bias, and it explains why, from the same fact, a "book" lawyer will try one case, and a "people" lawyer will try quite another. The case we "see" is inherently autobiographical. That's why we use concept focus groups to learn what case the jurors will "see."

What Jurors Believe: Their (Prejudices) Outcome-Determinative Values

Jurors, individually and collectively, represent all the messy stuff that makes us the people we are. This includes our biases, sympathies, and prejudices—the very attributes courts direct every juror to ignore. The legal system's answer is that fairness is produced by allowing all sides to question prospective jurors, and then eliminate the extremes on both ends by exercising challenges. The result is a committee of the community our culture deems to be "fair."

We also know all sides are trying to obtain a jury that is biased in their favor. This is as it is intended, as the adversary model assumes justice will result when opponents vigorously pursue self-interest within this system. Because of this process of exclusion, I think of voir dire as a system of juror deselection," rather than selection.

It is important to understand that biases involve what people believe and that these biases foreshadow jurors' votes. We all know the court instructs the jury not to be influenced by "bias, sympathy, or prejudice." If these mandates were self-fulfilling, we wouldn't need jury selection. Examples include any tenants of the tort reform agenda or arguments like:

- "Money won't do any good because it's not going to bring back the dead."
- "It's blood money!"
- "A rich person may be legally entitled to a verdict, but not need the money as badly as a nice defendant who owes it."
- "Jurors are not to consider race, gender, or religion, etc."

These are some of the concerns attorneys for both sides must explore. A good way to identify these outcome-determinative attitudes is to ask yourself, "Later, when the jury retires to deliberate, what is the first thing they are going to talk about?"

There's no one way to articulate the embedded biases every plaintiff faces when they are claiming somebody else is responsible for what's happened to them. Bossart, Cusimano, Lazarus, and Wenner offer four generic biases.[3] These core biases are enduring and appear and reappear under different labels and masks:

- *Suspicion:* Jurors are suspicious of everyone in the courtroom, particularly the plaintiff, the plaintiff's attorney, and the plaintiff's claims.
- *Victimization:* Jurors are worried that they or others will somehow be victimized by the outcome of the trial.
- *Personal Responsibility:* Jurors are not going to hold a defendant responsible if they feel the plaintiff has behaved irresponsibly.
- *Stuff Happens:* As the facts of the claim become more complicated, it becomes easier for jurors simply to write off an act of negligence that caused very real harm to the plaintiff as just another one of those unfortunate things that happen in life.

---

3. Bossart, Cusimano, Lazarus, and Wenner, *Winning Case Preparation.*

Additionally, each of the following beliefs is introduced by title with a brief explanation, followed by a paragraph captioned "Application," which discusses the concept's use in the courtroom:

- **Blame the plaintiff.** This is part of the belief that the civil justice system is broken, and its closely related to the next belief (the anti-lawyer bias). These are planks in the conservative tort reform agenda and the "there are too many (frivolous) lawsuits, lawyers, big verdicts, and punitive damages awards" arguments.
  - » *Application:* Don't bother trying to defend the McDonald's hot coffee verdict. Differentiate your client from the jurors' perceptions of how plaintiffs who file frivolous lawsuits might act. If your opponent wants to talk about frivolous lawsuits, then you might discuss frivolous defenses. Ask the jurors if that's possible, and if so, what might it look like?
- **Anti-lawyer bias.** Many voters like their congressional representatives, yet distrust Congress. Many people like their lawyer, yet dislike lawyers in general. This is why lawyers should avoid any behavior that conforms to jurors' preexisting negative stereotypes of attorneys, such as looking or acting slick, being contentious, or pandering to the jurors' emotions. This assures you will fail the jurors' citizenship test, and thus fail to earn their trust.
  - » *Application:* Similar to how the anti-plaintiff bias was processed.
  - » *Example:* I ask the jurors what I, as an attorney advocating before them, can do to earn their trust. They always tell me to be honest, never exaggerate, and if I make a mistake, to own it. Every experienced trial lawyer will tell you the most important attribute is credibility. Why? Because, without it, it doesn't matter what you say.
- **The "Just World" hypothesis.**[4] This is when a juror says "If you play with fire, then you're going to get burnt!" It relates to peoples'

---

4. N. J. Finkel, D. S. Crystal, and H. Watanabe, "Commonsense Notions of Unfairness in Japan and the United States," *Psychology, Public Policy, and Law* 7, no. 2 (2001): 345–380.

emotional need to believe that the world is an orderly place and that everything happens for a reason or "bad choices produce bad results."

» *Application:* To the jurors, conclusions flowing from a just world hypothesis are old-fashioned commonsense. Such conclusions are so organic to the jurors' values that jury selection neutralization techniques aren't very effective. A peremptory strike is usually necessary. Given that each side has limited peremptory strikes (usually three), then this is why motivating a prospective juror to recuse themselves is so important.

» *Example:* Similar to the format used earlier with confirmation bias, try to entice jurors to request that the judge allow them not to serve on this particular case. Because of their strongly held opinions, by their own admission, it will be difficult for them to be completely fair. This line of questioning helps neutralize the issue for both the individual jurors and the panel at large. It is my sense that it is easier to neutralize confirmation biases than conclusions flowing from a just-world hypothesis. Revelations of strongly held (adverse) beliefs on matters central to your case help prevent the disclosing juror from later sneaking up on the other jurors during deliberation with an undisclosed agenda. I think of this as a "wolf in sheep's clothing." This is because before the trial began, the entire juror panel knew what that biased juror believed.

Next are processing errors or heuristics:

- **Sequencing.** Solomon Asch, an eminent social psychologist, demonstrated the importance of the order of proof, or sequencing, in an experiment.[5] In the study, subjects received the following statements and then were asked to rate the person:

---

5. Solomon Asch, "Forming Impressions of Personality," *Journal of Abnormal and Social Psychology* 41 (1946): 258.

» Steve is intelligent, industrious, impulsive, critical, stubborn, and envious.

» Steve is envious, stubborn, critical, impulsive, industrious, and intelligent.

The two statements contain the same words, simply in reverse order. What Asch found was that Steve was rated more favorably when he was described with positive traits first.

- **Availability bias.**[6] Whatever most occupies the jury's attention during trial will influence what jurors focus on during their deliberations. Why? Because people mistakenly equate the availability of information with frequency, probability, and causality. For example, many assume that murder is more common than suicide, even though it occurs almost 50 percent less often. The reason for this assumption is that murder is widely reported while suicide is under reported. Thus, murder is more available in our memory. Another example is that when the public is bombarded with information about frivolous lawsuits, people understandably assume such cases are common even when, statistically, they are not.

  » *Application:* Think about the sequencing of your proof. Seize the initiative. Keep the focus on the defendant's misconduct. When I began practicing law, the prevailing thought was to begin the case by first calling the plaintiff, thereby introducing the plaintiff to the jury as a real person. The insights of trial consulting changed this. Opening with the defendant's misconduct defines what the case is about, in other words, the plaintiff could have been anyone.

- **Belief perseverance bias.** This bias refers to jurors' tendency to cling to a story once adopted, even in the face of conflicting evidence. Think here of your opening statement…

  » *Application:* An (early) adopted trial frame or story becomes a conceptual template or lens the jurors use in interpreting and

---

6. L. Waddington and S. Morley, "Availability Bias in Clinical Formulation: The First Idea That Comes to Mind," *The British Journal of Medical Psychology* 73 (Pt. 1) (March, 2000): 117–127.

understanding later evidence. Jurors do not continually update an adopted trial story as new evidence is introduced. Consistent evidence strengthens an adopted trial story, while inconsistent evidence is critically scrutinized and often ignored.
- **Primacy.** Information presented early tends to be remembered best, and therefore it has an inordinate influence, particularly when grounded in values. Primacy reinforces the potency of both the availability and belief perseverance biases. The power of primacy applies not only to the entire trial but to every part thereof.
  » *Application:* Begin and end each witness with strengths and begin and end each day, and each part thereof, with your best points.
- **Recency.** The last thing jurors hear is more easily remembered. Combining primacy and recency, it follows that your "weakest" evidence should be buried in the middle of the trial. This is a reason why defense counsel will often request the court instruct after the closings rather than before; this avoids the jury retiring to deliberate with the plaintiff's rebuttal argument ringing in their ears.
- **Preemption.** This involves being the first to present negative material. Preemption is done not only to preserve credibility but also to reduce the impact of any unfavorable facts. Use preemption during the jury selection and opening statement. The emotional result of effective preemption is called "deconditioning." The more one is exposed to a particular stimulus, the weaker the response becomes. The repetitive playing of the videotape that showed the police beating the defendant in the initial Rodney King state court criminal trial is a good example. The videotape was played to the prospective jurors more than sixty times during jury selection and the opening. The arresting officers were acquitted. At a personal level, each of us can see the effect of this deconditioning in our own responses to violence in the media.

  Before using preemption, ask yourself how you can turn your case's weaknesses into strengths. Once again, the "as is" or previous infirm condition, is a good example: "The more fragile the plaintiff was, the less trauma it took to injure him."

How Jurors Think: Information Processing Behaviors

A number of these "biasing errors" are similar, however depending on the facts, there can be real differences. I'll discuss six major ones in some detail, then list additional ones you should be familiar with.

- **Confirmation bias.**[7] This is at the heart of processing information inductively. Jurors will search for evidence that confirms their pre-existing beliefs, critically scrutinize evidence that is contrary, and interpret ambiguous evidence consistent with their preexisting beliefs, i.e., "I told you so…" or "I knew it…"

    Beliefs are primarily driven by life experience. This is why it is imperative to fully explore life experiences during the jury selection. A core belief will prevail over evidence that challenges it. Core beliefs and values must be identified, discussed, and neutralized during jury selection. If not confronted during voir dire, it will be too late when the jury retires to deliberate.

    » *Application:* This is what jury selection is all about: identifying the outcome-determinative attitudes each of the jurors possesses that foreshadow their ultimate decisions. Stated differently, how a juror finally votes is often determined by their preexisting values. When unfavorable to you, these attitudes need to be clearly identified, acknowledged, and, to the extent possible, neutralized. Legal directives rarely negate a bias; however, skilled jury selection can reduce it. Emphasize the prohibition against "bias, sympathy, and prejudice" and "conjecture, speculation, and guesswork." If a copy of the instructions goes back to the jury room, it will continue preaching during the deliberations.

---

7. Daniel Kahneman, Paul Slovic, and Amos Tversky, eds., *Judgment Under Uncertainty: Heuristics and Biases* (New York: Cambridge University Press, 1982).

Consider making the effort to prepare a copy for each juror, it's the court's discretion.

» *Example:* During jury selection, I write the outcome determinative attitudes that scare me on a pad or an easel in large letters. I label these as biases. This begins a candid discussion along the following general format. I begin with the general statement that we are all biased in some way, and I invite the jurors to admit they, too, have strongly held beliefs on topics that are relevant to this case, such as tort reform. And given these firmly held beliefs, it will be difficult for them to begin the trial being completely impartial to both sides. I then progress to the question in each juror's mind, given their strongly held beliefs and the facts of this particular case, "Is this the right case for me (this particular juror) to serve on?" If they decline my invitation to voluntarily ask the judge to excuse themselves, I then inquire how they are going to prevent their strongly held beliefs from contaminating their decision making. The magic isn't what the juror you're questioning says; it is the rapt attention the other jurors are paying as they listen to the comments of their fellow jurors. This starts a kind of group inoculation against biases.

- **Fundamental Attribution.**[8] This refers to the tendency to over attribute to people the influence of "internal" factors, (i.e., personal responsibility, individual choices, etc.), yet when it comes to themselves, the same people flip-flop. They will under attribute the influence of their own actions or choices, and over attribute causality to external or situational factors, such as the acts of others. For example, most parents are very proud of their children. If their child is sitting on the bench in athletics, it's because the coach is bad. If the same child were playing more, then it's because they're so talented. If your child gets an A in school, it's because they're smart; if they get an F, then it's because your child has a lousy teacher.

---

8. Daniel R. Stadler, "Does Logic Moderate the Fundamental Attribution Error?" *Psychology Reports* 86, no. 3 (July, 2000): 879–82.

In a car wreck, a juror will look at the plaintiff and say: "You dumb driver, you were not paying attention." However, if the same juror is later in a wreck, then they will idealize themselves and say, "I am a good driver, my brakes failed, the other driver wasn't paying attention and that's what caused the collision!"

> » *Application:* Try and present your witnesses as someone the jurors will like. Why? Because if the jurors positively relate to them, they might see themselves in the shoes of that witness and identify with them. The jurors will then attribute the favorable internal presumptions (I think of this as a halo) to that witness; the opposite is just as true if the jurors don't like the witness.

- **Hindsight Bias.**[9] This is nothing more than Monday morning quarter-backing, however, it smells a little like confirmation bias. Hindsight simply allows one to interpret the past because you know the outcome. Because of hindsight biasing errors, jurors skip the analytical questions of foreseeability and go straight to the conclusion of fault, answering "yes." This bias can favor an injured plaintiff because you can argue that because of the defendant's choices, "this was an 'accident' waiting to happen." Stated slightly differently, "There was no doubt someone was going to get hurt, the only question was not 'if,' but 'who' and 'when.'" The defendant will conversely use hindsight bias to their advantage when arguing comparative fault by emphasizing any choices the plaintiff made.

  > » *Application:* I like to point out that the defendant is responsible not just for what they actually knew, but also for what they reasonably should have known. In other words, ignorance is no defense.

---

9. Christopher W. Williams, Paul R. Lees-Haley, and Richard S. Brown, "Human Response to Traumatic Events: An Integration of Counterfactual Thinking, Hindsight Bias, and Attribution Theory," *Psychology Reports* 72, no. 2 (April, 1993): 483–494; Suzanne C. Thompson, Wade Armstrong, and Craig Thomas, "Illusions of Control, Underestimations, and Accuracy: A Control Heuristic Explanation," *Psychological Bulletin* 123, no. (March, 1998): 143–161; Ulrich Hoffrage, Ralph Hertwig, Gerd Gigerenzer, "Hindsight Bias: A By-product of Knowledge Updating?" *Journal of Experimental Psychology: Learning, Memory and Cognition* 26, no. 3 (May, 2002) : 566–581.

> » *Example:* Invite the jurors to think of an instance where they already know the outcome of an earlier choice, and then later criticize it. It's easy to know the answers to the test questions when you have the answer sheet. How many of us are quick to criticize earlier investment choices based on what we later learned in the Wall Street Journal?

- **Defensive Attribution.** At a deep psychological level, when jurors are anxious because they feel threatened, they will tend to blame the injured person as a way of addressing their own emotional discomfort. Then when jurors imagine themselves confronting the same situation the plaintiff did, they ask themselves how their "ideal self" would have behaved, not "Have I ever acted like that?" This explains why jurors who are mothers so harshly judge other mothers in child dart cases, especially those mothers on the jury who have never left their child unattended—not even for a second.

    If the hindsight errors can favor the plaintiff, then defensive attribution favors the defense. This heuristic is vexing because it operates unconsciously, most lawyers will think they want a juror similar to the plaintiff, yet paradoxically, this similarity can be what prompts frightened jurors to idealize themselves and apply defensive attribution fault. This is an instance where instincts and commonsense can betray you.

Counterfactual Reasoning: Applying Biasing Errors to the Issue of Causation

There is a good reason why the LSAT specifically tests our analytical skills. Learning to "think like a lawyer," in large part, involves refining your ability to understand and communicate why a particular event has occurred. Typical examples of causation arguments include "The plaintiff would never have been injured if . . ." and "Yes, it might be true, but . . ." What we lawyers call "causation" jurors understand as an explanation.

Consultants teach lawyers that in determining "the" cause of an outcome, jurors instinctively construct alternative scenarios that might have led to different results. This process is called "counterfactual" reasoning. The easier it is for jurors to imagine a different sequence of events producing a different result, the more likely jurors will focus on the interchangeable element as "the cause" of the result in question. Illustrating with a basic slip-and-fall case, if jurors can comfortably construct an alternative scenario to what actually happened, such as the plaintiff traversing a different route into the building, then they are likely to conclude, "Had the plaintiff just gone the other way, the accident wouldn't have happened." This is another reason you want to keep the focus of judgment on the defendant and away from the plaintiff, ergo increasing his responsibility. If jurors construct an alternative scenario that includes the building custodian placing a "slippery when wet" sign at the base of the stairs, the jurors are likely to conclude, "Had the building custodian just put up a sign, the accident wouldn't have happened." Thus, the building management becomes the focus (remember the availability bias), thereby increasing the defendant's responsibility.

Experienced lawyers sweep up and down the facts of the case, both before and after the moment of the plaintiff's injuries, searching for the best spot possible, or "causation event," from which to either attack or defend. When defending, they look for something unique that happened that might explain the bad outcome. This works because if an unusual event explains what happened, then the suggestion is it probably will not happen again. This means the world is a safe place and there is no need for the jury to educate the defendant with a large plaintiff's verdict to prevent a similar injury from recurring. The plaintiff, on the other hand, wants to assign fault to an event, or nonevent, which can be characterized as a choice, as early and as often as possible.

Additional psychological principles to bear in mind include:

- *Repetition, visual and oral:* Repeat your frames and themes.
- *Naïve Realism:* People believe they "see the world as it really is."
- *Risk Aversion:* People avoid risk when they are gaining.
- *Loss Aversion:* They are willing to take more risks when they are losing.
- *Irrational Escalation:* Sunk costs can compel continued funding of losing struggles, i.e. "throwing good money after bad."
- *Framing:* Many equivalent offers are accepted or rejected depending on how they are presented, i.e. framed.
- *Reactive Devaluation:* Things that are offered are worth less than things that are not offered.
- *Reciprocation of Concessions:* People feel obligated to reciprocate acts of goodwill, even when it has no value, and was never requested or desired.
- *Later Cognitive Dissonance (commitment bias):* Once you've said no, it's harder to later change and say yes.
- *Authority:* The perception of authority can impact decision making.
- *Certainty and Possibility:* People value changes from impossibility to possibility, and from high likelihood to certainty, more than equivalent changes elsewhere.
- *False Uncertainty:* People are reluctant to make decisions when awaiting the outcome of a preliminary matter, even if the event is analytically irrelevant to the decision.
- *Scarcity or Deadlines:* Fleeting offers or disappearing commodities seem more valuable than if it is abundant or available, i.e. this is a "limited time offer…"
- *Fairness as a Decision-Making Criterion:* People will reject deals that leave them better off if their ideas of fairness are violated by accepting the deal.
- *Availability:* People fail to distinguish their cases from notorious cases.
- *Anchoring:* People tend to overvalue opening numbers, and will view them as starting points or brackets. Your damages request is an anchor. This is also referred to as "priming."

- *Construal Biases:* People think that others' views are more extreme than theirs.
- *Optimistic Overconfidence:* People tend to optimistically assess uncertainty levels, in other words, they believe they know more than they do.
- *False Consensus Bias (projection):* People believe others think the way they do.
- *Base Rate Neglect:* People tend to over-rely on misleading information when it appears to be particularly relevant, and they undervalue objective data about similar cases when it's not obvious.
- *Ellsberg's Paradox:* People are more comfortable with known risks than unknown risks, even when their familiar preferences yield worse results.
- *Illusion of Control:* People think they can control and predict the future better than they can, and better than others do.
- *Positive Illusions:* People believe their contributions are more valuable than they actually are.
- *Inertia of Preferences:* People will fail to take simple steps to further their interests if there is a familiar preexisting methodology that offers a second-best alternative.
- *Endowment Effect:* A thing owned is more valuable to the possessor than to the market.
- *Mental Accounting:* Arbitrary mental divisions of categories of similar assets limit the ability to trade.
- *Liking:* People say "yes" more to people they like.
- *Social Proof:* If everyone's doing it, then it must be okay.
- *Fixed Pie Bias:* People tend to view situations as "zero-sum," even when there's room to create value.
- *Perspective Bias:* People evaluate information in accordance with their partisan roles.

Whatever frames an attorney decides to build their trial story and themes around, it must align with community values, namely fair play, aka commonsense. The art is in selecting the right issue(s) on which to try your case. The tactical high ground you choose to try your case on should be driven by the controlling community values, as revealed in your focus groups.

Trial effectiveness requires that a lawyer be able to anticipate the core issues of the opponent's case. This knowledge allows you to preempt and neutralize the opponent. This does not mean you should allow an opponent to dictate how you try your case; however, it does allow you to begin the process of preemption by framing the contested issues in a light most favorable to you.

Once you anticipate the issues or "high ground" the opponent will try their case on, then ask yourself, "What credible responses are available?" Jury consultants will tell you in medical negligence cases that even if liability is clear, the defense still can win by focusing on the separate issue of causation.

Consider having the court reporter transcribe your opposing lawyer's opening. This provides you with their road map. If they vary from it during closing, remind the jury of your opponent's "promises" by reading, verbatim, what they promised during the opening.

Conclusion

Heuristics are available to all lawyers in all courtrooms. Think of each concept as a tool. The more knowledgeable you are about the tool, the more effective you can be in its uses. Understanding the psychology of human behavior improves your jury selection, can alter the order of your proof, and helps you develop your case frames, story, and themes.

9

(Pre)Trial Checklist

This checklist, with its suggested table of contents, is primarily for a lawyer who has little experience with jury trials—especially trying them solo. I imagine we're sharing lattes and I'm walking you through a jury trial, discussing each of its steps, how they interrelate, and the common mistakes many lawyers make. If you've done criminal work, either prosecution or defense, and now you're trying your first personal injury claim, I provide insights on what's new and different. For more experienced attorneys looking to improve their skills, I offer suggestions on what excellence can look like at each step.

There are a number of good books written to guide lawyers through their first trials. I recommend the following:

- Daniel Small (editor), *Going to Trial: A step-by-step guide to trial practice and procedure* 2nd ed. (ABA Press, 2003).
- Rick Friedman and Bill Cummings, *The Elements of Trial* (Portland, OR: Trial Guides, 2013).

- Mark Mandell, *Advanced Case Framing* (AAJ Press, 2019).
- David Bossart, Gregory Cusimano, Edward Lazarus, and David Wenner, *Winning Case Preparation: Understanding Jury Bias* (Portland, OR: Trial Guides, 2018).
- Nash Long III (editor), *Trying Your First Case: A Practitioner's Guide* (ABA Press, 2014).
- Elden Rosenthal, *The Plaintiff Lawyer's Playbook: Insights and Recommendations on How to Prepare for Success in Settling and Trying Cases* (Portland, OR: Trial Guides, 2019).

Trial Notebook

There's no one way, paper or electronic, it's your choice. I'm an old paper dinosaur, so I discuss a trial notebook that uses three-ring binders and index tabs. In bigger cases, I often have many binders. In product liability cases there are many well-indexed books for the experts, research, and authorities; of course, the same is true in medical negligence cases.

A generic format is a trial notebook with the following sections:

1. To-Do list
2. Then include this master checklist
3. A trial (witness list) schedule
4. The (current) pleadings or pretrial order
5. Case frame, trial story, and themes
6. Jury instructions and verdict form
7. Trial memos and bench memos
8. Law (important cases) divided by case or subject
9. Important pretrial motions and rulings
10. Witness lists for both plaintiffs and defendants
11. Deposition summaries, indexed by witness
12. An exhibit list of all parties, with folders for key documents
13. Voir dire sheet with jury box seatings
14. Opening

15. Direct exam by witnesses with exhibit references
16. Cross-exam by witnesses with impeachment documents and deposition summaries
17. Closing–save a few key points for rebuttal
18. Indexes of the important medicine, science, or authorities

(Pre)Trial Idea List

In this list, I highlight some of the big ideas. I start with general strategy and then divide the list into each stage of a jury trial.

I've moved instructions to early pretrial because it's a legal roadmap of what you must prove. I've also included two sections on knowing your trial judge. The first identifies questions about how the judge conducts voir dire; the second involves the judge's preferences concerning trial procedure and evidence. To the extent possible, study your trial judge. Try and watch them pick a jury, and maybe even preside over a day of evidence. I know that often you may not know who your trial judge is until you receive an assignment from the presiding judge, maybe the morning of trial.

There is some intentional repetition, such as my emphasis on liability, and occasionally there will be clear connections between successive parts, such as jury selection and closing.

Plaintiff's cases are won with a persuasive case-in-chief and direct examinations. You can win a criminal defense case on your jury selection, cross, and closing but not in plaintiff's work. You're the only one who must overcome the burden of proof. Another big difference in plaintiff's work is that once you rest, you will face a blizzard of creative defense motions to strike the allegations of your pleadings for a failure of proof and a directed verdict against each of your causes of actions arguing there's an absence of sufficient proof on a necessary element. Did you use all the "magic" words that are legally required to make jury questions? Your opponent will argue that because of an absence of one or more of these crucial words, the jury is being forced to speculate.

I repeatedly characterize liability and negligence as "choices." Why? Because this increases culpability, and big liability is a key to winning big damages.

Frame your case with conservative jurors in mind. They are rule based. They believe in public safety, personal responsibility, and accountability. They expect people to keep their word, and to honor their (social) responsibilities.

Your job is to learn the facts, the rules necessary to get the facts into evidence, and the principles of persuasion to make them memorable. You must answer three overlapping questions:

1. What's my legal theory? (This is why the law says my client can win.)
2. What's my factual story of the case? (This is what we say happened, and why it's probably true.)
3. What's my moral theory of the case? (This is why it's right that we should win.)

Remember to be accurate, brief, and clear, and follow the KISS rule: "Keep It Simple Stupid." Be respectful of everyone, all the time. Keep a clean counsel table. Be "bilingual," and speak legalese to the judge but plain English to the jury.

1. Strategically develop your trial frames, story, and themes.
2. Follow David Ball's excellent seven-step formula for your opening statement.[1]
3. Liability provokes damages. Much of the following is taken from Don Keenan' and David Ball's *Reptile*, later renamed *The Edge*:
    a. Characterize the rules that were broken as safety rules. Emphasize:
        i. How likely it was that someone was going to get hurt.
        ii. How what happened to the plaintiff was not only foreseeable but could have been much worse.

---

1. David Ball, *David Ball on Damages* 3rd ed. (Portland, OR: Trial Guides, 2013), 117.

  iii. Generalize your liability, what's similar in the jurors' lives?
  iv. Look for institutional or systemic failures, inadequate training, or a lack of supervision.
  v. Explain what the defendant could and should have done differently, and why. Did the defendant save time or money by cutting corners?
  vi. Look for maximum culpability. It should be egregious enough that the jurors will want to banish or drive the defendant out of "our tribe."[2]
4. Make your case about correcting an injustice, rather than furthering justice. Justice invites a contemplative response, we're all wired to react to injustice, meaning we "know it when we see it!"
5. Stories need a hero and a villain. Present your liability proof in a manner that enhances culpability, making it more than mere negligence. Have a clear timeline that emphasizes the various choices the defendant made that ultimately led to the plaintiff's injuries. Motive isn't an element in negligence claims, however, it's where jurors instinctively go in their attempts to construct a narrative of "what (really) happened." What happened is important, but why it happened is much more important.
6. Search for betrayal, be creative, and don't quit early. If you can't find it, then at least show how and why the plaintiff reasonably trusted and relied upon the defendant.
7. Relentlessly keep your focus on the defendant and their choices and off the plaintiff. Why? Because that way it could have been anybody, thus turning your case into a de facto "class action." It also minimizes the three defense heuristics of counterfactual reasoning, defensive attribution, and the jurors engaging in their "idealized self."
8. What are your best (see *Advanced Case Framing*) "I can't get over it facts?"

---

2. This is something I learned from trial consultant David Clark, from Omaha, Nebraska, his email address is clarkdavid5@hotmail.com.

9. People think in terms of pictures, not words. Show, don't tell. Paint a clear picture without irrelevant detail. Physical evidence the jury can hold or touch is gold.
10. Use rhetorical questions in your closing that anticipate your opponent's best facts and arguments, which you then directly answer with clear references to the testimony and exhibits.
11. Reframe your opponent's best facts, or at least "put them in context."[3]
12. Framing the "as is," "thin skull," or "previous infirm condition" damages instruction into what's "big to the plaintiff, but little to the world?" Think about shifting from a quantitative (objective) measure of damages to a qualitative (subjective) standard. This is important because beginning lawyers rarely get objectively large damages cases, such as burns or amputations.[4] Consider Moe Levine's arguments, such as, "If you take away half, who has lost more, the millionaire or the beggar?" or "It isn't what you take from them, it's what you leave them with."
13. Find lay witnesses who can powerfully testify to the changes in the plaintiff.

Trial Strategy

Jury trials are three competing stories: the plaintiff's, the defendant's, and the jury's. Your job is to tell the jury's story—in the plaintiff's voice, that way the jury will recognize your trial story as their view of the world. Within the blizzard of facts, what's your compelling trial story?[5]

---

3. *See* Keith Mitnik, *Don't Eat the Bruises: How to Spoil Their Plans to Foil Your Case* (Portland, OR: Trial Guides, 2015), chapter 13.

4. William A. Barton, *Recovering for Psychological Damages,* 3rd ed. (Portland, OR: Trial Guides, 2010), chapter 2.

5. Concept focus groups can teach you the jury's story, and you can then shift to structured focus groups to help identify and refine your most persuasive facts and arguments.

You want the jury to accept you as their guide on your shared legal journey, however, you must earn their trust.

I've discussed heuristics and biases before this checklist. Don't let your legal training and "uneducated" intuitions betray you.

Trial Frames, Stories & Themes

Framing is finding a favorable perspective or lens that embraces all the evidence, both good and bad. A trial story is a brief elevator speech of what happened, themes are phrases that favorably capture what the case is about. You want a compelling trial story summarized with memorable themes. You have grafted the keywords and ideas from the important instructions into your trial frames, story, themes, and closing argument. This is what "cloaking yourself in the dignity of the (judicial) robe" looks and sounds like! If the jurors adopt your case frames, thereafter they will tend to accept what's consistent and reject what isn't.

Don't unnecessarily object. Trials aren't law school evidence exams. The jurors will think you are an obstructionist who is trying to keep something from them, and in a sense, they're right Be aware of your nonverbal behavior. How you say what you say is even more important than what you say.

Jury Instructions

Begin at the end. One of the first things you should do is generate a draft set of instructions.

Common Mistakes

- Relying only on standard uniform jury instructions.

What Excellence Looks Like

- Submit important special instructions with authority.

Liability

Trying to identify some form of betrayal, splintering your negligence allegations into choices (the earlier the better) motivated by profit or self-interest, and polarizing your case when the defense suggests your client or you are fudging. Also looking for systems failures, a breakdown in communication, or a lack of supervision and training are ttried and true strategies.

Again, I emphasize liability. When your opponent wants to sanitize your proof by admitting liability, work to get most of your liability proof in on the issue of causation. Examples of this could be how long the plaintiff was looking in her rear-view mirror prior to the impact, how violent the impact was, etc. Be creative.

Generate a list of (Rick Friedman's) Rules of the Road.[6] "Rules" for your case are sayings or statements that are:

1. A requirement that the defendant do, or not do, something.
2. Easy for the jury to understand.
3. A requirement the defense cannot credibly dispute.
4. A requirement the defendant has violated.
5. Important enough in the context of the case that proof of its violation will significantly increase the change of the plaintiff's verdict.

---

6. Rick Friedman and Patrick Malone, *Rules of the Road: A Plaintiff Lawyer's Guide to Proving Liability*, 2nd ed. (Portland, OR: Trial Guides, 2010).

Common Mistakes

- Not making your liability story big enough or, in other words, showing how culpable the defendant is. Does your liability involve betrayal or is it merely benign neglect, which we're socialized to forgive and forget? After all, that's what "bad things happening to good people" is about.
- Becoming so client-centered that you mistakenly make the case about your injured client instead of the defendant and their bad choices. The plaintiff could have been anybody, including the jurors and their families. The defendant's conduct was a threat to all of us.
- Not generating a case-specific list of "Rules of the Road."

What Excellence Looks Like

- Own your opponent's best facts and turn them to your advantage through smart case framing or at least put the bad facts in context.

Investigation

Hire an investigator to locate and talk to all the potential witnesses, good and bad. Visit the scene early, hopefully at the same time of day or night and in similar weather. Take advantage of technology to remotely access distant witnesses and video record your depositions.

Common Mistakes

- Not hiring an experienced investigator to conduct a prompt investigation.
- Not nailing down early the key witnesses and proof necessary to win your case.
- Not perpetuating aged, infirm, or out-of-state witnesses.
- Not getting out of your office and finding great lay damages witnesses.

What Excellence Looks Like

- Do a thorough two-sided investigation that allows you to anticipate the defenses and frame problems to your advantage.
- When developing your damages, spend quality time with your client and their family, getting up close and personal.

Focus Groups

There are two kinds of focus groups, concept and structured. First, do one or more concept focus groups[7] where you learn the jurors' general values and assumptions in your type of case. You have a kind of conversation where you discuss the key facts of the case and ask for their reactions, and then ask them why or to explain their finding. You're looking for the five anti-plaintiff biases: suspicion, victimization, personal responsibility, stuff happens, and blame the plaintiff.[8] Next, you follow with structured focus groups[9] wherein you actually present your specific case and look for the group's reactions, good and bad. Think of these as mini-trials, or "clopenings" (an abbreviated opening statement-closing argument), and argue for a verdict.

Focus groups don't have to cost much. You can do your own and have a friend help you with the understanding that you will return the favor. You want to learn the "jury's story," of what they think is important and why. Focus groups are also good for spotting any comparative fault issues, whether plead or not. What caught the focus group's attention, good or bad, big or small?

---

7. David Bossart, Gregory Cusimano, Edward Lazarus, and David Wenner, *Winning Case Preparation: Understanding Jury Bias* ((Portland, OR: Trial Guides, 2018), 89.
8. Bossart, Cusimano, Lazarus, and Wenner, *Winning Case Preparation*, 8.
9. Bossart, Cusimano, Lazarus, and Wenner, *Winning Case Preparation*, 91.

Your job is not to win the first focus group. It's to lose it, and in the process learn all your (potential) problems. In later structured focus groups, test and refine your best responses.[10]

Common Mistakes

- It's natural to want to win the first (concept) focus group. Don't.
- Not recruiting conservative or defense-oriented jurors to serve on your focus groups is a mistake. You want to hear all the bad stuff now.
- Not welcoming the opportunity to be the lawyer for the opposing side in a later structured focus group.
- Not sufficiently preparing to ensure focus group results are valid.

What Excellence Looks Like

- Welcome the opportunity to argue the other side, and do it with great gusto and preparation.
- Have a talented lawyer play the part of opposing counsel in your final structured focus groups.
- Carefully prepare and test your arguments and trial exhibits in structured focus groups, and energetically advocate the best of both sides so the results are reliable. Make it real!

Your Opponent

Ask around about opposing counsel. What's their reputation? Do they have habits, good or bad, such as a heavy-handed cross, questionable ethical behavior, routinely accusing the plaintiff of malingering, or

---

10. For a good reference, see David Ball and Artemis Malekpour with Debra Miller, *Focus Groups: How to Do Your Own Jury Research* (Trial Guides, 2008), DVD and On Demand.

personally attacking their opponents? Do they usually hire the same IME doctor(s)?[11] Forewarned is forearmed.

You may not know who your judge is going to be, but you sure know who your opponent is. How can you turn their predictable behaviors to your advantage? As the plaintiffs' lawyer, you must always wear the whitest hat. Don't succumb to "fighting fire with fire," and again remember that only you have the burden of proof.

Pretrial Motions *In Limine*

Short, concise memos get read; long ones, not so much. Be familiar with any pretrial motions to exclude expert testimony, or FRE 401-403 motions to exclude. 401 is for a lack of relevance, and 403 is for even when relevant, the evidence still should be excluded because of undue prejudice, confusion, or delay. If your trial judge hears the motions, you will learn whether the judge is a gatekeeper or tends to let it all in and let the jury shake it out.

Common Mistakes

- Not filing your pretrial motions in a timely manner.
- Not requesting a continuing objection when the judge allows matters into evidence over your objection.
- Not asking for an early assignment to a trial judge because you will be filing early pretrial motions, which should be ruled on by the same judge who hears the case. This also allows you to watch your assigned judge pick a jury.

---

11. *Recovering for Psychological Damages*, chapter 13, 177–201, lists generic questions from which you can modify 4 or 5 to fit your facts.

What Excellence Looks Like

- Your trial brief should succinctly state the legal questions, support your requested special instructions, cite the controlling law, and distinguish any contra authority.

Learn Your Judge's Jury Selection Habits

Watch your assigned judge select a jury:

- Before jury selection begins, some judges will want you to give a brief (two to three-minute) mini-opening that (non-argumentatively) states your case.
- Are there any explicit or implicit time limits for jury selection?
- Does the judge ask the lawyers to submit a list of proposed questions which the court then discusses with the jury, and thereafter leaves some time for the lawyers to ask (brief) follow-up questions?
- Does the court invite questions of all the jurors at once, or is it one at a time in the order they are seated?
- How many peremptory challenges do you have?
- Know the difference between peremptory challenges and challenges for cause (when the judge should excuse a juror because, as a matter of law, they are disqualified).
- How willing the judge is to excuse jurors for cause, and how much proof do they require before excluding a prospective juror for cause? How much rehabilitation do they allow in support of a party's challenge for cause?
- How are the peremptory and for-cause exercises handled? Are they in open court, at a sidebar with the judge, or in chambers? You usually make your for-cause challenges in open court.
- What's the judge's procedure to fill the empty seat of an excused juror? I prefer next in line, because then if I choose to exercise my

last preemptory challenge, I know who will fill that empty seat. This allows me to make a somewhat educated choice between two jurors.

Learn Your Judge's Trial & Procedure Preferences

Any special court rules or local practices? Ask the judge's clerk.

Have a jury selection sheet with separate spaces or boxes for each of the prospective jurors and alternates.

It's your job to earn the "long half" of all the judge's nonreversible discretionary rulings. You do this by earning their trust.

Visit the courtroom. Study the courtroom, courthouse hallways, entrance, and exterior. Are there any inspiring art, sayings, or symbols?

You have multiple audiences: the jury, the judge, and potentially an appellate court. Think of your trial judge as a thirteenth juror. Always respect the robe. Like in the military, you salute the rank and not the person holding the rank: "yes, your Honor," "no, your Honor." There are no exceptions.

- Which seat do you want at the counsel table? Why? Secure your preferred seat during the pretrial hearing. Get there early in the morning of the trial and further nail it down.
- Are you allowed to move around the courtroom, or are you limited to the counsel table or a podium?
- Do they instruct the jury before or after closing?
- Does the judge tolerate speaking objections? Speaking objections are considered sophomoric and a bad habit. Stand, say "objection," and succinctly state your legal basis. If the judge wants your argument, they will ask for it.
- When it comes to evidence, is the judge a "gatekeeper," or do they tend to let everything in and then let the jury shake it out? You can learn the answer to this question by filing pretrial FRE 401 and 403 motions to exclude evidence.

- Does the judge allow continuing objections?
- When offering exhibits, does the court also want its own "bench" copy? (Assume yes.) A courtesy copy should be provided to opposing counsel.
- Does the judge allow jurors to submit witness questions? View their questions and the witness's answers as gifts. Remember their questions when preparing your closing.
- On cross-examination, does the court allow witnesses to explain their answers to simple, one-fact, "yes or no" questions? If explanations are allowed, it limits your ability to control the witness and thus the type of cross you can effectively conduct.
- If you call a witness adversely, how much of a "hostility" foundation does the judge legally require before allowing you to ask leading questions during direct?
- Does the judge allow recross, and if so, how much?
- Will the judge allow rebuttal if you could have presented the same evidence during your case-in-chief? Don't assume it.
- Does the judge welcome special or personalized instructions? Many newer judges don't like them.

Jury Selection

What did you learn from your focus groups about the type of juror you want, or don't want, and why? A primary purpose of jury selection is learning enough about prospective jurors that you can intelligently exercise your challenges.

Identify the bad jurors. Try to save your limited peremptory challenges by inviting the jurors to exclude themselves, having the judge excuse them for cause, or maybe getting lucky and having your opponent strike them. The question of whether to use your last peremptory challenge is an enduring problem.

When the lawyers are picking the jury, the jurors are picking a lawyer. Not only must you prepare your client for the jury, but you must also prepare the jury for your client. Lawyers generally talk too much and don't listen enough; it should be at least 30/70 or 20/80 in favor of the jurors doing the talking. Honor each juror with some questions and show respect for their answers. *Listen.* Jury selection is your only chance to have a conversation with them. Try to build rapport.

Do you want jury alternates? If so, how many? If you run out of alternates during the trial, is the defense willing to proceed with a smaller number? Probably not.

Know the law when it comes to challenges for cause and *Batson* challenges.[12] In difficult cases, consider asking the judge to have prospective jurors fill out supplemental written questionnaires.

Use a flip chart to list or write out your problems, and (strategically) show your fairness by also discussing what the other side is worried about.

Later during closing, show the jurors the same "list of worries" you wrote during jury selection. Remind the jurors that when you began the trial everyone agreed that no verdict would be based upon "conjecture, speculation, or guesswork," or "bias, sympathy, or prejudice," and yes, that's what your "worry list" consists of.

Look at the jurors when you are talking to them. Eye contact is essential. You can't win your case during jury selection, but you can lose it.

Common Mistakes

- Avoid premature advocacy or arguing your case too early. You can and should, however, begin the process of introducing your case frames and winning credibility.

What Excellence Looks Like

- Promptly and candidly talk about the really big outcome-determinative issues.
- Be up front about the weaknesses and problems in your case.

---

12. *Batson v. Kentucky.* 476 U.S. 79 (1986) for race, ethnicity, or sex.

- Introduce your case themes.
- Personalize your client by introducing them to the jury; place your hand on their shoulder. During the trial, give your client a pen and pad of paper to take notes on, which you frequently review. This shows you respect your client and their thoughts.

Your Opening Statement

Opening statement is the most under-utilized part of a jury trial. Going first allows you to frame the case and make it about what you want it to be about. David Ball's seven-step formula is gold.[13]

What's your trial frame, story, and theme? By the end of the opening statements jurors may not have decided who's going to win, but they've probably got an idea of who they want to win!

Define any important terms, be a teacher or a trustworthy guide. Don't tell, instead share. Analogies and stories are effective because they avoid the pushback the "paradox of persuasion" provokes.

Use an outline, but don't read. When important, be specific but don't get lost in the weeds. Maintain eye contact with the jurors, and remember that you can only make real eye contact with one juror at a time.

Practice in front of a video. Tighten it up. Use a timeline to simplify and organize. Confusion always favors the defense.

Your trial story doesn't have to be chronological. If you're going to tell a story, ask yourself where it should start, why, and from who's perspective, or "voice," it should be told. Start with a crisis, and draw the jurors in.

Common Mistakes

- "Premature advocacy," meaning you are arguing too early.
- Promising the jurors something you can't or don't prove or deliver on.

---

13. David Ball, *David Ball on Damages*, 117.

What Excellence Looks Like

- Keep the jury's attention on the defendant and their culpability, the choices they made, and explain their motive.
- Anticipate, preempt, and frame the best of your opponent's case to your advantage.

Direct Exam

Plaintiffs' lawyers must excel at direct. It's often the last trial skill they master, and the average ones never do. Unfortunately, we prepare more for cross than direct. Why? The media glamorizes cross. And when cross goes badly, you look bad. However, if your direct is lousy, then the witness looks lousy. When done well, direct looks natural. It's not![14]

All my plaintiffs are brave. They never whine, and they are grateful they weren't hurt worse. Jurors already know the plaintiff's hurt, but deep down they really want to know who the plaintiff is–as a person. Direct can be a powerful glimpse of the plaintiff's character, maybe even their hero(ine)'s journey.

A common mistake (especially beginning) lawyers make is to ask leading questions on direct. The problem isn't that your questions suggest the answer, it's worse. Your leading questions prevent the witness from telling their story. You're doing the testifying. It also suggests you don't think the witness knows the correct answer without you having to tell them. Many defense attorneys don't object when a plaintiff's lawyer leads on direct. Why? Because it shows you either didn't take the time to properly prepare your witness or you don't know how to; but even more, they know it's not effective lawyering.

A blunt way to think about each witness is to ask yourself "Who are they? What do they have to say? Why should the jury care?"

---

14. Consider the paragraph method of direct in *McElhaney's Trial Notebook*, 3rd ed. (ABA Press, 2003), chapter 4, "Simple Direct," and the technique of bracketing on page 419.

Being truthful, and appearing to be truthful, aren't the same. Our job isn't to tell people what to say, it is to help them to say it credibly and effectively. Visual aids and photographs help.

Prepare and practice—again, and again.

Make sure each witness understands their place in the larger trial story. Have them look at the jury when answering your questions. If permitted by the judge, it's helpful for you to stand on the far end of the jury box. That way the jurors seated between you and the witness will be able to clearly hear both of you, plus it assures that the witness is looking towards all the jurors when answering your questions.

Include the judge, even if it's discretely. Gesture "tell us," with your hands while looking at the jury—and judge. When your opponent objects to evidence based on relevance, if the judge is interested then the jury will hear it.

Begin and end with strong witnesses. Your experts should be great teachers. Get them out of the witness box and down standing next to an exhibit in front of the jurors, and hope the jurors ask questions,

Do you want to call a defendant adversely? If you want to play portions of their deposition, then be sure and submit the proposed sections to opposing counsel and the court to review for any objections.

Check with the clerk before you rest to make sure all of your exhibits have been formally received into evidence, and that the clerk's record indicates it.

Common Mistakes

- Not spending enough time preparing your case-in-chief and the direct examination of key witnesses.
- Too many leading questions. The witness needs to tell their story, not you.
- Not getting out of your office and finding a few great lay damages witnesses.
- Not spending quality time with your client and their family in their home, getting to know them up close and personal in their lives.

- Not knowing what your client's hero(ine)'s story is. What's intimate, personal, poignant, and provides a glimpse of character?

What Excellence Looks Like

- Have your witnesses testify in the present tense. Set the scene. Ask the witness to "paint a word picture for us (the jury)." Have them tell where they ("we") are, and what can they ("we") see, hear, and smell. Have them testify as if it's happening now.
- Brief lay damages witnesses are gold.

Defense Motion(s) after You Have Rested

Once you rest, you will face a blizzard of creative defense motions to strike allegations of your pleadings for a failure of proof, and a directed verdict against each of your causes of actions arguing there's an absence of sufficient proof on one or more essential elements. Did you correctly use all the "magic" words that were legally necessary to make jury questions?[15] Your opponent will argue because of an absence of one or more of the keywords, the jury is now being forced to speculate.

What Excellence Looks Like

- You have anticipated and prepared for all the defendant's predictable motions when specific words were legally necessary. You have used the magic words and have kept track of them.
- Any offers of proof to make a record?

---

15. For more on this, *see* chapter 10, "Legal Foundations & Magic Words."

Cross-Examination

You should be in control. You (can) pick your fights by the questions you ask, the topics you select, and the order in which you ask them. Think of cross like a rifle with a scope, it's not a shotgun. Pick your best points, look for clean shots, and get out. Impressions are everything, particularly in long trials. You don't win if you look bad in the process of making a witness look bad. All ties go to the witness.

Start with constructive cross and then shift to short, one-fact-at-a-time questions, to which there should only be three possible answers: "yes," "no," or "I don't know."[16] Of course, it must be obvious that these questions can, and should, be answered with a "yes" or "no." Yes-no "questions" can actually be short declarative statements that end up sounding like questions. Stating a simple fact with a rising intonation at the end dynamically turns your "statement" into a question.

Prior to questioning, give the witness a copy of their deposition for reference. This makes you appear evenhanded, plus it's a good way to control the witness. Direct their attention to particular pages and lines.

Use looping with its repetition.

Don't forget McElhaney's self-accrediting cross.[17]

Don't cross the other side's experts on points your own experts are equally vulnerable on. An obvious example is if they're out-of-state experts when yours are too.

You set yourself up to fail when you are aggressive with too many opposing witnesses. Save your righteous indignation for the important ones, the ones the jury will think have earned it. Even then, keep it professional and never be snarky, snide, or personal.

What if a hostile witness refuses to respond to your yes-no questions with a simple answer and the judge lets witnesses ramble and explain their answers? (By the way, you should have known this was the judge's

---

16. *See* chapter 11, "Different Types of Cross-Examination."
17. James W. McElhaney, *McElhaney's Trial Notebook*, 4th ed., "The Real Purpose of Cross" (Chicago, IL: ABA Press, 2005), 441–447.

inclination before trial.) Embrace it, besides, you don't have much choice. Turn lemons into lemonade. When the witness rambles on, let them finish, then pause and politely suggest that maybe your question wasn't clear (when you and the jurors all know it was!) and then again repeat your short, simple question while impatiently glancing at your watch. The witness then drones on again. Repeat this one more time. The witness is self-impeaching by their obvious bias. Caution—this only works if your questions are short, and obviously can and should be answered with a brief yes or no. All the jurors must know the answer is a simple yes or no. Pause after you receive a great answer; allow the silence to emphasize its importance.

On redirect, expect competent opposing counsel to clean up or address any adverse inferences you may have raised in your cross. This calls into question Irving Younger's advice that we should save our last point for closing.

Contrary to popular lore, you should never vanquish a witness–even when the jury gives you permission. When you beat a witness up, there's nothing left for the jury to do. It might feel good, but it's not smart lawyering. Your job is to judge acts, not people. Judging people is the jury's job, and the size of their verdict will reflect their view.

Common Mistakes

- Cross doesn't have to be "cross." The first person to become angry usually loses.
- Repeating areas of your opponent's direct exam that hurt you.
- Being rude, snarky, or heavy-handed with any witness.
- Interrupting a witness.
- Not listening to the witness's answers.

What Excellence Looks Like

- You know the answer to all twelve pretrial questions concerning the judge's preferences.
- You extract all the concessions in the form of a constructive cross-exam that the opposing witness must concede.
- Destructive cross consists of short, one-fact-at-a-time, yes or no questions that answer themselves.
- Start strong and end strong. Impressions are everything.

Jury Instructions

I prefer the instructions to be given prior to argument, that way I can argue the law's application to the facts and thus explain why, in this particular case, the law is so important.

Carefully make your record to preserve any appeal issues if the judge denies any of your important requested instructions; make sure you have taken legally sufficient exception to any of the opponent's instructions you claim are errors. Check your state's law, but generally, prior to the instructions you must clearly and specifically state exactly what you are objecting to, and why.

Closing

The special verdict and its questions are a guide for your closing. Stress the importance to the community of the jury's verdict, and how a verdict in your favor protects all of us.

The real purpose of closing isn't to persuade individual jurors during your argument; rather it's for you to arm your favorable jurors with the arguments and evidence they can later use during their deliberations to convince opposing jurors.

You should be able to give eighty-plus percent of your closing before the trial begins.

Show the jurors the same "worry" list you prepared during jury selection and remind them of their oath not to allow "bias, sympathy, or prejudice," or "conjecture, speculation, or guesswork" any place in their deliberations.

Organize and touch on the important exhibits, and explain why they're important.

Don't argue that a verdict in your client's favor will improve the community's standard of care. It's not effective. Instead, argue that it's the defendant who wants to lower what is reasonable and expected. It's called the endowment bias, or the "bird in hand." Jurors will want to protect something they already possess.

Mention any of opposing counsel's failures of proof, misstatements, illogical inferences, or poor citizenship; however, always keep it clean–nothing personal.

If there are comparative fault allegations, when appropriate, be prepared to admit some culpability. Explain that the jurors are still required to award full damages, and then later the judge will reduce the damages total by the percentage of the plaintiff's fault before entering the judgment.

Apply the damages law to the facts. Itemize the claims of damages with a credible explanation to support your numbers. Your prayer is an anchoring number, and don't forget life expectancy.

Again, big liability makes for big damages!

Common Mistakes

- Not being organized.
- Being undisciplined or, worse, calling a witness a liar. If it's obvious then you don't need to say so; if it's not obvious then it's too risky.
- Not being comfortable talking about money for pain and suffering or the loss of life. You should have discussed this with the jurors during voir dire.

- Wasting the jurors' time by repeating the evidence. It's a closing argument, not a summation! Explain its significance and importance.
- Asking the jurors to put themselves in the shoes of the plaintiff. It's called the "golden rule" argument and it is improper.

What Excellence Looks Like

- Explain and apply the favorable law to your facts (cloak yourself in the dignity of the robe).
- Be persuasive in your request for damages. Review the inventory of arguments I have included and select the best. Ask the jurors: if this case isn't worth _____, then how much more does the plaintiff have to suffer before it is?

When all the parties have rested, the defense will once again "make their record" and repeat the earlier motions to strike and dismiss that they made after you rested.

You will often have many of the past verdict motions from after you had rested repeated again in the form of a judgment notwithstanding the verdict.

10

Legal Foundations & Magic Words

This chapter is born from my teaching of entry-level lawyers and the kinds of mistakes they make frequently. It includes a lot of evidentiary odds and ends that might seem not all that important, but they are. These are necessary terms and elements of proof, the absence of which will result, after you have rested, in a successful defense motion that will get you thrown out of court. When doing plaintiffs' work, you will have to know not only the law and how to use it to your advantage, but also how and when to use technology in the courtroom.

Motions in Civil Cases

When you start doing plaintiffs' work, you'll find a couple of surprises. First is the motion practice, particularly at the end of your evidence or case-in-chief, and then a second time at the close of all the evidence. If you're not careful to dot your i's and cross your t's, then you can easily have the court dismiss parts or all of your claims for a failure of proof. It's best to review the pleadings at the end of each day and check off the elements you have offered proof on during that day. Be prepared to remind the judge of evidentiary specifics in the record. Before you rest, ask the court for a recess to permit you to review your complaint. Make sure you have sufficient proof in the record on every element of each of your causes of action. If you've missed something before you formally rest your case, ask the court for permission to recall a witness to fill in any gaps in your proof. Having a claim stricken on a defense motion for a "directed verdict" is embarrassing and unnecessary.

Second, know the "magic" legal words your experts must use in order to meet the minimum legal standards on both liability and damages. These buzzwords may seem arcane, but a failure to use these specific words or phrases can result in a defense motion to strike your claim for a failure of proof. This means there's insufficient evidence to make a jury question a necessary element of your claim. Think of these important words as *terms of art*, and don't be dismissive of their legal importance.

Before I get into the foundational words and questions, I want to explain that under Federal Rule of Evidence 703, any expert can refer to the types and kinds of records that experts customarily rely upon in providing professional services. FRE 703 states:

> An expert may base an opinion on facts or data in the case that the expert has been made aware of or personally observed. If experts in the particular field would reasonably rely on those kinds of facts or data in forming an opinion on the subject, they need not be admissible for the opinion to be admitted.[1]

---

1. Federal Rules of Evidence 703.

This allows your medical experts to review your client's treatment records and then offer professional opinions based upon them.

Back to the necessary questions and key words. We'll use a simple personal injury claim with the four elements:

1. Duty
2. Breach
3. Injury
4. Causation

This involves the proof of medical causation for the injuries you've pled the defendant is responsible for. These might include past and future medical expenses, lost wages, past and future impaired earning capacity, and a permanent injury. Additional areas of compensation might include an enhanced susceptibility to future injuries or medical proof of adverse reactions to medications. While we're talking about the importance of talismanic words, note how, in the example questions that follow, I don't refer to an auto wreck as an *accident*. The word *accident* suggests a lack of fault. Use the neutral terms *collision*, *wreck*, or *crash*.

Questions for Your Experts in Personal Injury Cases

These are damages questions for your retained medical experts in personal injury cases. Keep this list of medical questions handy for reference. I've put in italics the key legal phrases you must use. For brevity, I've generally left out the doctor's responses where it's obvious. I placed suggested responses and my comments immediately after some of the questions.

> Q: Doctor, were you retained by my office to assist this jury in answering various medical questions involved in this lawsuit?
> Q: Have you been provided and have you reviewed the various health-care records generated by the plaintiff's injuries and her resulting care?
> Q: Are these the type of records experts, such as you, customarily rely upon in the rendering of professional opinions and services?

Rule 703: Have your expert identify the records they reviewed.

> Q: Doctor, I'm now going to ask you a number of questions. To the extent you offer *professional opinions*, will you please limit your answers only to those which you hold to a *reasonable medical probability*?

This is important and eliminates the necessity of repeating before every question that elicits a medical opinion that it is to a *reasonable medical probability*.

> Q: Was the auto collision of [date] a *substantial or material cause of injury* to the plaintiff? (Use the exact terms of your uniform civil jury instruction on causation, such as "but for")...
> Q: Doctor, would you please describe the specific injuries that you believe were caused by the collision of [date]. Are these *injuries* (scars) *permanent*?
> Q: Are the *limitations* of motion in the plaintiff's [body part] *permanent*?

> **Q:** At the time of the collision on [date], did the plaintiff have any *preexisting condition(s)* that rendered them *more susceptible to future injury*? Explain.
>
> **Q:** Did the collision aggravate any *preexisting conditions* the plaintiff had? Explain.
>
> **Q:** Doctor, please accept that this list of medical or health-care expenses were incurred by the plaintiff after the collision and prior to trial.

Have an itemized list of the medical expenses for the care the plaintiff has received as a result of the collision. Have it stamped and marked as an exhibit. Most of the time pretrial, the defense will agree to the fact that your list of medical expenses has been incurred and that the costs are reasonable while reserving the question of causation. If they haven't agreed, then you must prove that 1) the services were actually provided, 2) that their cost was reasonable, and 3) that they were medically necessary to treat the injuries the defendant caused.

> **Q:** Based on your care of the plaintiff and review of the records, do you have a professional opinion whether these medical expenses *were caused* because of the collision that occurred on [date]?
>
> **Q:** Were the medical services reflected in these bills *reasonably necessary* for the plaintiff's care and treatment resulting from the collision on [date]?
>
> **Q:** Doctor, are you familiar with the *reasonable and customary charges* for treatment of injuries such as those incurred by the plaintiff set forth on Exhibit [___]?
>
> **Q:** Doctor, have you reviewed the medical bills set forth in Exhibit [___], which total $[___]?
>
> **Q:** Are the charges set forth in Exhibit [___] *reasonable and customary* for the services rendered?

Remember the big three on all specials:

1. The services were actually provided.
2. The costs for the services were customary and reasonable.
3. This treatment was medically necessary.

Lump-Sum Method

The lump-sum method I use in the example questions is preferable to reviewing each bill in the record, live, during trial. Consider offering a total under FRE 1006, the voluminous records rule.

At least thirty days before trial, I give my opposing counsel a letter with all of the medical bills attached. In the letter, I ask that they agree that these bills were actually incurred, reasonable in cost, and medically necessary. Opposing counsel will almost always agree to the total if you ask them in plenty of time before the trial starts. Often, however, they want to reserve the legal question of *causation*—Were the medical bills necessary because of the defendant's fault? Doing this in advance of trial will speed things up. If you fail to do this in advance, you will waste the court's time and annoy the jury by having to go through every medical bill during trial. Waiting until just before trial to ask for opposing counsel's admissions suggests a lack of preparation on your part and is an invitation for an opportunistic opponent to put you to your stumbling proof. Submitting your lump-sum total with the attached bills as a formal request for admission will allow you to later petition for attorney's fees. Remember, we talked about trials being close-quarters combat. Don't be at a disadvantage because of a lack of timely preparation. Calling the other side sooner rather than later helps you avoid having to ask for what should be an unnecessary favor. Don't be caught short; it's always your fault if it could've been avoided.

Then at trial:

1. Show a summary of the bills to your client.
2. Ask if this is the total of the health-care bills that they received.
3. Get your expert's testimony that the costs were reasonable.
4. Get your expert's testimony that the services were medically necessary for treatment.

Confirm All Agreements in Writing

Confirm all agreements in writing. Do this for anything that requires an element of proof. This is nothing personal; it's just smart and professional. File your request for admission early enough that you'll have plenty of time to muster your proof if your opponent doesn't agree. In most jurisdictions, there's a thirty-day time to answer requests for admissions. Get your ducks in a row, in a timely fashion. It shows you're prepared and you know what you're doing. If your requests for admission are standard, reasonable, and *pro forma*, and the defense denies them, then you can later request an award of attorney's fees.

> Q: Will the plaintiff probably have *future pain and suffering* as a result of the collision? Why?
> Q: Will the plaintiff probably require *future medical treatment* as a result of the collision?
> Q: What is the *present value or cost of these future health-care services*?

Remember, it's the *present value* of any future medical services because the money is being awarded today, even though the costs will occur in the future.

> Q: Is the plaintiff's future ability to work (earning capacity) impaired as a result of injuries he received from the collision? Explain.

If you need a follow-up to any of these questions, it can be one word: *explain*. This invites a narrative response, which is always more persuasive than yes or no answers. Treating doctors can't be offering opinions outside their area of expertise. So, the loss of future earnings is generally within the purview of a vocational rehabilitation expert, and the reduction of the losses to present value varies. Most vocational rehabilitation experts can do this. Some judges will require an economist, and some states and federal courts say reduction of future losses to their present value is within the expertise of a jury and requires no expert testimony.

Research your jurisdiction's rules on the admissibility of collateral sources, such as insurance and disability payments. File a motion *in limine* to exclude all evidence of collateral sources, and request a continuing objection. Your client is usually entitled to recover the full value of the health-care costs, even if the insurer has applied an internal or administrative discount. This will allow you to place the full amount of the value of the plaintiff's health-care costs into evidence even if an insurance company received and paid a discounted rate.[2] There are also probably subrogation liens that must be protected.

---

2. *See White v. Jubitz*, 347 Or 212, 219 P3d 566 (2009).

Foundation Liability Questions in Professional Negligence Cases

We're jumping here from personal injury damages elements and proof to professional negligence cases, which can be quite complex. We're also jumping from damages into liability. These are more challenging cases than auto wrecks and standard PI cases. If you're less experienced, consider associating with a more experienced lawyer (see chapter 19, "When and How to Refer Your Case," for information on this).

In a professional negligence claim, such as medical malpractice, you'll need testimony from a qualified medical expert on the applicable standard of care. When proving a breach of the standard of care, use the following questions with your experts in direct examination.[3] Be sure to read your statute on the duty of a medical doctor. In Oregon, they must exercise "care, skill, and diligence."[4] Note that I include here, again, the presence and importance of *magic words*. The correct term of art is *professional negligence*. In the following example, the expert will be an orthopedic surgeon in a medical negligence claim; however, the formula and magic words are generic. It could be an architect, accountant, psychologist, or what have you.

Begin by establishing the credentials of your expert:

> **Q:** Doctor, without undue modesty, tell the jury about your professional experience, training, and background.

A copy of the expert's CV or resume isn't admissible because it's hearsay. Review their resume for the material most relevant to your case so you'll know later what to emphasize for the jury. This can include

---

3. The common term *malpractice* is actually slang.
4. OR ST § 677.095

board certifications, fellowships, teaching appointments, and publications. Explain what they stand for and why they're important given the injuries in this particular case.

> **Q:** Did my office retain you as an expert to assist the jury in evaluating my client's claims of injury?

Establish what records your office has previously provided to the expert and then any research the expert did to prepare to testify in this case. Again, advise the doctor, to the extent they offer professional opinions, to please limit them only to those they hold to a *reasonable medical probability or certainty*. When your expert is through testifying, the defendant will have an opportunity to review the records that your expert reviewed or relied upon in forming their opinions. This means *your expert should bring all their files to court with them*. Even if the files weren't subpoenaed, be sure they bring them anyway. If they don't, the judge might make them go back to their office and return with their complete files and then allow the defense the opportunity to conduct their cross another day. Most trial judges direct all parties to notify the opposing counsel, at the close of each day, which witness they plan on calling the next day. As for experts, they also must provide copies of all their files for review overnight. This allows opposing counsel the opportunity to thoroughly review the files that evening in preparation for cross-examination the next day.

The following are a series of questions and answers you can use with your retained expert:

> **Q:** Are you familiar with the *standard of care,* or the *methods of customary and proper medical treatment in this or a similar community of a reasonable and prudent orthopedic surgeon*?

This is the generic boilerplate. I also add the exact terms of our statute—*care, skill, and diligence*, of the Oregon statute.

> A: Yes, I am familiar with the *applicable standard of medical care*.
> Q: Explain to the jury what the applicable medical standard of care is.

Some jurisdictions require that the expert actually spell out the standard of care. It's the level of medical care, meaning care, skill, and diligence, that a reasonable and prudent provider would render in the same or similar community at the relevant times in question.

> Q: Do you have a professional opinion whether the conduct of the defendant was careful, skillful, and diligent and, therefore, met the applicable medical standard of care?
> A: Yes, I have an opinion.
> Q: What is your opinion?
> A: My opinion is the defendant's conduct (was not careful, skillful, or diligent) fell below the applicable standard of care.
> Q: Please explain.

Once again, many jurisdictions require that the expert specifically point out the deviations from the standard of care.

Practice Comment

I like to enlarge the allegations of negligence from my pleadings and mount them onto a foam board for use as a demonstrative exhibit.

I then have the expert review each allegation in order and explain how and in what particulars the defendant was negligent, meaning how the defendant failed to meet the applicable medical standard of care—that is, was not *careful, skillful,* or *diligent*. As they complete discussing each successive allegation, I then have my expert witness place a check mark or, better, their initials, next to the allegation they've just testified to—using the foundations and necessary magic words. The poster board becomes a giant checklist and reduces the risks of a directed verdict for a failure of necessary proof.

Once I've completed liability, I then shift my questions to damages and causation. I generally limit the treating doctor to questions on damages and permanency. This makes sense because most general practitioners probably aren't competent to offer opinions on the standard of care in medical specialties, such as anesthesiology, neurosurgery, or orthopedics. In addition, it's not fair to ask any specialist the treating doctor referred their patient to, to testify against the original treating and referring doctor. The testifying doctor would never get another referral. That's why we use experts from out of state or have recently retired.

I then offer the exhibit of enlarged allegations as demonstrative evidence by asking the doctor if the use of this exhibit will "aid and assist the jury in understanding their expert testimony." Irrespective of whether the exhibit is received as evidence, this process makes a clear record.

David Ball, in *Damages*, makes a good point. When it comes to your experts, the preferred term is reasonable medical or professional *certainty*.[5] However, when it comes to the other side's experts, you should use the lesser term of reasonable *probability*. The point is obvious. Your expert's opinions are certain, which is more confident than just probable, or 51 to 49 percent. The bottom line is your expert's

---

5. David Ball, *David Ball on Damages*, 3rd ed. (Portland, OR: Trial Guides, 2013).

opinions must *probably* be true, also known as, *more likely than not*, meaning more than 50 percent true, and therefore are not "speculation, conjecture, or guesswork."[6]

If your lawsuit involves a nonmedical area of professional liability, include related code words. For example, ask the expert to answer all questions based upon a *"reasonable professional probability in* [insert the specialty—such as psychology, architecture, dental, and so on]."

Follow this formula and you won't have any problems when you rest and face the inevitable defense motions to strike each of your liability and damages allegations for a failure of (necessary) proof.

High versus Low Tech

This section is important because younger lawyers who are comfortable with technology can easily lose the human element in their presentations. When I confront a witness during cross-examination, I emphasize my point by holding any enlarged, inconsistent documents on foam boards, one in each hand. I fix my gaze squarely on the witness and ask, "Which is the truth?" I can't viscerally do this with a computer display. Much of the potency of this type of cross-examination comes from its presence and physicality.

With that said, a good computer "tech" can quickly present multiple documents on a split screen and achieve the effect almost as well, just differently. Your choice. I often have quite a few background exhibits, but only a few that are really important. For that reason, I only enlarge and mount the key ones on foam boards. Sometimes, I'll have a jury notebook for each juror, containing copies of the important exhibits. The rest are in the custody of the clerk. All this is, of course, subject to local practice and your judge's discretion.

The level and type of tech equipment that courts provide varies from the latest to just blackboards with chalk and flip charts with

---

6. James W. McElhaney, *McElhaney's Trial Notebook* (Chicago, IL: ABA Press, 2005).

highlighters. In federal courts and high-tech state courtrooms, jurors often have individual viewing screens on the back of the jury seat in front of them. Lawyers can use electronic monitoring (ELMOs) or laptops to present documents with selected portions highlighted for emphasis. You may have to bring your own computer or ELMO. Check out your courtroom and talk to the judge's clerk. Which side of the counsel table do you want, and why? Walk the courtroom; get a feel for its dimensions, content, and spacing. Technology can be well and good, particularly in document-intensive cases, however, the intimate and personal aspects of your proof can quickly become lost.

Think about the level of person prominence you want in court and remember the distinction between you "testifying" on cross and "disappearing" on direct. What are you comfortable with? Once you've answered these threshold questions, then you can work backward and start making good decisions about the role you want technology to play in your trials. Your answers will almost certainly change as you become more and more confident in yourself and comfortable with the latest technology.

All technology discussions ultimately lead to the larger question of how to present your case most persuasively and cost-effectively. This then segues into the use and, in my mind, the potential misuse of technology. Even if you can afford the technology, it doesn't necessarily mean it's to your advantage; it's more how you use it.

You can decide the role technology should have in your next trial by breaking the question down this way:

- **Will it help?** Even if you can afford it, ask yourself how much you think technology will improve your presentation. Look for ways you can dramatically frame competing positions, such as "he said" and "she said." Also be thinking about the generation of powerful demonstrative exhibits that communicate your key points. Round up a few friends to be a mock three-person jury, then make a high-tech and low-tech presentation. Inconsistent tech material can be compared and contrasted on a split screen. This is effective, but so are enlarged exhibits mounted on foam board. In closing, you can

replicate the same dramatic comparisons you did in trial. Check your state's rules of evidence to determine whether demonstrative exhibits go back to the jury room. However, even if they don't, you can almost always use them in your closings.
- **How much will it cost?** Estimate the cost of the hardware, the software, the time to create your exhibits, the ability to download depo transcripts and videos for trial retrieval, plus any other technology, including the expense of a computer tech to help you in the trial if you need it. Then total all the costs. There are lots of competent freelance techs who will be happy to give you a bid.
- **Analyze.** Next, using a cost-benefit analysis, decide if the advantages of the technology outweigh its disadvantages. I routinely agree to split the cost of a standard high-quality technician with my opponents.

In document-intensive cases, you can't afford *not* to use technology. In the old days, there were stacks and stacks of unwieldy foam boards scattered all over the courtroom. Now there's a tech sitting in a corner who, in seconds, can pull up any page from any document, and then enlarge or highlight the exact parts that you want and present them on a split screen. It's very impressive.

Technology Can Fail

It doesn't always go so well. Here's where a competent techie is so valuable. If you're going to do it yourself, be sure you practice. Remember, you're an "unsworn" witness, and as McElhaney pointed out, you're constantly either accrediting or discrediting yourself during the entire trial. Good luck on that when you're fumbling about, wasting everyone's time.

You're More Important Than Technology

Or at least you should be more important than technology. Remember earlier I said you were the most important (unsworn) witness the jury will see and hear? The problem with some lawyers, and it seems truer the younger they are, is that technology becomes more an end than a means. In my trials, the focus is always on real people; it's my nature. Maybe it's because I live in a small town and try to convey an unpretentious openness, or perhaps I like the appearance of being the little guy or underdog. The truth is I'm a tech-challenged dinosaur. Jurors smile when I pull out my foam boards. I relish the contrast when my opponent is obviously more sophisticated. If my father's funeral had been with a closed casket, I wouldn't have the one poorly fitting sport coat I own.

So far these questions about technology are pretty straightforward, but there's a bigger question lurking in the background, and its answer can trump a yes to all earlier questions. A retired judge made this point nicely when he told me of a commercial case in which the plaintiff, a small upstart business, claimed that a large business competitor improperly used their dominant market position to drive them out of business. The big defendant hired a big law firm from the big city that used lots of impressive technology. In the very process of defending themselves, the defense unwittingly proved the plaintiff's case. Think about it. How did high-tech defenses by lawyers dressed in expensive suits play into a small-town plaintiff's trial themes? I always ask: is there a low-tech way to accomplish the same task? This way, I never wander far from the heart of my case and my essence, which will always be people and our shared human drama.

Each year the state bar sponsors a CLE at the federal courthouse in Portland. The courtrooms in the new courthouse are all loaded with the latest technology. One year, the presiding judge, Owen Panner, was discussing all the technological benefits available to lawyers trying cases in the new courthouse. He humorously pointed to me in the back and told the group the technology was there just for me, a small-town lawyer, in order to level the playing field when I went against the big downtown firms. I politely responded, "Thanks for nothing your Honor. A level playing field is the last thing I want. I'm not interested in a fair fight. I'm here to win!"

Conclusion

Legal foundations aren't very sexy. It's hard for beginning lawyers to appreciate their importance. Nobody gets sued for a weak cross-examination or bad opening statement. However, you can be sued for failing to ask the right questions with the correct words, resulting in your case being dismissed.

11

Different Types of Cross-Examination

Cross is generally more suicidal than homicidal.

Herbert Stern[1]

Lawyers have developed a number of approaches in pursuit of the "perfect" cross-examination. I know at least five, each with its advantages. As with a baseball pitcher, the more effective pitches—fast ball, change up, curve, and slider—you have in your arsenal, the more potent you will be. All of my comments are offered in the context of IA and mindful professionalism. Like jury selection and closing argument, cross-examination is one of those places in the trial where the lawyer's personality clearly intersects with content and delivery. Cross-examine in a measured way, carefully picking your fights, always with an eye to winning. You get to pick the topics and select the exact words you use in the questions you ask. You're supposed to be in control. Be

---
1. Herbert Stern, *Trying Cases to Win: Cross-Examination* (Wolters Kluwer, 1993).

surgical with your indignation; it's more often a matter of tone than content. When pursuing destructive cross-examination, be firm and professional, and never sarcastic or rude. I've quoted examples from various authors that illustrate their distinct approaches. I've sprinkled the material with my thoughts in brackets.

Start with Knowing Your Judge

Many lawyers think judges just call balls and strikes. I disagree; "equity is the length of the Chancellor's foot." Ponder the ramifications of the answers to these questions:

- Is the judge a "gatekeeper," meaning exclusionary when it comes to the admissibility of evidence, or *inclusive*, thereby allowing the jury to hear most everything that's arguably admissible, and then letting them shake it out? Pretrial motions *in limine*, (FRE 401 and 403 motions) to exclude otherwise relevant evidence on grounds of prejudice, confusion, misleading, or cumulative, or *Daubert*-type motions, will quickly answer these questions. I think a judge's discretion as similar to a basketball ref's "calling it close" or "letting the players play…"
- Will the judge strike a witness's gratuitous explanations as nonresponsive and instruct the witness to answer your thin-sliced, one-fact, yes/no questions with yes/no answers?
- Conversely, does the judge routinely allow witnesses to explain their answers?
- What threshold of adversity does the judge require before declaring a witness to be legally adverse or hostile, thereby allowing you to use leading questions on your direct exam?
- Does the judge allow re-cross or does the testimony stop at redirect, as sometimes happens in federal court?
- Are the jurors allowed to ask questions of the witnesses?

A Note about Anger

Nobody likes angry people. Gerry Spence has said most of our cross-examination sounds like arguing. He's right. He's also talked of the *magic mirror*, saying, "When you point your finger at a witness, you're pointing three fingers back at yourself." You can win the battle but lose the war. You lose that exchange, and you look bad even though the witness may have looked worse.

Next, I want to add that at no time should you call a witness a liar. If it's obvious the witness has lied, then you don't need to say so; and if it isn't obvious, then it's too risky. It's just that simple. Sure, you can talk about *bias*, *interest*, and *motive*—please do. But once again, your job as a lawyer is to *judge acts, not people*. Judging people (witnesses) is jury empowerment, it is their job, and is one they're well equipped to do.

Alternative Cross-Examination Styles

As I present your alternatives, I'll discuss the benefits and burdens of each style with contrasting opinions of respected authorities. I begin by observing that criminal defense tends to be very robust, and its elite practitioners are some of the best cross-examiners. Think about it. If they don't call the defendant (which many don't in high-end cases), then they've got to rely on their cross-examination. In plaintiffs' work, a strong cross won't save you if you don't have a compelling case-in-chief.

No Questions, Your Honor

I begin by asking a threshold question of whether you should cross-examine the witness. Irving Younger maintains that if the witness hasn't hurt you, simply waive cross-examination.[2]

You don't have to cross-examine every witness, particularly if you're more likely to hurt your case than help it. Jeffrey Kestler explains why with a helpful inventory of considerations. Ask yourself the following questions:

- How badly has the witness damaged your case?
- Will the jury perceive a failure to cross-examine as a concession or a sign of weakness?
- Do you have enough material to conduct an effective cross-examination that does not actually meet the harmful testimony head on?
- Does the witness have favorable testimony (also called *constructive cross*, which we'll get to later in this chapter) to provide?
    - »If so, is this witness the only source of this information?
- Did the witness appear credible?
    - »If so, what are your prospects for destroying that image?
- What impeachment material do you have available?
    - »Would it be more effective to confront the witness with this material or to introduce it as part of your case?
- Can you show that the witness has misstated or overlooked certain important facts, or taken them out of context?
- How will the witness react under the pressure of your questioning, and how will this affect the jury's assessment of the individual's credibility?
- What are your chances of convincing the jury that the testimony is insignificant or cumulative if you waive cross-examination?

---

2. Stephen Easton, *Revisiting Irving Younger's 10 Commandments of Cross-Examination* (Burnsville, MN: The Professional Education Group, 2021), DVD.

Unfortunately, you must sometimes make your decision whether to cross-examine in the time it takes you to rise from your chair after your opponent states, "No further questions."[3]

For a contrary view, Judge Stern advises you never waive cross-examination.[4] If the case is triable, there is at least something to be done with any witness called by your adversary. Maybe you cannot impeach them as a liar, but there may be some way to limit or blunt their thrust. If not that, or in addition to that, they probably have at least something to help you. If a witness called by your adversary offers nothing to you by way of any of these avenues, then I have to question the viability of your case. And then, putting aside the question of what you are doing trying such a case, you simply have nothing to lose by cross-examining because you are going to lose anyway![5] More and more authors suggest that at least some cross-examination is expected. I'm in the minority here and tend not to cross-examine without a good reason.

Style 1: Constructive Cross-Examination

Most lawyers think of cross-examination as destructive and impeaching. However, an often-overlooked purpose of cross-examination is to extract favorable concessions from an opposing witness. Judge Stern refers to this as *hitchhiking,* and you should use it at the beginning of your cross-examination. Why? Because once you're hostile to witnesses, they're less likely thereafter to concede points. Also, it allows you to begin in a friendly manner, and once you have extracted everything favorable they have to offer, then you shift to a firmer tone. It's called

---

3. Jeffrey L. Kestler, *Questioning Techniques and Tactics* (Colorado Springs, CO: Shepard's/McGraw-Hill, 1992).

4. Herbert Stern, *Trying Cases to Win: Cross-Examination* (Wolters Kluwer, 1993).

5. Stern, *Trying Cases to Win*: *Cross-Examination*, 334.

hitchhiking because you're gaining favorable concessions from an opposing witness and piggybacking on them to further your case.[6]

Ask what parts of your opponent's direct examination helped you. What aspects of your case can this witness corroborate, what must this witness admit, and what should the witness concede under Stern's *rule of probabilities,* that is, what do we already know that our common sense tells us is true?[7]

Mauet suggests that if you've gained favorable admissions from a particular witness, you may want to omit any later discrediting cross-examination of the same witness.[8] He explains that jurors might be skeptical if you argue that only testimony favorable to your side should be believed, while the rest should be disbelieved. In other words, a subsequent destructive cross may undermine the value of prior concessions. I disagree and am comfortable mixing constructive and destructive.

Style 2: Younger's Yes/No Ten Commandments

In the late 1960s, Irving Younger established the gold standard for destructive cross by positing single facts offered as declarative statements in the form of questions. Never let the witness explain an answer and leave your final point for closing argument. This is often referred to as the *yes/no* approach and permits only one of four possible answers:

1. Yes.
2. No.
3. I can't answer the question with yes or no.
4. I don't know.

Younger's famous Ten Commandments are:

---

6. Stern, *Trying Cases to Win*: Cross-Examination, 13.
7. Stern, *Trying Cases to Win*: Cross-Examination, 177.
8. Thomas A. Mauet, *Trial Techniques and Trials*, 9th ed. (New York: Wolters Kluwer: Law & Business, 2013).

1. Be brief.
2. Ask short questions; use plain words.
3. Ask only leading questions.
4. Ask no question to which you don't know the answer.
5. Listen to the answers.
6. Don't quarrel with the witness.
7. Don't let the witness explain.
8. Don't rehash the direct examination.
9. Don't ask one question too many.
10. Save the explanation for the final argument.[9]

No problem if the witness answers your yes-or-no question with the expected yes-or-no answer. If, however, the witness insists on gratuitously offering (rambling) explanations, then you have the following choices:

- If the judge will direct the witness to answer your question as yes or no, then you have the option of moving the court to strike the witness's uninvited explanation as nonresponsive to your yes-or-no question, instructing the jury to ignore the witness's explanation, and directing the witness to answer your question with a yes or no.
- If the judge allows witnesses to explain their answers, then consider my *chaos model*, which I'll develop a bit later.

Younger says if you're well prepared, then you should be able to give 80 percent of your closing before the trial ever starts (I agree) and that the most valuable purpose of cross-examination is to set up the arguments you wish to make during closing. He suggests you limit your cross-examination to three points with each witness. Fifty years ago, he claimed that it takes about twenty-five trials for a lawyer to become reasonably competent at cross-examination (fat chance today given the

---

9. Summarized from *The Art of Cross-Examination* by Irving Younger. The Section of Litigation Monograph Series, No. 1, published by the American Bar Association Section on Litigation, from a speech given by Irving Younger at the ABA Annual Meeting in Montreal, Canada in August of 1975.

success of mediation). While most of us can become reasonably competent, he adds it takes real God-given talent to excel at cross-examination and that only seven or eight lawyers in the history of the English common law have been blessed with that gift.[10] Wow!

The durability of Younger's Ten Commandments isn't a function of its correctness; it's more a credit to Younger's energetic presentation and catchy simplicity. It's easy for academics with little or no clinical experience to teach. I find the yes/no method is helpful but overrated. On redirect, skilled opposing lawyers will clean up any confusion spawned by your cross-examination, thereby blunting the larger points you developed for closing. It can also make you look overtly partisan, meaning you're not interested in the "whole truth," which is at the center of every witness's oath.

Being an obvious advocate may at first seem to be exactly what our jobs are; however, under IA, there can be excessive partisanship. Thus, if you're striving (as a lawyer) to be the most credible (unsworn) witness that the jury hears, yes, you can have too much of a good thing. I want the jury to see me as pursuing justice, not just winning. What I'm advocating is a tempered approach.

There are many criticisms of Younger's Ten Commandments. For instance, Stern asserts that they are fear-based. He argues that they derive from "…fear of what witnesses may say, fear that we cannot deal with what they will say…" and that they are "…designed to protect advocates from witnesses…" He goes further, stating, "But these rules counsel folly. Every seasoned cross-examiner breaks and dishonors them regularly."[11]

The Art of Cross-Examination: Essays from the Bench and Bar is an insightful criticism of Younger's rules and their reasoning. It politely and correctly debunks most of "Moses's Commandments."[12]

---

10. Easton, *Revisiting Irving Younger's 10 Commandments of Cross-Examination.*
11. Stern, *Trying Cases to Win: Cross-Examination*, 23–28.
12. Charles Gibbons, ed., *The Art of Cross-Examination: Essays from the Bench and Bar* (Chicago, IL: ABA Press, 2014).

Pozner and Dodd have authored an excellent supplement to Younger's yes/no approach in *Cross-Examination: Science and Techniques*. They hold that there are only three rules:

1. Use leading questions only.
2. Use one new fact per question.
3. Break cross-examination into a series of logical progressions toward a specific goal.

Pozner and Dodd acknowledge the limitations of any cross-examination that saves the last point for closing. Your opponent can simply clean up any misleading impressions on redirect that were created by your thin-sliced, one-fact question, and it can hurt you by making you appear overly partisan. They advocate a chapter method of cross-examination that is topically driven, and they discuss various techniques, such as the advantage of looping and speaking in threes.[13]

Looping

Looping involves repeating a favorable fact that an adverse witness concedes in each later question. Following is an example:

> **Q:** Describe the violence of the impact when your car struck Mrs. Jones.
> **A:** It was *terrifying*. [or any other helpful adjective…]
> **Q:** After this *terrifying* collision, did you accurately describe this *terrifying* collision to the investigating police officers?

---

13. Larry Pozner and Roger J. Dodd, *Cross-Examination: Science and Techniques*, 3rd ed. (New York: LexisNexis, 2018).

Speaking in Threes

People find it easier to remember ideas when packaged or presented in threes. Examples are General MacArthur's speech on "Duty, Honor, and Country" or the "lookout, speed, and control" example in chapter 15, "The Craft of Storytelling."[14] In my sex abuse cases, I describe the abuser's act as an "abuse of trust, an abuse of power, and a violation of human dignity."

Questions in Short Statements

A familiar technique in cross involves presenting your questions in the form of short declarative statements, with a rising intonation at the end. It's amazing how a transcript will reflect your cross as a series of declarative statements, yet in real time they sound like a series of questions. Pause at the end of each statement with an affirming nod (as if to say: "isn't that true?"), and the witness will then respond with *yes*. Once again, the key is short, tight, declarative statements consisting of one true fact per question. An example follows:

> **Q:** You met my client on February 23?
> **A:** Yes.
> **Q:** At 3:30 p.m.?
> **A:** Yes.
> **Q:** At a coffee shop?
> **A:** Yes.

MacCarthy on Cross-Examination is a solid yes/no work. It insightfully emphasizes the importance of the lawyer looking good and/or

---

14. General MacArthur's Farewell Speech—Duty, Honor, Country (May 12, 1962). The address by General of the Army Douglas MacArthur to the cadets of the US Military Academy in accepting the Sylvanus Thayer Award on May 12, 1962.

the witnesses looking worse. He cautions that the lawyer looking bad far outweighs any benefits of the witness looking bad. Strive to look good because impressions can be, and often are, more important than substance, particularly the longer the trial lasts. By the time of closing, few jurors remember exactly who said what, but they all will remember their impressions of your cross-examination, and, thus, of you. I agree.

MacCarthy's focus on looking good is consistent with IA's focus on always wearing the whitest hat, although with IA, it's not just about looking good—it's about being good.

Don't waste time in meaningless pleasantries, begging, or viciously attacking witnesses. You always lose when begging or beating up witnesses, even if you occasionally gain something of value. By focusing on looking good, you start to correct some of the bad habits assertive yes/no cross can encourage.

MacCarthy's formula for a successful cross is:

SHORT + STATEMENTS = CONTROL

This formula holds that control of the witness is your objective, but even more—if the witness wants to argue with you and thereby deny you control, the witness will look bad. By using short (declarative fact) statements, you will either gain witness control or the witness who denies you control must, by necessity, look bad. Either result is favorable for you.[15]

Per MacCarthy, cross-examination resembles a child's teeter-totter with the lawyer beginning in the down position and the witness in the up position. The object is to reverse positions by creating a positive impression.[16] I like MacCarthy's emphasis on the impressions we create.

---

15. Terence MacCarthy, *MacCarthy on Cross-Examination* (Chicago, IL: ABA Press, 2007), 39.

16. MacCarthy, *MacCarthy on Cross-Examination*, 42–43.

Style 3: Storytelling Cross-Examination

This approach views cross-examination like every other part of the trial. It's one more chance to tell your trial story. That's why it doesn't matter what the witness says. Once again, you're *testifying* during cross-examination.

Gerry Spence's Storytelling Cross-Examination

Gerry Spence took storytelling to new heights when he welded psychodrama with storytelling. Spence's use of psychodrama's structured development of the trial story and witness preparation generates his compassionate or *soft cross-examination*. Many experienced trial lawyers intuitively understand the psychological levers that motivate human behavior. However, good instincts are not the same as the material generated by psychodrama with its structured format.

Psychodrama is action, not words. You don't talk about an event. Instead, you truly re-create it to refresh the witness's memory of the original event with the full emotional experience present at the time. When you approach a set of facts this way, it accesses and releases a powerful story in real time.[17]

Psychodrama is a process involving a cluster of techniques that reveal the deepest aspects of human nature. Some of the forensic tools include role reversal, doubling, scene setting, and soliloquy. The lawyer asks questions to which the witness's answers really don't matter because every juror knows what really motivates the witness and, therefore, already knows the true and unspoken answer. The questions have a sensitive feel that says to the witness (and jury), "Yes, you fudged, but we understand." I stand high on my tiptoes in praise of psychodrama.

The April 1999 issue of *Trial* contains an informative overview of psychodrama and powerful examples of its application. This is what I

---

17. James D. Leach, John Nolte, and Kaitlin Larimer, "Psychodrama and Trial Lawyering," *Trial* 40 (April 1999).

call a *soft* cross-examination. At the end, the jurors will all understand why the witness turned state's witness. The alternative is *hard* cross, wherein a snitch is the scum of the earth:

> For example, in preparing to cross-examine a physician who does a large number of independent medical examinations (IMEs), the director asks the lawyer to take on the IME's role. The lawyer may learn that a true story the doctor is not telling—and that the lawyer on cross can tell—goes something like this:

> "I became a doctor to relieve human suffering.... When I was approached to do a defense medical evaluation, the feeling was different.... I make a lot of money doing these evaluations and by testifying for defendants. Practicing medicine is far more difficult.... I realize that the defense attorney evaluates whether my testimony helps the defense and that there are other doctors waiting to take this work if the defense attorney doesn't choose me in the future."

> Alternatively, in preparing to cross-examine a former confederate of a criminal defendant who testifies against him in exchange for a greatly reduced sentence, the lawyer is directed to take the role of witness. The lawyer may learn that a true story the witness is not telling—which the lawyer on cross-examination can tell is the following:

> "I was facing years in prison. I was afraid of being separated from my children and of them growing up without me.... I have no privacy, even for the most basic of human needs. I hate it."

The jurors can see the true motivation of the witness and understand that the witness is not objective or unbiased. The lawyer's humanity and credibility are strengthened in the eyes of the jurors, and the witness is discredited.[18]

Spence did both civil and criminal trial work at the highest levels and always told a story of betrayal. Graduates of the three-week Trial Lawyers College program learn to view trials as competing stories. In 2007, I attended the three-week program. I unabashedly endorse it.[19] It takes a lot of preparation, skill, and presence to deftly present Spence's soft cross-examination. The line of inquiry (remember, you're actually testifying through your questions) you pursue must be true. That's why it doesn't matter how the witness answers. The jury already knows the truth through what you're saying.

Herbert Stern's Cross-Examination & Its Offspring

Judge Herbert Stern's five-volume magnum opus, *Trying Cases to Win*, has one volume dedicated to cross-examination.[20] Stern says a credibility attack is not the purpose of cross-examination; instead, it's one of three cross-examination techniques. The purpose of cross-examination is the same as opening argument and direct examination: to argue your case to the jury. You argue *through* the witness, not *with* the witness. You make all the statements *through* the witness *to* the jurors and, thus, communicate directly to the jurors. You testify *through* your questions. I consider this a close cousin to Spence's storytelling cross-examination, so I've included it as an alternative or variation.

These are the three purposes and techniques of cross-examination:

1. To impeach.
2. To get help *hitchhiking*, meaning extracting favorable concessions from your opponent's witness.

---

18. Leach, Nolte, and Larimer, "Psychodrama and Trial Lawyering."
19. Trial Lawyers College, http://www.triallawyerscollege.org.
20. This section is a comment on Herbert Stern's *Trying Cases to Win: Cross-Examination* (Wolters Kluwer, 1993).

3. To demonstrate that the witness's testimony doesn't matter (in other words, the witness's testimony and cross-examiner's theme and theory of the case can live together in the same lawsuit).

Whenever we attack the credibility of a witness and fail, we self-impeach. Whenever we make an assertion of truth in the form of a question that the jury rejects, we self-immolate.

Stern believes whenever we try to force a witness to answer in just one word (yes or no), we send an unmistakable signal to the courtroom that we are afraid of the witness and what the witness has to say about the case. And that is no way to signal that we are truth givers interested in justice, rather than game players interested only in winning. This method is a clear rejection of the single fact yes/no approach.

When your statement to the jury through the witness and the witness's response don't agree, the tribunal votes on the question and answers immediately. The jury either agrees with your assertion or the witness's denial. No one waits to vote.

Stern advocates the *rule of probability*. Here, he recommends that you make an assertion crafted to go as far as possible in your favor, but not one whit farther, that the witness must agree with at the pain of being disbelieved. Stretch the rule of probabilities too far, and the jury's common sense will side with the disagreeing witness. There's an obvious double hit in these situations. The selection of the lawyer over the witness, or vice versa, implies a rejection of the other, and this is toxic to a lawyer's credibility.

Determine your cross-examination topic by your ability to make a point, and then to win any ensuing confrontation. Decide this by the material you have available to cross with. These are the tools of cross-examination.

Stern doesn't think cross-examination should avoid the central issue of the case. He further disagrees with the yes/no teaching where you save the last point for closing and, thus, try the case to win it in summation. He argues that it is too late by the time of summation. Jurors have already formed their opinions, and your arguments won't change them. Instead, closing's focus needs to be on arming those jurors who are on your side with the facts and arguments they can later use during deliberations to convince opposing jurors. Do this using rhetorical questions. For example: "During deliberations some of you may wonder why the doctor didn't [fill in the blank]? Well, now we know. The answer is found in exhibit five, on page two."

McComas's Dynamic Cross-Examination

Criminal defense lawyer, James H. McComas, in *Dynamic Cross-Examination*, offers his own take on Judge Stern's approach.[21] He begins with the premise that traditional yes/no type questioning won't cut it; something much more vigorous is required. It is far more important to identify why witnesses "…made contradictions, inconsistencies, omissions, and 'mistakes' in a way that supports our plausible reality of innocence…"[22]

McComas uses the term *levers* to denote anything persuasive that can be used to impeach a witness. This may be a prior inconsistent statement, a fact, or a plausible argument that's inconsistent with what the witness is contending. He refers to the witness as your "dance partner or boxing opponent" and cross-examination as a "fight or dance." It's a dialogue that goes far beyond yes/no questions. McComas encourages you to use open-ended questions to coax answers from witnesses that expose who the witness really is and what truly motivates their testimony. Gone is the safety net that comes from never asking a question you don't know the answer to. McComas suggests that the risks are greatly overstated, and the ultimate weapon is your case theory.

This approach can be unsettling at first because it suggests that you aren't in complete control, but you remain in control by the choice of topics and the ability to use the answers to advance the case theory. The heart of *Dynamic Cross-Examination* is in developing proof and

---

21. James H. McComas, *Dynamic Cross-Examination: A Whole New Way to Create Opportunities to Win* (Portland, OR: Trial Guides, 2011).
22. McComas, *Dynamic Cross-Examination*.

arguments that answer the "why" questions to each side's outcome-determinative points to your client's maximum advantage.

You prepare a list of psychological motivations (the witness's probable agenda), distinct topics on which to cross-examine, and the specific factual leverage points you can quickly refer to in controlling the cross-examination. You also regularly will shift your level of intensity by topic.

McComas doesn't plow new ground. Stern suggests using the same techniques while exposing witness motivation in a manner similar to how Spence does it in his soft cross-examination. Because there are no discovery depositions in criminal cases, McComas relies on raw talent—intuition, instincts, and experience—rather than the techniques of Spence's psychodrama to generate his cross-examination material.

Style 4: Self-Impeachment for Obvious Partisanship

A big problem with Younger's Ten Commandments is rule number seven: *Don't let witnesses explain their answers*. When Younger developed his Ten Commandments in the late sixties, most judges didn't allow witnesses to explain answers. Today, however, this isn't uniformly as true. If your judge allows explanations, then consider continuing to repeat your short, clear, yes/no questions. However, if the judge is willing to let you control the witness, then, as mentioned earlier, you may ask the judge to instruct the witness to answer your yes-or-no questions with "yes" or "no." Then further move the court to strike the witness's prior explanation as nonresponsive, and further instruct the jury to disregard it. This invites the jury to devalue the witness for their clear partisanship in not answering your accurate, brief, and clear (ABC) question with the obvious, self-evident answers.

Every teacher of cross-examination supports this approach. However, most writers don't encourage asking the judge for help by either instructing the witness to answer the question or by striking the nonresponsive answer. They say this makes you look weak when you want to appear to be in control. I think it's more nuanced and depends on the judge and context. Jurors respect the judge as the courtroom boss. Therefore, I submit you don't lose anything if you know the judge will authoritatively rein the witness in. But you need to know the judge's inclinations and likely rulings, lest you appear not just weak but also incompetent.

I call this my *chaos* model because, unless done well, everything soon goes to hell. When the witness keeps rambling on and refuses to answer your (ABC) short and simple question, your response should be to firmly keep repeating your thin-sliced, declarative, one-fact, yes/no statement (question), while impatiently looking at your watch. If you're lucky enough to still have a court reporter, instead of electronic recording, about the third time the witness fails to answer your question, ask the court reporter to read the last question back to the witness. You get it. Again, this impeaches the witness for bias, because each time they refuse to answer your short (ABC) yes-or-no question, with the obvious yes-or-no answer, they are demonstrating their obvious bias in favor of your opponent.

If you're going to impeach a witness for factual inconsistencies, make sure it's on something important. Don't waste time on freckles. These are the staples of most cross-examinations:

1. Impeachment of a witness's conclusions, particularly an expert's, for having ignored or for not being aware of underlying inconsistent facts.
2. Impeachment for partisanship shown by the witness not answering your accurate, brief, and clear (ABC) questions.
3. Impeachment for prior inconsistent statements on a subject that's important.

Newer lawyers become frustrated when witnesses don't answer their short ABC simple questions. Stop whining, and instead view their non-cooperative partisanship as a gift. The question now becomes: How do you take maximum advantage of their obvious bias?

Using jury empowerment techniques requires judgment and involves some risk. You must know your judge to correctly assess your options and risks. These suggestions are somewhat counterintuitive because, as in martial arts, they offensively use an opponent's aggression against them. The engine for Younger's Ten Commandments yes/no cross-examination model and my chaos model is the simplicity and clarity of your questions and the obvious answers.

Here's an example of an IME doctor:

> Q: Isn't it true that you saw the patient on one day?
> A: Yes.
> Q: For half an hour?
> A: Yes.
> Q: It's now three and a half years after the car wreck?
> A: Yes.
> Q: And you're in court offering opinions about the rest of their life?
> Q: What advantages does a treating doctor who has seen the plaintiff multiple times have over a hired expert who only sees the plaintiff one time?

Style 5: "Self-Accrediting" Cross-Examination

In *Trial Notebook,* 4th ed., Jim McElhaney says, "the real purpose of cross-examination is to show the judge and jury that you are the better witness."[23] This means that the purpose of cross-examination is to self-accredit yourself, rather than discredit the witness. McElhaney is the only author who offers this as a primary basis for cross-examination. It doesn't take much to do the job and to do it well. Consistent with IA, McElhaney emphasizes that, while never under oath, you are functionally testifying during cross. This approach can be little more than a subtle

---
23. James W. McElhaney, *Trial Notebook*, 4th ed., "The Real Purpose of Cross" (Chicago, IL: ABA Press, 2005), 441–447.

shift in emphasis. You ask the questions in a nonconfrontational, almost friendly manner. It's in keeping with the best of IA and grounded in McComas's emphasis on the importance of making a good impression.

McElhaney explains this style best himself:

> Once you start looking at cross-examination as the time to show you are the better witness, you will see opportunities everywhere. Every group of questions is like a volley between you and the person you are cross-examining. How you handle yourself determines the score:
>
> - When you try to make too much of a point, you lose that volley. The jury can't trust your view of the facts.
> - Quibbles are costly. The quibble is the lowest common denominator. It says this is the best you can do.
> - If the jury sees you check a fact when you ask a question, you win at least part of that volley. It sends the message that you are careful.
> - If the witness forgets something and you remind him, you win that volley.
> - If the witness can't find something in a document and you show her where it is, you win that volley.
> - Don't take it personally if the witness evades your questions. Rejoice. It means she doesn't want to answer your question, and it gives you a chance to show that to the jury. "Dr. Maxwell, is there some reason why you don't want to tell us whether you did that test?"
> - If the witness says, "If you say so," you win that volley. Like the dog that rolls over on its back in doggy surrender, the witness is saying, "I give up."
>
> You can still show the jury you are right. So, you say, "Not if I say so, Mr. Sisson, that's what it says in your letter. True?"

By the time you've finished cross-examination, you want the jury to think that you are:
Careful.
Fair.
Honest.
And you know the facts better than the real witness does.[24]

Use What Works for You

Try all of the cross-examination styles. We all fear failure; however, growth demands pushing yourself. When your only tool is a hammer, every problem looks like a nail.

My Approach

I start with *hitchhiking*, or helping my opponent's witnesses to help me. Then I switch to yes/no. This can be soft when I want to accredit myself, or hard if I want to discredit the witness. I sometimes use Spence's soft cross. I watch my tone and try to always stay on the high ground by keeping it more in the "I understand" delivery. It's easy to slip into an aggressive and destructive mode when you intend to go soft. Don't allow your anger to trump your better judgment. I save my yes/no destructive cross-examination for the witnesses I know I can score clean, important shots on. If I'm going to pick a fight, then I must be sure it's one I can win.

I don't look at the witness when asking hostile or destructive questions. I stand directly in front of the jurors and ask my questions of the witness while keeping my gaze fixed on the jury. I use notes sparingly. I'm testifying to the jury through the witness. During closing, I further reiterate my best points by standing in the exact spot I was when I did

---
24. McElhaney, *Trial Notebook*, 447.

my earlier cross-exam. It's called anchoring. When done well, this is powerful, that's why I save it for important points on key witnesses.

Further Reading

Cross-Examination Handbook is a great primer on cross generally and is chock full of examples. You can't do much better in one book.[25] Judge Stern has reduced his five-volume set to a one-volume edition of *Trying Cases to Win*.[26] It's a great read.

Conclusion

You have lots of choices when deciding how to cross-examine. Test all of these options for your comfort and effectiveness. Practice cross-examination in your mind; walk through it a number of times. What are your most important points? Have your key questions (ABC) clearly in mind. Know your judge. What are you going to do if the witness wanders and tries to explain their answers? Are your impeachment documents ready? It's always about credibility—not just the witness's, but yours.

---

25. Ronald H. Clark, George R. Dekle, and William S. Bailey, *Cross-Examination Handbook* (New York: Wolters Kluwer, 2014).
26. Herbert Stern and Stephen Saltzburg, *Trying Cases to Win: In One Volume* (Chicago, IL: ABA Press, 2013).

12

Framing Your Damages
Qualitative Arguments

Every case has problems, especially the ones that get tried—that's why they get tried. I'm going to offer you ways to reframe your problems so that they become assets; that is, your deficits become strengths. Be creative. You can maximize recoveries in your smaller personal injury cases with what I call *qualitative damages arguments*. The big idea is to shift the jury's damages analysis from an objective or numeric one of subtracting losses to a more subjective and intimate view of what the particular loss means to this specific plaintiff. Rather than computing before-and-after differences, we focus instead on where the plaintiff is presently, following their injury, and the importance of what was lost to them. IA's qualitative approach keeps the spotlight on the individual plaintiff rather than on the plaintiff as a subset of the larger community. A big shout-out to Keith Mitnik's *Don't Eat the Bruises*, chapters 13 and 14, where he offers a wonderful three-step approach to turning problems into advantages.

I have placed this chapter at this point in the book to help you think about creatively applying damages rules. Those are the rules on *as is* or previous infirm conditions, multiple causation, and enhanced future susceptibility. Use them as a theme. Carefully read law and the instructions in this chapter with an eye to developing your trial theme or story from their key words.

Quantitative Analysis for Damages

During the first weeks of torts class in our first year of law school, we learned that four legal elements must occur in order for a tort or civil wrong to exist:

1. A duty.
2. A breach of that duty.
3. An injury.
4. Causation, meaning the injury was caused by the breach of the duty.

When facts support these four elements, then a *tort* or *compensable loss* has occurred. This means that the injured person can sue the wrongdoer and seek a verdict for their resulting losses. There is an easy way to express this algebraically:

$$\$ = (A - C) \times B$$

Let me explain. The formula involves two axes.

FRAMING YOUR DAMAGES

Horizontal Axis

The first axis goes across the top of the page from left to right and involves a time continuum from the past, or pre-injury, to the present.

- A is the plaintiff's pre-injury status.
- C is the plaintiff's present condition or post-injury state.
- B is somewhere along this timeline when the liability event occurs, which causes injury to the plaintiff.

Our time continuum appears horizontally as follows:

(A) Plaintiff before Injury   (B) Liability Event(s)   (C) Plaintiff's Current Condition

This model is generic and fits all situations. The liability breach can be anything from a one-time failure to heed a stop sign to multiple ongoing allegations of misconduct, such as sexual harassment or toxic pollution. If there are many liability events, then we express this as B (x), with x being the number of discrete wrongful acts.

Vertical Axis

Our second axis is vertical, or up and down on the left side of our page and expresses the extent of damages.

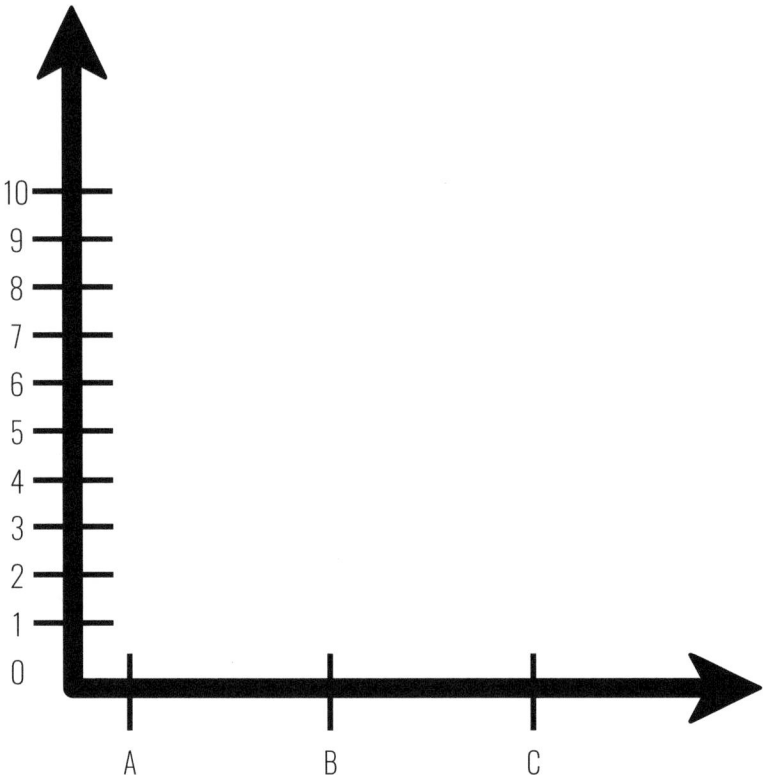

Assume we have a health scale (A, before, and C, present, in our model above), which ranges from 10 to 0. A person who is a 10 is in great health, and at the opposite end, a 0 means death. Most people have average health and fall somewhere between a 4 and 6.

Applying the above model, assume that the plaintiff is walking down the street in generally good health (say A = 6). We then have a clear breach of duty when the defendant blows a stop sign, B, striking the plaintiff in a crosswalk. The injuries caused by the defendant's conduct reduce the plaintiff's health from 6 to 2 (this is the plaintiff's condition immediately after the event). After a year of rehabilitation, the plaintiff reaches maximum medical improvement and is at a 4. Thus, the difference between before the event, A (6), and after the event, C (4), expresses the plaintiff's permanent damages. This is expressed as follows:

$$\$ = (6 - 4) \text{ B or } \$ = (2) \text{ B}$$

Causation is expressed by the liability event, meaning B, being placed outside of and after the bracketed damages proof. Our formula is obviously oversimplified, and the final subtraction within the damages is a measure of permanency. You can apply this conceptual model to any kind of case, be it personal injury, commercial, or what have you.

Traditional Law-School Model

This model, with the two axes, is the traditional law-school model that assesses each person's damages in the context of the larger community and defines losses by reference to how the community or tribe values similar losses among its members. This is a deductive or right-brain way of seeing things. It is illustrated in every insurance company's formulaic approach to valuing losses. This is the adjuster's mindset when saying, "My company won't pay general damages of more than three or four times the specials." Other examples include scheduled losses in workers' compensation claims and tort reformers' attempts to reduce exposure by imposing caps on damages awards.

This limiting approach reduces the economic consequences of wrongful conduct, and so reduces the financial incentive to avoid harming others. The Ford Pinto litigation in the 1970s is a good example of this problem. Ford was aware of a dangerous fuel tank issue with their Pinto, where a minor crash could cause the car to explode, but they decided it was more cost-effective to settle lawsuits than to institute a simple and inexpensive safety change. It is against this kind of calculated behavior that uncapped punitive damages find their most persuasive arguments. It explains why businesses and manufacturers welcome punitive damages being limited to single-digit ratios.[1] Limited consequences generate increased predictability, which increases the

---

1. This is based on the *State Farm Mut. Auto Ins. Co. v. Campbell*, 538 U.S. 408, (2003). This case federalized punitive damages by holding the Due Process Clause generally

incentive for irresponsible corporations to pursue measurable profits. Consumer injuries are a calculated cost of doing business. As you can see, these are policy-laden macroeconomic issues. It's one more reason why civil jury trials in our American common-law tradition are at the intersection of community values, economics, and rights.

The Alternative: Qualitative Thinking

In contrast to the traditional quantitative model we just discussed, IA says we are *all* unique and special, and holds that when the rights of the least among us are fully protected, then the rest of us are beneficiaries as well. The reasoning is that when we protect the rights of those on the fringes, then we are necessarily protecting the rights of all of us who are closer to the center. The economic consequences that follow when anyone breaks the community's rules means the larger verdicts you can generate in "smaller" cases promote safety and deterrence.

To illustrate the differences between a quantitative and qualitative approach, consider the different responses to the simple question, who has lost more? Assume we have two people: one is a millionaire, and the other is homeless and has only a dollar. Take away half from each and now ask: Who has lost more? Under a quantitative model, it is obviously the millionaire because he has lost $500,000, which is much more than 50 cents. Now let's shift the focus with the same question to a qualitative analysis by asking, Which loss means more to each of them? Thinking of it this way, 50 cents means more to the homeless person than $500,000 means to the wealthy person. When you only have a little, then a little means a lot. As Moe Levine said, "It isn't what you take from them, it's what you leave them with."[2]

---

requires a relationship between the amount of the underlying damages awarded and the size of the punitive damages.

2. Moe Levine, *Moe Levine on Advocacy* (Portland, OR: Trial Guides, 2009).

These values are expressed in our American common law in the standard uniform *as is* or *previous infirm condition* civil jury instructions, which generally reads as follows:

> If you find the plaintiff had an emotional or physical condition that predisposed him to be more subject to injury than a person in normal health, nevertheless the defendant is liable for any and all injuries and damages that may have been suffered by the plaintiff as the result of the fault of the defendant, even though those injuries, due to the plaintiff's prior condition(s), may have been greater than those that would have been suffered by another person without those infirmities under the same circumstances.[3]

This instruction essentially says that wrongdoers take their victim *as is* and, therefore, cannot defend based on their victim's prior infirmities or shortcomings. *The law protects the weakest among us.* Philosophers agree. Protection of person and property is the primary purpose of laws. Pause and reflect on this. The bully doesn't need help. It's the weakest among us who most need the protection of the law.

It is true that "the law is the law" and that the jury is to apply the rules as charged by the court, but this is only the start of advocacy. The law doesn't come to life until a committee of the community, meaning a jury, actually applies it. This is what Oliver Wendell Holmes Jr. meant in the opening paragraph of *The Common Law*, when he said, "The life of the law is experience, not logic."[4] Jury verdicts are the energizing headwaters of our common-law tradition. This is why understanding the moral and policy reasons for a rule is so crucial. That's why we plaintiffs' lawyers really are social engineers and yes, artists operating in the medium of the law.

---

3. Uniform Civil Jury Instruction in most states.

4. Oliver Wendell Holmes, Jr., *The Common Law* (New York, NY: Dover Publications, Inc., 1991).

Applying Qualitative versus Quantitative Thinking

Of course, if the injuries are serious and self-evident, such as fractures, burns, and amputations, then there's no reason not to use the traditional extrinsic, or subtraction-driven analysis; after all, you've got *objective* facts like X-rays, photographs, and great input from treating doctors. But, even here, there is often a place for combining quantitative with qualitative.

The qualitative model is effective in situations where the plaintiff was disadvantaged or had less than what is considered normal before the liability event occurred. Included are people with shortened life expectancies, substance abuse issues, or other preexisting life challenges. This includes many problem clients—those with prior injuries or challenges that blur medical causation. Examples range from alcoholism, chronic injury or disease, prior criminal convictions, suicide attempts, domestic issues, poor parenting choices, bankruptcy, and just about anything else the defense can muster in an attempt to devalue the plaintiff's character and deservedness.

I know how important it is to have a presentable or "good" plaintiff, and, if you are fortunate, you might also have a target defendant. Cases with great plaintiffs are rare, and when they occur, they usually settle for obvious reasons. The more likely scenario involves an unattractive plaintiff with modest objective injuries. Here's where IA's qualitative approach shines.

Unappealing Plaintiff with Limited Losses

Let's consider an unappealing plaintiff with limited objective losses. For example, imagine a plaintiff who is a chronic alcoholic and can't hold a job, and who was injured in a crosswalk by a speeding motorist.

Many cases in every beginning lawyer's inventory fit this description. Applying the formula, if the plaintiff was a 2 or 3 in their overall health before the B event, and they suffered a modest objective loss of perhaps ½ or 1 because of the defendant's misconduct, then this is not a big case under qualitative analysis. The losses just aren't that much.

Don't get sucked into playing the subtraction game. Don't forfeit your and your client's credibility by trying to stretch the difference *before* and *after* in an attempt to maximize the injuries and thus your client's damages. Instead, consider focusing on what your client has been left with, not what they lost.

Start with the A list—what the client began with—and be creative. Rather than trying to stretch your client's pre-injury health to a 4, 5, 6, or 7, instead honor all their foibles and challenges by being honest about their pre-injury condition of say a 2 or 3.[5] In other words, *generate credibility by embracing the real person and the whole truth*. Sometimes I ask my clients, "What is big to you but little to the world?" I learn about their gardens, their grandchildren, their pets, and walking in parks.

I ask jurors in jury selection the same question. What is big to them, but unimportant to others? It's a way of introducing your (as is) case theme during jury selection. This is an example of where less becomes more. It's counterintuitive. Much of a defense lawyer's effectiveness in cross-exam is generated by plaintiffs' lawyers and clients stretching the facts. Even small misstatements can backfire on you, and besides, there's no need for that with the inherent honesty of the qualitative approach.

Once you have accurately positioned your client on the pre-injury A list, then assess their losses. If the losses aren't much objectively, that's ok. Say so. Be comfortable in telling the jury the truth. Honesty is always a great start. The losses may be small and not much to others, but

---

5. This argument was perfected by the late Marvin Lewis of San Francisco. He was a president of the California Trial Lawyers Association, Western Trial Lawyers, and the American Trial Lawyers Association (now known as the American Association for Justice). Marvin is known for *Gloria Sykes v. San Francisco Municipal Railway* and his 1975 book, *Psychic Injuries*, coauthored with Robert Sadoff. I always visited Marvin when I was in San Francisco. My book, *Recovering for Psychological Injuries* stands on his legal shoulders. Thank you, Marvin.

they're important to your client. If they don't have much, then losing even a little means a lot. It's all about the composite credibility of you and your client.

Think Qualitatively about Disabilities

Think qualitatively when arguing the importance of your client's disability. *Impairment* is an objective assessment of a loss of some bodily function, such as range of motion, while a *disability assessment* applies those losses to the life and activities of a specific person. For example, two people can have exactly the same objective injury or impairment, yet it can have dramatically different implications for their disability assessment. If a professional baseball pitcher with a ninety-four-miles-per-hour fastball loses 2 percent of the range of motion in his pitching arm, then, as a professional baseball player, he is probably 100 percent vocationally disabled. Yet, to the rest of us, the same impairment would merely be an inconvenience.

You can easily see how a treating doctor who is familiar with a patient will have greater insight into the disability implications of what a minimal or mild impairment means to your client. Compare this to the defense attorney's hired defense expert, who examined the plaintiff only once, a year after the B event. I have a bad left knee that would disable me if I were a police officer or firefighter, yet it is merely an inconvenience to me as a lawyer.

One technique I use is to ask my clients for about three or four of their most embarrassing moments since the incident changed their life. I also ask them for the most difficult moments for them since the incident. If a friend, relative, or neighbor was there, I ask them to describe the moments too. It can be quite moving. To draw out further information about how their life has changed, ask about moments of attempted intimacy between married or long-term partners.

Disability versus Impairment

Have the treating doctor testify about the impact an otherwise modest impairment has had in the life of your specific client. Doing this shifts the focus from the extent of impairment to its impact on this particular person, meaning the extent of disability. A modest range of motion limitation, also called *minimal or mild impairment*, can have a significant impact on the life and work of your client. Who better to explain this profound disability than the treating doctor who has seen and treated this plaintiff multiple times.

Remember the two examples that make the point: an injured knee might be an inconvenience to me but would disable a police officer or a firefighter; just as a minimal impairment to my dominant arm might be an inconvenience to me, but would 100 percent disable a professional baseball player.

The defendant says the plaintiff suffered only minimal impairment. Show why and how this nominal loss has resulted in a substantial disability to this specific person.

Explain the *As Is* Rule

Qualitative arguments are not appeals for sympathy; rather, they are an invitation for the jurors to apply the law and their common sense. You will receive compromise verdicts until you begin effectively communicating why the ideas behind the *as is* instruction are so important. This is why it's vital to understand the reasons for a rule of law. Your arguments are legitimate because the *as is* rule is the law the judge instructs jurors to apply. Ask the judge to not just orally instruct the jury but also provide them with the instructions in writing. I even go so far as to offer to propose a separate set for each juror. This is within judicial discretion and emphasizes how important the law is to each of the jurors.

I also like to have the judge instruct the jury before my closing. I then enlarge the *as is* instruction and argue its importance.

Clients appreciate when you deep dive into their lives and share what's really important to them. Explain the *as is* rule to your clients and their families and the reasons for the rule; then review the kind and type of arguments you will be making on their behalf. You will find the plaintiffs and others in their lives can offer many details that highlight the importance of otherwise modest losses. The personal nature of otherwise "ordinary" losses is a lot like spices, a little goes a long way.

Find Lay Witnesses

Have friends and neighbors provide insights that only those close to the plaintiff will know. *There is nothing better than lay witnesses*—a hunting partner, carpool rider, fellow church member, AA sponsor, neighbor, or best friend—to share these private moments. If you haven't found others to speak for the plaintiff, then you haven't worked hard enough. You're not done until you're done.

I like to have the plaintiff go easy when describing their injuries. I have my plaintiffs begin by expressing gratitude that they weren't hurt worse. I often have them express the positive value of what they have lost (like the value of a good back or a good night's sleep), rather than complaining about their present circumstances. I leave the intimate details of the devastating impact otherwise "minor" injuries have upon my client's life for my lay damages witnesses. Remember it's the *quality* and not the *quantity* of your damages proof.

Vary Arguments for Each Jury

Vary your arguments to fit each jury. Ask during voir dire if any of the jurors have suffered a loss of something that may be small to the world but big to them. Learn what is personal and important for each juror.

What are their hobbies? What do they enjoy doing in their private time? Each of them will understand how diminished their lives would be if they suffered the loss of something they valued that may be minor to others. Examples include gardening, picking up a grandchild, going for walks looking for agates on the beach, and so on. On a deep, personal level, the jurors will understand why the law protects the weakest among us. This legitimizes your arguments for large money damages for each juror. Every juror is different, but in a larger sense, we're all the same. Little things can mean a lot, particularly when you don't have much to begin with.

Try to access each juror's sense of *vulnerability*. Everyone resists this, because no one welcomes feelings of weakness. Remind the jurors that no matter how healthy they may be now, should they live long enough, they too will become old, infirm, and powerless.

Ask yourself what the defendant has left the plaintiff with—and without. Is there a loss of pride, honor, or dignity? Is the plaintiff alone? When you're at or near the bottom, seemingly small losses can be everything. Extrapolate from the impairment-disability model. Don't be linear and self-limiting. Get up close, intimate, and personal with your client; by the time of closing, you will also be close and personal with your jurors—your neighbors.

Good lawyers instinctively work within the generic formula of

$$\$ = (A - C) \times B$$

to develop case strengths, which then become their case themes and trial story. Damages arguments based on subtraction can be sterile. With the qualitative approach, the equation and arguments are much more intimate and elastic.

Qualitative Thinking & Variations on Damages Arguments

Consider which is more important: an attractive plaintiff or a target defendant. There's no one answer to this enduring question. There are two tenets of advocacy lore: big fault provokes big damages, and its corollary, damages provoke liability. Why are these true? Because the

$$\$ = (A - C) \times B$$

formula expresses an elastic and dynamic process. These insights generate many creative variations from a rote subtraction formula. The following sections offer several examples.

Liability Provokes Damages

When liability is aggravated, focus on the fault or liability event (b). We'll express this by using an uppercase *B* when the defendant's misconduct is offensive or quasi-punitive and a lowercase *b* when the defendant's misconduct is more benign. Thus,

$$\$ = (A - C)\, B$$

when aggravated, or

$$\$ = (A - C)\, b$$

when ordinary negligence.

For example, in a case involving the sexual exploitation of a child, ask, "If this case isn't worth $3 million, then how much more did the plaintiff have to endure before it is?" This nonlinear argument shifts the focus from trying to measure the actual consequences to the plaintiff, meaning A – C, to the vulgar nature of what the defendant did to her, that is, B. A large or powerful defendant also helps me keep the jury's focus of judgment on the defendant and their misconduct rather than the plaintiff.

Damages Provoke Liability

Serious damages invite us in; we want to know how and why this happened, and what can and should have been done to prevent it. There's no need to shift to a qualitative model when big damages are self-evident; the extrinsic or traditional quantitative model works nicely. When there are large objective injuries, you can easily answer what they took from the plaintiff. With these damages, the formula is:

$$\$ = (A - C) \times b$$

That usually means the internal difference between the before and after on our 10 to 0 scale is at least 3. The larger the difference between before (A) and after (C), the bigger the damages, and thus the greater the case value. A real challenge in big damages cases is to not over-try them. Burn cases are an example. Also, don't forget to emphasize hope, be it in medical advancements or emerging technology. The plaintiff's resilience and character should always be front and center.

A Fragile Plaintiff Can Help Explain Causation

In this situation, a small liability event, even a tiny one, can still produce devastating consequences to a vulnerable plaintiff. It is akin to how "a straw can break the camel's back" or why "one person's meat is another's poison." It is important to understand and emphasize your jurisdiction's favorable multiple causation rules. Some are similar to this: Many factors may operate either independently or together to cause injury. In such a situation, each factor may be a cause of the injury, even though the others by themselves would have been sufficient to cause the same injury. If you find that the defendant's act or omission was a substantial factor in causing the plaintiff's injury, you may find that the defendant's conduct caused the injury even though it was not the only cause.

You don't need to prove b was the (only) cause—legally, b was simply one of the (one of many) legal causes. As an analogy, talk to the jurors about accomplice liability in criminal cases. In a bank robbery, everyone is legally responsible for the acts of all the others involved: the person with the gun on the teller, the second person guarding the door, and finally, the accomplice parked outside driving the getaway car. In the eyes of the law, each is equally responsible. I also think of a double play in baseball, short to second, and then the throw to first. In the score books, it's 6-4-3. The first baseman receives equal credit in the score book even though they caught an easy throw from the whirling second baseman. Research any tort reform modifications to your state's common-law rules of joint and several liability. An example might be minimum percentages before there is joint and several liability for noneconomic damages, say 26 percent, or perhaps the plaintiff can't be more than 50 percent at fault and still recover. Contrast the multiple causation rule (*a* cause, not *the* cause) with some states' more limited "but for" rule.

Ground Your Case Themes in Desirable Community Values

Suppose you have a dispute arising over the meaning of an oral agreement, confirmed only by a handshake. An attractive case theme might be, "Let's put honor back in a handshake."[6] Find a venerable value in

---

6. Harry Mills, *Artful Persuasion, the New Psychology of Influence: How to Command Attention, Change Minds, and Influence People* (New York, NY: American Management

which you can ground your trial themes so the jury affirms the importance of these values when it returns a significant verdict for your client. Jurors are hardwired to sniff out hypocrisy. When suing an institution, look for promotional statements of lofty goals and corporate culture, and then compare them with how it actually treated the plaintiff, and so on.

Keith Mitnik's *Don't Eat the Bruises* is a major contribution to plaintiffs' jury trial work.[7] In particular, I want to direct your attention to the following two big ideas.

In chapter 13 of *Don't Eat the Bruises*, "Owning Their Favorite Facts," Keith refers to "hijacking" the defense's best facts. Think of this as a form of prevention, meaning going out in front on some of their best facts and using them to your advantage. He invites you to take a key fact the defense is relying on and attempt to reframe or own it. If the fact was a foreseeable consequence of their negligence, then they can't profit by their own wrongdoing; in other words, the outcome was foreseeable, and the defense is now trying to forsake that responsibility.

He follows with chapter 14, "In Context Versus Out of Context." If you can't eliminate the bad facts with an FRE 401 and 403 pretrial motion *in limine* or own those facts to your advantage, then place them in context. Imagine you had a rebuttal opening statement. What would you stand and respond with that mitigates or explains their best facts? Then merge this new rebuttal into your opening. Season your comments with a little righteous indignation. After all, you should be upset when the defense unfairly tries to opportunistically take advantage of a fact.

Association, 2000); see *In re Central Ice Cream Co.*, 59 B.R. 476 (1985). This is Gerry Spence's argument in a case he tried in Chicago for a small family business who sued McDonald's for breach of an oral contract.

7. Keith Mitnik, *Don't Eat the Bruises: How to Foil Their Plans to Spoil Your Case* (Portland, OR: Trial Guides, 2015), 159–169, 171–185.

Keith offers the following on the concept of a lead-in to opening statement:

The lead-in to this final phase of your opening is as follows:

> In life, it is never good for things to be taken out of context. In a courtroom, it is doubly important that things be put in context. Before I sit down and the defense gives their opening statement, I want to talk to you about some of the evidence they will tell you supports the defense. I won't get a chance to get back up and put things in context, so I will do that now.
>
> So let me talk to you about some of the evidence I expect the defense will talk about, so I can put it in context.

A generic comment like this will bring to the forefront the importance of putting things in context and the dangers of allowing them to be taken out of context. You should not accuse the defendants of taking things out of context, because it will draw an objection. It is not necessary to cross that line to make the general point that it is the jurors' responsibility to keep a close eye on the totality of the evidence and your responsibility to make sure it is presented *in context*.[8]

Effective Damages Proof & Arguments

Lawyers ask me how to maximize damages, thinking I've got a magic formula or incantation that will spin straw into gold. Yes, there are techniques and arguments that give you your best chance for a good result; however, this problem didn't appear just before closing; it's been around since the client signed your fee agreement. Developing

---

8. Mitnik, *Don't Eat the Bruises*, 173–174 (emphasis in original).

damages and persuasive arguments for the number you're requesting can't be an afterthought.

Anchoring

The idea of anchoring is synonymous to connecting or tying your damages request to something else, be it the exact words of the instruction, another number, or even a subject. Try to frame or make your case about something large that's morally important. Damages arguments are always made in a larger context. Where's your moral high ground? Where is your opponent weakest? Arguing damages in this larger context will access the jury's positive values. Arguing big money for pain and suffering is a lot easier with the wind at your back.

Advocacy professor Jim Wren says it well:

> Substantial verdicts for damages, particularly intangible damages, spring from the desire of jurors to make a statement that stands for what is right and for what really matters. What matters to jurors? Their perceptions of what matters to their families and their communities (or at least that part of the community whose opinions are important to those jurors).
>
> Jurors may start a trial (and if never engaged, may end a trial) with only the desires to make a right decision as efficiently as possible, and to go back to their lives. But engaged jurors start to grasp a more powerful desire, the desire to take the heroic path as a protector of right, family, and community. When that desire and self-image kick in, damages become the means for saying what matters and how much it matters.[9]

This is a ringing endorsement for jury empowerment.

---

9. Jim Wren, *Proving Damages to the Jury* (Costa Mesa, CA: James Publishing Inc., 2011), 56.

Link your pain and suffering damages number to a concrete amount, such as multiplying the specials by a certain factor, or perhaps a per month or per annum argument.[10] I like to tie it to the plaintiff's life expectancy. It's too abstract and difficult to think of what it means to have thirty-five more years of pain and suffering, so try going back thirty-five years and be specific.

The Law/Instructions

I start with two large legal notions: *all parties are equal before the law* and *no verdict is to be based on bias, sympathy, or prejudice*. No one needs the protection of the law more than the weakest among us, and that especially includes those who are emotionally vulnerable. To treat their injuries as being less serious than physical injuries violates the law and is, therefore, a form of implied bias or prejudice. Start with the exact words of your state's uniform civil jury instructions for pain and suffering, which are often labeled "noneconomic" damages.

The words of the court's instruction provide judicial directives that respond to many jurors' understandable concerns about money. Of course, pain and suffering are subjective and, therefore, highly personal; and yes, there's no exact formula available, such as adding up numbers in economic losses. Judges also instruct the jurors to use their common sense and good judgment.

Pain is when you burn your finger on a hot stove; suffering is when you cry yourself to sleep. Carefully think about this distinction. Shame and humiliation are entitled to be compensated the same as broken bones, and, yes, people really are more than skin and bones—that is exactly what the judge is telling them. Finally, the law even respects "inconvenience and interference" and directs the jurors to compensate for this too.

When you anchor or ground your damages request to the exact terms of the instructions, you're borrowing from the dignity of the

---

10. Check your state's rules. Some states don't allow a *per diem* argument.

robe (judge). Consider enlarging the verdict form and actually fill in the spaces with the amounts (the prayer) you're requesting for damages. Don't order or command the jurors; this invites the *paradox of persuasion* and an understandable backlash. You're a guide or teacher, not a drill instructor; tone it down.

Giving the jurors a specific number helps frame their discussion and is psychologically known as *bracketing*. Build your closing toward the verdict through the instructions. Finish with the verdict form—that's what the jurors are going to do. Think of the jury's answers to the questions on the special verdict to be your report card. Yes, the jurors get to "grade your paper."

Setting Your Damages Theme during Jury Selection

During jury selection, individually ask the jurors about some small and personal interest each of them may enjoy that would be a serious loss if it were taken. Have any of them ever had a soft tissue injury or emotional loss? Have them describe the experience. This conditions the jury for the kinds of losses they will be hearing about later, and invites them during this deliberation to compare their potential losses to those of the plaintiff. I mention the "amount in controversy," meaning the prayer. Without having heard any evidence, does the amount put a bee in their bonnet?

Be creative in generating exhibits that bolster your pain and suffering arguments. If you have physical injuries, use them as a jump-off point (akin to anchoring) for your transition to pain and suffering or injuries no one can see. It might be a medical illustration of injuries to the muscles that an X-ray won't show in a soft tissue injury case. Photographs of the plaintiff's physical injury can speak far more eloquently than any words. In unusual cases it may require enlarging pages from the *DSM-5* containing the diagnostic criteria for post-traumatic stress disorder.[11] The foundation for your demonstrative evidence is simply whether it will "aid and assist the jury…"

Your Confidence

Don't be tentative or hesitate when arguing your damages number. Even if you really aren't so confident or sure, you need to deliver a compelling argument. That's your job, and it won't happen by accident. It takes thought, preparation, and then practice standing on your feet and delivering your argument. You're not ready until you can give the jurors reasons for your suggested conclusion. Look them each in the eye. Volume and repetition have nothing to do with quality. Ask and answer the hard questions you know the jurors are going to be asking. Your best answers are always better than ignoring the obvious questions.

I videotape my preliminary opening and closing and review them with others. How can both be better? What's missing? Is it focused?

One legitimate approach is to *under-try* the damages in serious injuries that are straightforward and self-evident. Examples include burns, amputation, or, in the domain of the emotional, perhaps an event that meets *DSM-5* criteria A for post-traumatic stress disorder involving actual or threatened death, serious injury, or a threat to physical safety.[12] In these specific circumstances, developing the damages proof to its outer limits may be counterproductive.

Under-trying damages must be a carefully calculated decision. On first blush, you might think trying a minimalist damages case would be easy because you're putting on less evidence; however, it's actually more difficult, requiring deft judgment and nuanced advocacy.

---

11. American Psychiatric Association, *Diagnostic and Statistical Manual of Mental Disorders Text Revision: DSM-5-TR* (Arlington, VA: American Psychiatric Association Publishing, 2013), 271–280.

12. American Psychiatric Association, *DSM-5*.

Why do all my injured clients try their best to return to work? Why do I discourage my clients from behavior that might appear to be whining and complaining? Why do I want them to share with the jury all that remains in their lives they're grateful for? Intuitively you know the answer. Themes of stoicism and gratitude are grounded in community values and are what many jurors want to hear. Yes, jurors are responsible for awarding an amount of money that fully compensates for the plaintiff's losses, but at some point, it's not necessary to hear more about the plaintiff's pain and suffering. At some point in the trial, the jurors get it—the plaintiff is seriously injured. If they don't get it, piling on the proof probably isn't going to help much and, at some outer point, can actually boomerang. In other words, *less can be more.*

When analyzing a case, I start with the liability. Is it aggravated such that "liability provokes damages," and how likable is the defendant? Next is the plaintiff's decency factor, which I also call their citizenship or ethos. This involves the jurors' emotional response to the plaintiff, which is textually different from sympathy. The plaintiff's appeal includes all the intangibles that make up your client's personhood. A likable plaintiff is essential in medical negligence cases, which are always uphill battles.

Most clients aren't good at talking about themselves. This is where careful lay witness selection, preparation, and tempered delivery are at a premium.

Reflect upon David Ball's advice:

> Jurors are like an audience reacting to a play. They make their decisions based on the information made available to them. So, you must control the proportion of time your trial spends on damages. Perhaps a third should be on harm, losses, and money.[13]

---

13. David Ball, *David Ball on Damages the Essential Update: A Plaintiff's Attorney's Guide for Personal Injury and Wrongful Death Cases*, 2nd ed. (Louisville, CO: National Institute for Trial Advocacy, 2005), 5.

After considering Ball's advice, review the proof you can muster with the traditional panoply of experts. Then impose my ABC test; that is, is your proof *accurate*, *brief*, and *clear*? The emphasis must be on quality, not quantity.

My Favorite Plaintiffs' Damages Arguments

Pick and choose the arguments that best match your facts.

1. Invite the jurors to value the plaintiff's injuries by considering the plaintiff's future as a job. Divide the prayer by the plaintiff's life expectancy and declare this to be the annual salary. Oh, by the way, there are a few conditions of the job: It's not for forty or fifty hours a week; it's for every hour of every day, 168 hours a week. The job also has no annual vacations or weekends off; it's every moment, for the rest of the plaintiff's life.

    There's one more provision: The plaintiff can't quit. They go to bed frightened and hurting. They sleep poorly, have nightmares, and wake up tired. They must forfeit most of the activities they used to enjoy the most. This is their future job. Is there any juror who would apply for it—at any price?
2. Illustrate how even a substantial verdict is modest compared to the price we pay for other things in our society that are obviously of lesser intrinsic value. Professional athletes, actors, and entertainers command multimillion-dollar paychecks. Racehorses sell for millions, and their seed alone sells for huge sums. Art sells at Sotheby's for millions, and it can't breathe or cry. Modern military equipment costs millions and billions of dollars. Maybe these are commentaries on our times and society's values, or lack of them. The plaintiff's losses compare favorably with the value of any of these.

3. When the plaintiff is aged, argue that our health and our loved ones are life's greatest treasures. If you have good health and are sixty or older, it's probably because you've earned it based on a lifetime of good choices and healthy habits. Good health is the investment of a lifetime.

    By injuring the plaintiff, the defendant has taken away the plaintiff's choices. They no longer can choose, and they never will be able to. They may or may not have ever pursued these lost options, but they sure can't now. Be specific. State exactly what the plaintiff can and can't do that they could do before, and then bring it home by explaining why this is so important to them.
4. Acknowledge any physical disfigurement. In our culture physical beauty is prized. Magazines endlessly tell us how to become more beautiful. Mrs. Jones's scars aren't going to be "air brushed" away. Time may heal all wounds, but wounds leave lasting scars.

Arguments against Businesses

Here are seven generic arguments that are effective against businesses or corporations:

1. Everything in the defendant's business life is a choice, Profit (business) versus Safety (consumer), with welcomed benefits and accepted burdens. The defendant's conduct that injured the plaintiff was a calculated business decision. The defendant chose to commit the acts (or *not* commit the acts, such as routine maintenance or safety checks) that led to the consequences. It may not have intended the effects, but it intended the acts that inexorably led to the effects.
2. The defendant will lose nothing by the jury's just verdict. The defendant made a choice to proceed with inadequate maintenance, which permitted it to profit outside the law. The defendant is now being asked to return its windfall profits to the public, meaning the

plaintiff. Instead, the defendant is now asking you to punish the plaintiff because he wasn't looking at his feet. The defendant is, in effect, saying that customers shouldn't assume a business's floor is safe. This business chose to compromise safety for profit.

3. We participate in a system where society distributes resources and money in accordance with previously agreed on ground rules. Anyone who ignores the community's rules, profits or gains an advantage against those who do play by the rules. In the process, safety and integrity are compromised.
4. To a business defendant, the plaintiff is merely a statistic, a cost of doing business. Only the names change. We wouldn't be here if the defendant had previously made the right choices, meaning properly balanced profit with safety.
5. The defendants don't appreciate that people aren't fungible or interchangeable; citizens aren't things. You don't treat people like common currency.
6. The corporation has one way of grading its proficiency—through its profitability. We already know that the defendant is profitable. We ask this jury, as the conscience of the community, to grade the defendant's citizenship, not its profitability.
7. Profits and safety aren't antagonists, but roommates. The consuming public rewards safety with patronage. If the defendant had made the correct choices, it wouldn't now be in the position of having to pay the innocent parties it has damaged.

Breach of Contract Arguments

There's a wonderful species of breach-of-contract-type arguments. Rick Friedman gives a good example in his book, *Becoming a Trial Lawyer:*

> A lawyer I know tries cases in a conservative area of Oklahoma. In this jurisdiction, arguing that the defendant was negligent in causing a traffic accident is a tough sell. The strong predisposition of jurors is that stuff happens, everyone makes mistakes, "There but for the grace of God go I," and the plaintiff should have been more careful. After attending a seminar on juror attitude, he learned that conservative jurors place a high value on contractual obligations. These jurors embrace the "sanctity of contract" with an almost religious fervor. In his next personal injury case, he reframed a traditional negligence case to address the jurors' values. He said something like:
>
> > When we get our driver's license from the state, we are entering into a contract with the State of Oklahoma and all other drivers who are legally on the road. The laws of the state are the contract we all agree to follow. Among other things, all of us agree to yield when the state put a yield sign up. A year and a half ago, at the corner of Elm and Shuster, Mr. Simpson broke that contract.
>
> His cross-examination followed up on this theme:
>
> > Q. When you got your driver's license, you were promising to follow the laws of this state?
> > Q. This was a promise made to all other drivers?
> > Q. You knew other drivers were promising the same thing to you?
> > Q. It is part of what made you feel safe on the road—the promises of these other drivers to follow the law?[14]

---

14. Rick Friedman, *Becoming a Trial Lawyer* (Portland, OR: Trial Guides, 2008), 123.

Along the same line, Jim McElhaney maintains that in a personal injury action,

> a theory of the case that is articulated as an obligation owed because of the wrong that was done—rather than as an appeal for pity because a person got hurt—is more likely to bring an adequate award.[15]

Conclusion

There are many benefits to my qualitative approach and Mitnik's instruction to own the defense's favorite facts. Using these techniques will enhance your credibility with everyone. Your trials will be shorter because you'll be up front with painfully honest assessments of the plaintiffs and their losses. Judges will welcome you back because you are accurate, brief, and clear. Using the qualitative approach will certainly help you win bigger verdicts in objectively smaller cases. Even more important, it will reduce the number of your losses and compromise verdicts where you had previously pushed the outer limits of the traditional subtraction game.

Many defense attorneys are so used to plaintiffs and/or their lawyers stretching the facts that when confronted with the potent honesty of qualitative arguments, they routinely overplay their hands and polarize their cases. This is what I had in mind when I discussed taking full advantage of an opponent's mistakes, but your client must be above reproach in order to take full advantage of these opportunities.

---

15. James W. McElhaney, *McElhaney's Trial Notebook*, 4th ed. (Chicago, IL: ABA Press, 2005), 21.

13

Mediation from the Plaintiff's Perspective

Most cases settle as a result of mediation. The skills necessary to be effective in trial and mediation overlap. In order to get the best results for your client, it's important to understand the psychology of the participants, develop solid negotiating skills, and be familiar with the structurally embedded aspects of the civil litigation process that favor each side.

Mediation versus Trial

I offer this chapter on mediation because the reality is that it's where most of the action is. Yes, jury trials are important—but the threat of a jury trial and verdict generating serious exposure is the engine that drives negotiation.

For beginning lawyers, good mediators tend to make sure that there's some congruence between the value of the case and the defense's final settlement offer. In smaller cases, the size of the defense's offer is driven more by the size of the case than the quality of the plaintiff's lawyer. This is because there isn't much potential or opportunity for a talented plaintiff's lawyer to enhance the case's value. Don't quibble about an experienced mediator's fees. All parties share the fees, and it's one place you can't afford a bargain.

Mediation comes with a few downsides. At the personal level, you can quickly get used to settling and thus lose your appetite for trial. There's no exact demarcation that says when you're crossing this line, but we all know it's a lot easier to settle than to start preparing for court. When you reject low-end offers and later competently try the case, you win credibility for future cases, even if you happen to lose.

Fewer and fewer civil cases are actually being tried because of mediation's advantages and effectiveness. With a growing number of highly competent mediators, it's easier and easier for inexperienced plaintiffs' lawyers to recommend that their clients accept the best mediated offer. We might soon reach a point where it's almost unethical for an inexperienced plaintiff's lawyer to go to court in an effort to improve on a tenured mediator's recommendation. The bottom line is this: mediators are getting better, resulting in more cases being settled, and plaintiffs' lawyers are getting less experienced. This is not good for the health of our civil justice system.

The Psychology of the Mediation Participants

Parties negotiate for two basic reasons. The first is to gain the satisfaction of a presently unsatisfied need. The second is fear of losing a presently satisfied need. Regardless of which is your primary motivation, the result is always the same: both are seeking to fulfill their objectives.[1] The plaintiff seeks to gain financial compensation for a past loss. The defendant's insurance carrier wants to avoid the future loss of its money. A significant plaintiff's verdict will reduce their finances; hence, the insurance company is negotiating to reduce its risk of a large future loss. From this elevated position, we can see that the negotiation process always comes down to the present satisfaction of the parties' needs.[2]

People act for *their* reasons—not yours. Work to understand and appreciate your opponent's perspective and motivation. Insurance companies have the money. Your job is to motivate them to deliver some of it to you and your client now. Before launching into a heated diatribe about why you think they should settle, reflect upon the primary reasons why they are even considering bargaining. Listen carefully as the negotiations progress. What are the key features of your case that appear to concern them? Is there anything unsaid that should be worrying them? Examples might include an adverse reaction to publicity if tried or a potential future bad faith claim.

There are some truisms of human behavior that operate in all negotiations. The first is that people who are about to *receive* money are risk-averse, meaning they are reluctant to gamble. Second, people who are about to *pay* money are risk-accepting, meaning they are more

---

1. Richard G. Halpern, *Plaintiff's Personal Injury Negotiation Strategies* (New York, NY: Wiley Law Publications, 1991), 1–2.
2. Halpern, *Plaintiff's Personal Injury Negotiation Strategies*, 3.

willing to gamble. Let's explore this idea. The following illustrates the psychological differences between the plaintiff and defense perspectives.

Assume I ask you to make a wager on a coin toss. You will flip your own quarter in the air and call heads or tails. If you call the coin correctly, I will pay you $5 million in cash within twenty-four hours. However, if you call it incorrectly, then you must pay me one-tenth of that sum, or $500,000 cash, within twenty-four hours. Would you accept the offer? Think about it. You know that this is an even money wager. It is your quarter, you are flipping, and you are calling the toss. The odds of a head or tail are exactly fifty-fifty. However, I have come along and offered you a ten to one payment. Would you take the bet? In his polling of people presented with this hypothetical bet, Richard G. Halpern found that less than 1 percent of people polled would take the bet.[3] The reason they decline the bet has nothing to do with whether or not the bet is fair, because it's obviously an excellent wager. The primary reason 99 percent of the people say no to this excellent offer is that there is a 50 percent probability that, within twenty-four hours, they are going to be $500,000 poorer, and most people can't afford a loss of this size.

Now, let's change the bet slightly. Everything I said before is still true, except now I am saying that we will sit here all day and you will flip your quarter one thousand consecutive times. We will keep score. The same 10:1 payment ratio per coin flip still applies, and we will settle up at the completion of the thousandth flip. Would you take that bet? Remember that the only change between the two offers is that we have increased the number of coin flips from one to one thousand. You are much more likely to accept the second offer because now the probability of you having to part with any money is in the range of trillions to one.

We can compare this example to the positions of the adversaries in tort negotiations. The one-flip example represents a typical plaintiff's position. This case, this trial, this negotiation is the only shot the plaintiff is going to have to be compensated. The thousand flips are analogous to the insurance company's position. They can afford to lose

---

3. Halpern, *Plaintiff's Personal Injury Negotiation Strategies*.

this one, or the next dozen, or more, because they will make it up down the line. The insurance company is in a position of basing much of what they do on statistics and amortizing losses. Because of this, the plaintiff starts the negotiation at a disadvantage. Plaintiffs and their counsel are emotionally and financially involved on a personal level in the outcome of this specific case. Defense counsel and the insurance adjusters are not. Once more, advantage to the defense.

Have the Right Mindset for Negotiations

Given the above insights, it's important that you, as plaintiff's counsel, and your client get into a proper mindset. When you cut through the rhetoric, you probably wonder how much of the insurance company's money your client is going to get. After all, it's only natural to be concerned about what the final outcome might be. The problem is that this fosters a weakened mindset. It's a perspective that has its own emotional inertia. It's a mindset with fear and vulnerability at its core. These unspoken feelings and resulting attitudes contaminate your ability to effectively negotiate.

If you're confident, it shows. If you're fearful, it shows. You and your client should do your best to communicate confidence, self-control, patience, and interest.[4] To draw upon a boxing metaphor, "Don't look for a place to fall when stepping into the ring." Measured optimism is the result of thorough preparation and careful analysis. Confidence isn't cockiness.

How do you avoid negative thinking? Let me suggest you change the questions. The focal point of the negotiation should not be the defendant carrier's money and how much they might be willing to pay your client. Instead, the focus should be on the plaintiff's release. The

---

4. Halpern, *Plaintiff's Personal Injury Negotiation Strategies*, 33.

question then becomes, how much is this insurance company willing to bid or offer in exchange for a release from your client? When entering negotiations, don't fret about how much of the insurance company's money you're going to get. Instead, know that you're either going to get X amount in settlement, or you're probably going to try the case.[5]

Here's another way to frame this process: Think of the settlement amount the carrier offers as one bid in the context of a bidding war. The amount that the carrier offers, or bids, is always done within the backdrop of a possible future jury verdict. Think of the future jury verdict as a sealed bid that has yet to be written by the jury foreperson and opened in court. Your present threat of what this future verdict might be is the primary driver of the insurance company's offer today. This is their present bid.

Remember that the insurance company is the only purchaser of your client's release. They are the only ones who want it. Their potential loss at a future trial determines the value of that release. Therefore, if they don't really believe that a trial will ensue, the present value of the release goes down. If they are convinced that you will take this matter to court, and you will try the case to its maximum value, then the present value of that release increases.[6] Of course, defense attorneys' billings and experts' fees are structurally embedded costs for insurance companies.

How to Respond to the Other Side's Arguments

You have choices in how you respond to the other side's negotiations. You can choose active listening, questioning, and of course,

---

5. Halpern, *Plaintiff's Personal Injury Negotiation Strategies*, 15.

6. Halpern, *Plaintiff's Personal Injury Negotiation Strategies*, 18.

affirmatively stating your case's strengths. I recommend you very attentively listen. I call this *aggressive listening*.[7]

Silence and pauses are powerful tools in all negotiations. It often makes your adversary uneasy. They feel a compulsion to speak. When the two of you are disagreeing, often neither of you is really listening to the other. Suppose you shift gears and simply attentively listen and don't respond. Maintain eye contact, but don't nod or speak. Your opponent is expecting a response, any response. When one isn't forthcoming, their natural reaction is to elaborate. Why? Because few people, particularly lawyers, can stand silence. Your adversary will likely continue telling you all of the areas in which they think that you have problems. This helps your situation. First, whether or not you really do have these problems, your adversary will detail them *ad nauseam*. This often provides you with additional information or insights into your case.[8]

The traditional approach is to respond with your pat arguments, which of course your opponent will usually reject out of hand. Consider making the same points by asking carefully crafted questions. Ask:

- "I wonder if…?"
- "Is it possible that…?"
- "Have you considered…?"

Before the negotiation, carefully craft a list of questions organized around the key topics that you want to focus on. Above all, don't say anything that you can't and won't back up.

Always be pleasant and professional. Negotiate on your terms. Try to be the kind of person that your opponent can both like and respect, while sensing at a deeper level that the polite, confident lawyer opposite them is honestly eager to go to court.

---

7. Halpern, *Plaintiff's Personal Injury Negotiation Strategies*, 114.
8. Halpern, *Plaintiff's Personal Injury Negotiation Strategies*, 115–166.

Thoughts on Mediation

Times are changing. Thirty years ago, there was virtually no alternative dispute resolution (ADR). Now it's common and often court ordered. In the past, negotiating on your own required different skills because most of it was done directly with the opposing counsel. Now there's a highly trained professional assisting all sides. Excellent mediators often achieve settlement rates of 85 percent and more.

It's the harsh economic reality that serious litigation isn't cheap. My view is that if you want a million-dollar verdict, then you have to try a million-dollar case. So much for the romanticism of law school. The market is economically blind, and contingency fees guarantee if you don't win, then you don't get paid. When you settle for amounts that do not truly represent the market value of the claim, not only are you doing your clients a disservice, but it's the most expensive money you'll ever touch. Why? Because with each claim, you are gaining a reputation as a negotiator. This happens quickly and without your permission. Your reputation soon is a tangible reality.

When I say *market value*, I mean the reasonable settlement value, factoring in all the transactional costs, such as attorney's fees and litigation expenses. An aspect that many lawyers do not sufficiently consider is the defendant's *composite exposure*. While this starts with the amount of money they will have to pay in order to "buy" a release, there are often nonfiscal factors, including the adverse publicity from public trials. That's why defendants want settlements confidential or sealed. Risk managers and institutional representatives are always mindful of these aspects.

Be respectful of your opponent and our shared profession. Demonizing the defendant or the insurance company makes no sense to me. They have the money. I choose to view my opponent as a potential ally with my job being to motivate the carrier to pay my client full market value.

Start by documenting every aspect of your claim and papering the adjustor's fees. Setting the reserves for your claim early and high helps the adjustor later help you. This makes it a shorter step for them to later write you a big check.

After Mediation

Once you have settled a case, don't later second-guess yourself with "buyer's remorse." I'm often conflicted about a settlement. A big part of me wants to go to court, and, yes, I believed I could have beaten an otherwise reasonable settlement offer my client accepted. We all know, however, it's the client's decision, and it's not helpful to hang onto regrets about what might have been. It's time to move on.

Why Mediation?

I recommend that you submit every case to mediation, particularly those you don't think will settle. Why? Because apart from the fact that you may be surprised, if you settle every case you mediate, then you can't expect anyone to take your threat of actually going to trial seriously. You have no credibility. When you leave a mediation headed for the courtroom, it creates an enhanced value for every future case you mediate. As bold as this statement is, it doesn't mean much unless you consistently obtain verdicts for significantly more than the carrier's last offer.

I don't believe that mediation with a skilled facilitator is ever a waste of my time, irrespective of whether the case settles. I almost always learn important things about my case, especially its weaknesses. The mediation process can be a good form of trial preparation. Your client probably has already given a deposition. This is the next stage. Carefully prepare clients prior to the mediation. Explain your game plan and strategies. Now is the time to reinforce your clients' confidence in you. Don't let the mediator sow doubt in your client's mind. All my well-prepared clients say four things to the mediator:

1. I trust my lawyers.
2. I trust the system.
3. I welcome a jury trial.
4. I am not afraid of an appeal.

Occasional mediation can assist in narrowing the issues and thereby shorten the trial. Just because a case doesn't settle pretrial doesn't mean it won't settle during trial.

I even go so far as to think that every case in my office is in some way connected, as in a web, with every other case I have or ever will have. My gestalt operates as if there is one huge insurance company—we'll call it the Holy Grail Insurance Company—that insures every defendant our office will ever sue. Under this view, my last offer in case A becomes the backdrop for my first offer in case B, and so on. Everything I do, at all times, is connected and occurs in the context of everything else. There are benefits to embracing this construct. Following are some implications of this belief system:

1. While I may be immersed in the specifics of today's case, our office always operates out of a set of core values that are consistent from case to case. We can do this because we thoroughly evaluate every case before we accept it, and are selective in the cases we accept. We are then committed to sinking almost unlimited time, effort, and money into developing our limited case inventory for trial. Finally, we really are excited to try the cases we have accepted.
2. "Sharp tactics" that may gain an immediate advantage in any one particular case, but are to the ultimate detriment of our reputations are out. Once again, this is a long view, and I think of it as *enlightened self-interest*.
3. In this business, credibility is the key to everything. I'm never negotiating from scratch. Why? Because my reputation precedes me in every new file I open. Of course, this is partially a fiction, but it's a useful one.

Structural Aspects of Mediation

Until payment, it is the individual plaintiff who bears the entire financial loss. The plaintiff isn't a big business that can amortize losses by spreading them over thousands of files, and the defendant knows this. This places the plaintiff at an obvious negotiating disadvantage, particularly with a trial in the distant future, followed by the threat of a lengthy appeal. This results in incredible economic pressure on serious injured plaintiffs. An aging plaintiff may not live to see the completion of a lengthy appeal. If they choose, the insurance company can simply hold on to the plaintiff's money, invest it, and later make a "reasonable" offer on the courthouse steps without the threat of prejudgment interest.

Multiple structural tort reform advantages also favor the defense. These include caps on public bodies, wrongful death claims, and noneconomic damages; modified joint and several liability; limits on interest during medical appeals; and so on.

A review of past verdicts doesn't include all those unreported cases that settled before or during trial and, by their settlement terms, are deemed to be confidential. As a generalization, it's the smaller cases and cases with big damages and questionable liability that end up actually being tried to verdict.[9]

When to Choose Mediation

In the abstract, you want to try your good cases and settle your bad ones. But in the real world, the opposite happens. If you settle all your smaller cases, where are you going to gain the experience that allows you to try your serious cases to their value?

It's okay to reject a nominal offer on a few minor impact soft-tissue cases (MIST). Try a few. Be upfront with your client, in a low offer case

---

9. Halpern, *Plaintiff's Personal Injury Negotiation Strategies*, 82.

they don't have much to lose. Pick a few cases with decent liability. You already have problems with your client who called a lawyer before they went to their chiropractor.

This is how you gain jury trial experience, otherwise it's not going to happen. Once you get the mechanics down, your comfort level will quickly increase. Prepare, bring your better angels, and consider my qualitative measures of damages. Everyone's nervous and scared at first; you'll soon get the hang of it.

Beware—settling out one defendant when there are multiple allows the remaining defendant(s) to successfully argue all sorts of empty chair defenses by pointing fingers at any defendant you have previously settled with. You might want to wait until after closing arguments to settle out one of multiple defendants. That way they had a lawyer during the trial to defend them from their co-defendants' predictable crossfire.

Distinguish between the exposure the insurance company is negotiating to avoid and your client's present financial needs. In a few big cases, mediators who were new to me asked my client a variation of, "What is your economic wish list?" In other words, "If you had a bundle of money, what would you do with it?" Most clients usually want to pay for all past and future healthcare needs, educate their children, and maybe pay off their house and car. The mediator can then argue that the amount that the insurance company is offering will address everything on the client's list, so what the client wants isn't just need, but greed. Then, rather than talking about the serious exposure the defendant has, the mediator shifts the focus and tries to characterize the plaintiff as being motivated by anger or revenge.

My response, apart from never accepting that mediator again, is that insurance companies are in the business of loss distribution. They pay to avoid exposure, nothing more and nothing less. The carrier will make a settlement offer based upon their assessment of their exposure. Perhaps my injured client is a millionaire with no financial needs. That doesn't necessarily mean the carrier has no exposure for a big verdict. Insurance companies are quick to take advantage of our clients' economic vulnerability when it's to their advantage. Yes, a client's financial needs are a factor, but the defendant's exposure is the bottom line.

Finally, in a serious case with an inexperienced plaintiffs' counsel, the defense is saying to themselves, "This lawyer has never tried a big case." They know that the lawyer probably isn't capable of fully bankrolling the case, and that this will place incredible pressure upon the plaintiff's lawyer, and thus their client, to settle.

Strategies for Negotiating

Don't negotiate until your client has reached maximum medical improvement (MMI). MMI is a plateau of stability for a sufficient time such that the treating doctors can reasonably forecast your client's future.

Negotiations are a waste of time unless you are talking with someone who has the authority to write the check. Cut out the middle people. Only a person with authority can make it happen. It's really the mediator's job to see that insurance representation with sufficient authority to settle the case are attending, or at least available.

Remember that you're never off the record. This means the dance of negotiation is always going on, whether in a bar or conference room. If negotiating before filing or discovery, there's no reason to withhold any information that the defendant is entitled to and will later receive during discovery. Consider checking for comparable verdicts with jury verdict research. When you reject an offer, carefully think about how you're going to say no. Both timing and content are implicated. There can be unintended messages within your response.

After years of negotiating, I have often observed an unwritten rule of thumb. I call it the *Rule of Halves*. Essentially, you can graph the time and dollar amount of both side's offers as a way of predicting the range and bottom line or final outcome.

Here is an oversimplified symmetrical example:

- (1:00 p.m.) Party A opens the negotiations with an initial offer of $10,000.
- (2:00 p.m.) Party B responds with its first offer being $4,000.
- (2:30 p.m.) Party A then counteroffers with $8,000.
- (3:00 p.m.) Party B responds with a second offer of $6,000.

From the above, you can predict that the case will settle in fifteen minutes for $7,000. I don't mean to suggest that the amount of each successive offer will symmetrically converge, such as in my example; however, there often is a slope or pattern.

Using the Rule of Halves always forces you to think ahead of your next offer by asking, *Where do I really want to be at the end of the day?* Said a different way, if you want to settle for a certain amount, then prior to starting negotiations, ask yourself:

- What should my opening offer be?
- What will they likely respond with?

and then,

- What should my first counteroffer be?
- Does the timing and amount of my offers and responses presage my ultimate number?

By the amounts of your first, second, and certainly third counteroffer, you are signaling the domain you are targeting. This kind of strategizing reduces the chances you'll later end up bidding against yourself. Avoid making two offers in a row without an intervening counteroffer from your opponent. Always be thinking at least two steps ahead of the present.

Even if negotiations break down, they aren't necessarily over. Your last offer, which the other side rejected, is a prologue to your next offer and counteroffer, which may (or may not) occur later, perhaps even during the trial.

I carefully chart all the settlement offers in writing. Use the court reporter if made during the trial. If you fail to document that you communicated the offer to your client and you later lose the case, you and the client may have forgotten the verbal communication of the offer. The same client might now be adamant that if only you had told them of the offer, they would have accepted it. Your next step will be a telephone call to your professional insurance carrier asking them to assign an attorney to defend *you*. This problem becomes even more dire if you happen to die before the statute of limitations runs, and then it's just your client's word. Your estate loses.

Give your client thorough procedures, alternatives, and risks (PAR) advice. This is drawn from the medical informed-consent model. Word your explanation so an eighth grader would understand it. Putting everything in writing protects everyone. It leaves no doubt about what was said, your explanation of what it meant, and your client's response. Write this letter as if it were an exhibit in a later malpractice claim by your client against you. Carefully written PAR letters soon become a smart habit.

In some bigger cases, I have hired an ethics lawyer to review my analysis and decision-making. These lawyers have occasionally recommended that I hire and pay for a third lawyer who is both conservative and unquestionably competent to persuasively disagree with me. At my request, this third lawyer then writes my client an opinion letter critiquing my analysis and valuation and setting forth their assessment and conclusions regarding the value of the case. I discuss this further in chapter 19, "When and How to Refer Your Case."

The work of this third lawyer usually costs me about $5,000. This process ensures that real informed consent occurs. I alone pay for the bills of the ethics lawyer and then the third (contrary-opinion) lawyer without passing the costs back to the client. I provide my client with this differing opinion for two reasons. First, it's the moral thing to do. Second, if we should lose the case, or if the jury awards an amount that's less than I had recommended my client settle for, this opinion letter is evidence that I not only met but exceeded the standard of care—I fulfilled my responsibilities to provide my client with real and informed consent.

Give your client bottom-line numbers. To do this, you must know what all your costs advanced are before you go into negotiations. After subtracting attorney's fees and costs, what will end up in your client's pocket? Is any of the recovery taxable? You must also protect your client against any liens. No surprises. Don't wait until after you've arrived at a settlement number with the defendant's insurance carrier to then approach lienholders and ask them to reduce their lien amounts. At that point, it's too late. Earlier, you still had the backdrop of a disputed claim when negotiating with a lienholder. Mediators and settlement conference judges can also be helpful at negotiating any outstanding liens.

Creative mediation suggestions include high-low bracketing and possibly shifting from mediation to an arbitration, often called a mediator's number. When both sides are still separated and can't close the gap, they can empower the mediator to render a binding decision by choosing a number in the gap. The mediator doesn't reveal whether the other side argued with the proposal. Preserving the possibility of a mediator's number is one of the reasons why mediators can be reluctant, at least early on, to tell either side what they believe the settlement value of the case is. By focusing on the process and acquiring the trust of both sides, the mediator's then in a position to later shift to a mediator's number if the parties agree.

The final word on whether to accept an opponent's offer belongs to the client. It's the client's case. However, during the first interview, I explain to prospective clients—before they ever see a fee agreement—exactly what our firm's negotiating philosophy is. We are aggressive, and if we do settle, then it's for top dollar. If the clients aren't comfortable with this philosophy, I encourage them to seek representation with another office. Don't agree to write a letter threatening litigation if a client's demands aren't me unless you're prepared to actually follow through on the threat. One more time, this has to do with your reputation.

Structured settlements have much to commend them, particularly for minors and the financially unsophisticated. When considering a structured settlement, first negotiate as if everything is cash up front. Otherwise, the negotiations will be contaminated with the inflated high of future payments, defendant's call this "funny money" and don't want to hear it. Once you arrive at that present value number, only then should you shift to discussing delaying payment through a structure into the future.

Consider your client's tax liability with any settlement or award. If there is punitive damages exposure, it may not be to your client's advantage to try the case and obtain a significant award for punitive damages. See if the terms of the settlement can be framed to shift the money from punitive to general damages, which generally aren't taxed. Once a verdict is entered for punitive it's often settled pre-judgment for a lesser amount of general damages, which won't be taxed.

If your mediation bogs down, ask if there's a legal question whose answer might break the impasse. If so, consider submitting the question to the court for disposition. If you are going to use this technique, I strongly suggest you have a written agreement of the exact question to be answered. You might want to have agreed upon numbers that both sides will pay. Depending on the answer, the agreement should be in writing or placed on the record with a judge or mediator specifically authorized to enforce the agreement. The case should be settled once you have agreed on the exact question and the consequences of a yes or no answer to that question.

Common Mistakes

- Allowing the mediator to drive a wedge between you and your client.
- Not writing carefully worded pre-mediation informed-consent letters to your client.
- Not educating your client on how much they will actually receive after attorney fees, costs, and the payment of any liens.

- Not communicating all offers and counteroffers, and not obtaining client consent for each of these moves.
- Not identifying and resolving all potential liens, if not before mediation, then certainly before a final agreement.
- Not making sure an insurance representative with sufficient authority to settle the case is readily available.

Conclusion

Listen a lot and seek to learn more than you reveal. You want the mediator to spend more time with the opponent than with you. Make sure you have (earned) your client's loyalty and support. If the case doesn't settle, be eager to try it and always strive to beat the defense's last best offer by an amount that justifies the trial. Arm yourself with the tools and knowledge of best negotiation practices. Understand what's at stake for all parties, and don't be afraid to go to court when appropriate.

14

On Personal Authenticity

As jury trial lawyers, we need authenticity for credibility, we need credibility for persuasiveness, and we need persuasiveness to be effective. Think about it. Without credibility, it doesn't matter what you say. Credibility comes from many sources, but it all starts with sincerity and caring. You, as a lawyer, are the most important (unsworn) witness the jury will see and hear.

Speaking from the Heart

Authenticity is related more to the speaker than to what is said. Speaking from the heart is easy to say, tough to do, and even harder before strangers in public. Perhaps one reason this is so challenging is because, at a deep level, all of us are frightened of rejection. Honesty demands vulnerability. The smarter we are, the more apt we are to think rather than feel. When left to our instincts, we lawyers analyze, categorize, rationalize, and intellectualize every minute aspect of our cases. Yes, we need to do this, and do it well, but this is the work of a legal technician. What's missing? It's that something extra, that potent passion that flows from deep within you, giving voice to your personal convictions.

How to Argue a Case with Authority

Begin by immersing yourself in the facts of your case. What resonates with you? What's compelling? Is it a sense of indignation generated by the liability or maybe the loss of something dear to your client? Spend time with your clients; get up close and personal. How have their lives changed? What's different? What's touching, intimate, personal, or poignant? What have the changes meant to your client? Talk to them about their hopes and dreams—the dreams they've lost and the ones they still cling to. How have their inner and outer worlds changed? Taste their emotions. Don't run from them; embrace them. Your clients are forced to live within their new worlds every moment of every day. Ask yourself, what aspect of your life allows you to empathize with your client? Might a number of jurors have had similar life experiences and feel empathy? This is expressed colloquially as "putting yourself in another's shoes."

Being authentic isn't about being maudlin or pandering. Good advocates know that. Even when sympathy is useful, it can quickly thin out in the jurors' minds. When something about your case naturally appeals to jurors, you don't need to pound on it. You will quickly lose ground because you might appear to be appealing to their emotions.

Convert sympathy into material that has more impact—that is, motivate the jury to administer justice with their verdict. Acknowledge the presence of natural feelings of sympathy for your client but remind the jurors no verdict is based upon sympathy. Explain that basing a verdict upon sympathy cheats not only the plaintiff but also the defendant. Injured people don't want sympathy; they want justice, which is also what the defendants should want. In the short term, it may seem that you're giving up something of value; however, from the strategic perspective of a longer view, you're forfeiting nothing. You are turning silver into gold. You are morphing sympathy into personal credibility and ultimately justice for your client.

Whenever you're talking from the heart, you're sharing something intimate and personal. It's your sense of decency and humanity shining through. You needn't raise your voice. When spoken with a quiet resolve, your truth will thunder.

Learning How to Speak "Heart Talk"

There are techniques that will assist anyone in locating and accessing the deep feelings that fuel heart talk. This process is divided into three stages: *identification*, *substance*, and *presentation*.

- *Identification* involves pinpointing the content you intend to share (this is most important).
- *Substance* is the content of what you say.
- *Presentation* is your delivery.

Content acquisition is a slow process that involves identifying which of your client's life circumstances resonate with you. What will allow you and the jury to emotionally relate to them? It starts with the plaintiff's new reality. Don't run away from your client, from their pains and experiences. Don't hide behind lots of words and trite phrases. Immerse yourself in their new world, be fully present. Sit quietly and listen to them breathe. Soak in the room, its atmosphere and ambiance. What's there to admire in your (wonderful) client? Have a cup of coffee with each member of the family. What were the worst of times? What were the best of times? Where is the pain and the joy to be found, and why? Little things mean a lot. I ask myself this: What's big to my client, but little to the world? Reflect on the plaintiff's new life and then harvest what comes to you.

For example, Jim was a career police officer who was seriously injured while on duty. He was retired with a full medical disability. He lost much of his physical ability. Later, he went in for a relatively simple back surgery that resulted in constant pain and partial paralysis in his legs:

> I admire my client's toughness. He always does the best he can. He begins each day saying, "Today I will walk," well knowing it will never happen. I sit and hold my seventy-three-year-old client's hand. He is alone and suffering, yet he is a shining example of courage and fortitude for his son, grandson, me, and yes, also for the jurors.

Heart Talk with Free Association

Another method to develop heart talk is called *free association*. It's a technique mental health professionals use. In this process, you go backward in your mind to emotionally access prior formative experiences. To free-associate, get comfortable, relax, and muse upon the case.

- What thoughts and images come to mind?
- What in your life has been similar?
- How was your experience the same or different?
- What feelings surface—good and bad?
- What is to like or admire about your client? Why?

Let your mind wander, but not too far. Gently bring your focus back to the facts of the case. You will gradually inch ever closer to the headwaters of your heart talk for this client and case.

Speaking from the Heart

Finally, you can generate respect and empathy by discussing the courage and fortitude your client shows in confronting the difficulties in their new life. When speaking heart talk, slow down and linger in the pauses. There's no reason to rush through the most important part of your presentation. Remember your jury selection. Eye contact with each juror is a must. It's a good time to lower your voice. This isn't about faking it; it's about effective communication, also known as *persuasive advocacy*.

Common Questions & Concerns about Heart Talk

Embracing heart talk is a challenge. Here are some common questions and concerns:

Heart Talk Is Really Nothing More Than a Performance, How Does It Enhance Credibility?

If words don't come from the heart, then you're just speaking with your lips. Credibility is driven by personal truths from deep within each of us. Here's an example of heart talk:

> **Mr. Barton:** I want to focus on my client, this one special person, who is largely unknown to the world. Indeed, she's a stranger to the world, but not to you, the jury. The courage that she shows in facing her life's new challenges, intimate but essential things such as her personal hygiene, being able to live independently in her own home, all matters each of us take for granted.

Heart Talk Seems to Come More Easily to Others Than to Me

Oddly enough, when heart talk arrives, it comes so quickly it can seem almost unnatural. At times, heart talk may emote, but it rarely comes easily. More often it is the result of quiet hours of thought and reflection. Insights harken in the small hours of the night, in the shower, at stop signs, in your sleep. Heart talk is often a flash of insight, the episodic result of a glacial process. Nothing coming to you? Go and be still with your client; just sit with them. If this feels awkward, arrange some kind of quiet activity with them, like feeding ducks in a park.

The Expression of Personal Opinions Is Ethically Prohibited

Be careful in your language. It's ethically improper to say, "I think…" Simply rephrase the material by dropping the words, "I think." If you really want to dot your i's, you can always say, "It's reasonable that…" Saying "I think" is just a bad habit you can easily correct. It allows your opponent to interrupt the flow of your argument with an objection, which they will win. And in the process, they can correctly accuse you of "unethical" behavior.

Can I Be a Good Lawyer without Heart Talk?

Yes. In fact, most trial lawyers never reveal much of themselves in court, and when they do, it's often in a snarling cross-exam, which is certainly not endearing. This is particularly true of attorneys whose practice is limited to emotionally sterile matters, such as patents, tax, and commercial matters. These lawyers argue the facts and law with great skill. However, they can never be more than competent technicians. Such attorneys aren't temperamentally comfortable discussing the real people behind the facts.

All This Heart Talk Would Be Easy If I Represented Victims of Sexual Abuse and Was Always on the Side of the Underdog

How do you do heart talk in commercial cases when you represent large businesses? My deceased friend, Richard Bodyfelt, used to represent all the Fortune 500 companies against product liability claims. During jury selection, when Dick was through introducing his client Ford Motor Company, I could hear Henry Ford chasing the American Dream out back in the tool shed, creating the first Model A. No matter whom Dick represented, no matter how big the corporation, somehow, he always represented real people.

Not Every Case Has a Client or Some Aspect of the Facts That Lends Itself to a Sense of Indignation. How Do You Generate Heart Talk under Those Circumstances?

Maybe you don't even like your client. Life rarely comes to us as cleanly or clearly as we would like. I am often in conflict, and I don't believe I'm always wearing the whitest hat in the courtroom. This is apart from the fact that I am running a business with a monthly overhead that in many ways runs me. How many young lawyers would rather be doing public-interest work, but have accepted the golden handcuffs of a big firm in order to pay their student loans? It's completely natural to be emotionally divided. Carefully think your way through every aspect of the conundrum. Frame the facts and case to your client's best advantage, and then put your full weight into your most persuasive facts. Don't beat yourself up by constantly revisiting your decision. The process of becoming an effective trial lawyer demands emotional discipline. Your name is on the pleadings. There's a yet-hidden story to tell for your client. Go find it, and then make it your own. Everybody deserves a lawyer who's in their corner. It's what we do, or at least what we should be doing.

Might I Be Perceived as Too Emotional If I Fully Embrace This Technique?

In other words, does the application or effectiveness of heart talk vary based on the lawyer's gender, or any other attribute? No, but there is a context for everything. Too much emotional content or appeals, too early in the case, will backfire no matter who you are. The short answer is that, because the heart talk comes from deep within you, there are no gender or disqualifying criteria. The question is whether it's congruent with you.

Conclusion

Law schools teach mechanics with a little technique. While advocacy requires hard work and basic skills, it appears lost on academics that, apart from thorough preparation, the most important attribute to effective advocacy is your authenticity. Most of us possess a strong personal ethos; however, law school and traditional litigation training can bleach our hearts and dry our souls. Find your "better angels," and then bring the very best of yourself to both the courtroom and life.

15

The Craft of Storytelling

Storytelling is as old as campfires, yet it wasn't until the mid-1980s that it finally crept into the legal profession's toolkit as an essential trial skill. Today it's almost passé: judges and advocacy teachers all encourage telling a good story. It allows you to teach without preaching. Stories are how we organize and make sense of the world. They are powerful weapons in the litigator's arsenal. Going first is a tremendous advantage that's rarely exploited by plaintiffs' lawyers.

Storytelling Is an Art Form

Storytelling in court is different than in theater and film. Unlike theater, there is no fourth wall in courtroom storytelling. Stage actors pretend the audience isn't there. In courtrooms, you talk directly to the audience, that is, the jury.[1] Another major difference between trials and theater, film, or novels is that in trials the jurors get to finish our story: their verdict writes the last chapter or ending.

Maybe you have pushback to the idea of storytelling, and think it's the stuff of bombast, the field of extroverts and raconteurs, or maybe you feel that's just not you. While the purpose of storytelling generally is to entertain, when applied in court, its mission is different—it's to persuade. All trial lawyers will improve their advocacy by studying and applying the forensic applications of storytelling.

Plaintiffs' lawyers are well-served by using the seven-step template on opening statements set forth in *David Ball on Damages*.[2] It's a well thought out formula that structures your opening and case.

Adapting Storytelling for the Courtroom

Most of the forensic literature on storytelling is generated by the plaintiffs' bar. There's a good reason for this. We go first. We decide who to sue, make the choices on venue, order the parties in the caption, frame the issues in jury selection, and, in opening, tell our arching trial story grounded in compelling trial themes.

When we see a persuasive story delivered, it looks, seems, and feels so natural, yet it's always the result of long hours of thought and preparation. It's a serious, sustained process of case evaluation, framing, and delivering that's creative and powerful.

Our job as trial lawyers is often compared to jobs in theater and movies; we create and select the trial story, do the casting (of witnesses), organize and direct the presentation, and produce it when we bankroll

---

1. Dominic J. Gianna and Alfred S. Julien, *Opening Statements 2D: Winning in the Beginning by Winning the Beginning* (St. Paul, MN: Thomson-West, 2004).

2. David Ball, *David Ball on Damages*, 3rd ed. (Portland, OR: Trial Guides, 2013), 117.

the case. We don't make the facts, but we decide which ones to present, their order, and delivery. And, yes, when it comes to demonstrative evidence, we create it.

Storytelling empowers you as the speaker. There's no need for notes. Why? Because you're actually living the story; you're speaking in real (emotional) time. Storytelling permits each of us to powerfully share from the inside out, rather than intellectually from the top down. Stories de-emphasize logic and reinforce the emotions and intuitions we humans all possess. Stories touch feelings in a way that sterile facts and statistics can't. Curiosity invites the listeners in; the storyteller uses words to paint images on the canvas of their minds. You and the jury share a story and, in the process, become emotionally immersed and bonded.

Elements of an Effective Trial Story

What are the ingredients of a persuasive trial story, and how do you deliver it? Foremost, it's not an argument: it's an organizing, motivational tool—a framing device. So, what does most good lawyering look like? See if you agree.

Good lawyers do the following:

1. State the issues(s) in the case.
2. List the witnesses.
3. Summarize their testimony.
4. Present within the context of an overarching timeline, and deliver with confidence.

Where to Begin Your Trial Story

Where you start your trial story can often be outcome determinative. You want the jury's attention focused on the defendant, not the plaintiff. Let me illustrate. Probably the most difficult case of my career took twenty-one years and involved seven appeals. It was an insurance bad faith case, *Goddard v. Farmers Ins. Co. of Oregon*.[3] In focus groups, I repeatedly lost the case when I started my trial with the events of the night when Farmers's insured, later convicted of manslaughter, killed my client while driving drunk. I only won by going back eight years earlier, when an aggressive Farmers Insurance agent sold a $100,000 policy to a man living in a dilapidated trailer house when Oregon's auto insurance minimum was only $15,000. The policyholder paid his premiums on time without a bounced check or claim. Then one night the unforgivable happened—he left a tavern drunk and killed my client in a head-on crash. That was an insurance bad faith case I could win.

The problem with starting with your client is that you're inviting the jury to constantly scrutinize your client's choices: psychologists call it *counter-factual reasoning*. The jurors will replay the liability facts over and over in their heads, coming up with all the ways the injury or event wouldn't have happened if only the plaintiff hadn't left for work early, or taken the elevator, or worn high-heeled shoes or perfume, and so on. The list never ends. This approach is also an expression of the *availability bias*, meaning, the way you frame your case makes the case what it's about.

Pick a point of view or person to tell the story from. Dramatize your direct examination. Make it happen… now! Invite the witness to "paint us a word picture," to "take us (the jury) back," to "set the scene for us" here in court. Where are we, who's sitting where, what can we smell? Your story should create vivid 3D color pictures (trial visualization), sensory impressions, and emotional reactions. Don't describe events; create images. Be sure to also include the judge in your eye contact and gestures. This is part of my viewing the judge as the 13th juror.

---

3. *Goddard v. Farmers Ins. Co. of Oregon*, 344 Or 232, 179 P3d 645 (2008). See *Goddard v. Farmers Ins. Co. of Oregon*, 202 Or App 79, 81–83, 120 P3d 1260, 1262–1264 (2005) for a recitation of the legal history of the case to that date.

> MR. BARTON: Jack, close your eyes and take us back to the kitchen the night of the shooting. Where are you sitting? What is cooking on the stove?
>
> MR. BARTON: Now, in slow motion, what happens next?

How to Dramatize Your Trial Story

How do you create a dramatic story the jurors want to solve in order to correct an injustice? A short answer is to provide a hero and a villain. Every case should be about righting a wrong—doing justice. Early on, the jurors want to decide who is to blame, who wears the black hat. This reduces their internal struggles. So, who's your villain, and why? Every case has one. I've seen investment cases between multimillionaires where the theme was "Risk is something we knew about, but nobody told us about the lies."

Only after focusing on the opponents' choices (wrongful acts) and their motives of self-interest do you then mention your client. Go back in time and explain how the defendant's previous bad choices brought your client to the courtroom, the place where your client has been forced to come to make the wrongdoer accept responsibility for their bad choices.

For example, I have sued interstate truck companies that set their speed control four miles over the speed limit, just enough that the police won't cite them, but enough to provide a competitive advantage against all commercial haulers who honor the speed limit.

Talk about Injustice

People are hardwired to react to injustice.[4] Talking about justice invites a contemplative and intellectual response; it's too abstract. This is a corollary to the idea that the plaintiff's story isn't big enough, meaning the

---

4. James W. McElhaney, *McElhaney's Trial Notebook* (Chicago, IL: ABA Press, 2005.)

defendant's conduct isn't aggravated enough to anger a jury—there's not enough injustice or betrayal that cries out to be corrected. This isn't to say that the plaintiff hasn't been wronged or isn't aggrieved, but that's the plaintiff's story, not the jury's. It's what McElhaney calls the "moral imperative."[5] This means that liability is big enough. Spence and David Clark refer to this as betrayal. When the plaintiff's story is big enough, you won't have to argue; the facts will do it for you. There's no need for you to belabor the obvious; the jurors will see it for themselves because they get it—it's now become their story, albeit spoken in the plaintiff's voice. Now that's a trial story that's big enough.

Skip all the adjectives and adverbs, just let the facts tell the story. Avoid the premature advocacy of turning an opening statement into a closing argument. As Sergeant Friday used to say, "Just the facts, ma'am."

Stories Are about Listeners

Is the story ultimately about your client? Yes and no. It's really more about the listeners—the jurors. Jurors may empathize with your client, but they are really rooting for themselves. I try to frame my case as a *de facto* class action, meaning any of us could have been the plaintiff. Jurors vote for their views. When we, as audience members, empathize with a character for our personal reasons, we are actually cheering for the character (ourselves) to overcome our own obstacles. Great stories are really about us, each of us. According to Steinbeck, "If a story is not about the hearer he will not listen."[6]

Jurors interpret trial evidence in the context of their life experiences, meaning their personal stories. They decide what happened by creating their own story of the events. Stories must answer the questions of what happened and why, and motivate the jurors to want to keep this from happening again. The message they are sending harkens from deep within themselves. Persuasion comes from the gut. Humans are moved

---

5. McElhaney, *McElhaney's Trial Notebook*.
6. John Steinbeck, *East of Eden* (New York, NY: Penguin Books, 2016).

by their deepest values, not messages received from a stranger paid to win a case. Jurors don't decide cases by who has the best lawsuit, but by deciding in their heads and hearts who should win, meaning who's right and wrong from the perspective of their commonsense.

Developing Trial Stories and Themes

The most powerful tools in your arsenal are a *winning trial story* unified with a *powerful theme*. The challenge is getting your trial story to align with the jurors' inner scripts. Your jury trial story consists of two major components:

1. Your trial story: Think of your trial story as an elevator speech.[7] It's a brief road map of who, what, when, and most important, why. It ties all of the facts of the story together in a short telegram-like statement.
2. Your trial theme: It's a phrase or silver bullet that connects complex evidence with the jurors' experiences, beliefs, and predispositions. Think of it as a mental handle. Scrutinize the key instructions and look for helpful words or phrases buried within them.

The trial theme or silver bullet provides the moral foundations for the jurors to convert their preferences into opinions and then to forcefully argue for their opinions during deliberations. Your theme must account for all of the evidence, and helps the jurors fit the story into the slot of their personal attitudes, beliefs, and values.

Develop your themes from case strengths. It might be something about the defendant's choices or motives, or a key phrase from the court's instructions. I struggle mightily to identify ways to turn bad facts into case strengths by creatively presenting them in light of favorable court instructions. There's plenty of time later to fine-tune the

---

7. John F. Romano, *Anatomy of a Personal Injury Lawsuit* (Portland, OR: Trial Guides, 2015).

particulars of your opening and closing. What are the "I can't get over it" facts, both for and against you?[8]

Good themes are often rhythmical. "If it doesn't fit, you must acquit." Repetition or parallelism (lookout, speed, and control) are helpful. Theme phrases in threes are easy to remember (care, skill, and diligence). Themes explain esoteric legal principles to a jury. Gerry Spence summarized the Karen Silkwood case, which involved exposure to radioactive plutonium and the legal principle of strict liability, to the jury in his trial theme: "If the lion (radioactive plutonium) got away, then Kerr McGee must pay." When the doctor isn't paying attention, I call it "ostrich medicine." When they misread the fetal monitor strips for the baby in utero, I call it "optimistic obstetrics."

How to Choose Your Trial Story & Themes

Out of the universe of possibilities, you'll select an arching yet simple trial story and themes that resonate with you.

We always bring something personal about ourselves to the trial of "our" lawsuits. Even a sterile stack-a-fact presentation reveals a lot about who you are—you're a technician and uncomfortable being real or vulnerable. Being a jury trial lawyer should be inherently autobiographical. It's personal and intimate, or at least, it can be. A big part of our professional journey involves weaving the best of ourselves into our trial presentations. What aspect of the plaintiff's plight grabs you? Are there any personal insights you can share that will bring clarity to the jury? I try to emphasize the power differential between the doctor and patient. Who had to trust whom? Who was charging for what services? How much trust did the patient have to give to the doctor?

This is just the first step. Next, you must be sure the jurors will recognize your story as theirs. Focus groups can help you identify and refine the collective story the jurors share. This gets back to asking if the

---

8. Mark Mandell, *Advanced Case Framing* (Washington, DC: American Association for Justice, 2019).

injustice is big enough. It must be an aspect of the case the jurors will instinctively recognize as not just wrong but, hopefully much more—a betrayal of deep trust.

Being Effective Requires Credibility

Jury trials are about generating, acquiring, and consolidating the intangible attribute of credibility. During closing, you use all your accrued credibility when you effectively argue for big dollars for pain and suffering. During cross-examination, when you politely correct an expert witness on misstatements in their reports, you are actively engaged in the process of generating and acquiring personal credibility.

Simplify...

If your case isn't simple, then you've still got a lot of work to do. Our jobs are always to simplify, simplify, and simplify. We must be able to say what our case is about in that short elevator ride. If we can't, then we're not ready. Simplifying is hard work. A quote attributed to Mark Twain says, "If you want me to give you a two-hour presentation, I am ready today. If you want a five-minute speech, it will take me two weeks to prepare." Lest I repeat myself, your mantra should be ABC, or accurate, brief, and clear.

What Are Your Rules of the Road?

Rick Friedman and Patrick Malone's book *Rules of the Road* is a major contribution to what we plaintiffs' lawyers do. Rick and Pat detail effective themes to weave into your trial story and anchor your depositions around. An example in a cancer case is, "early detection assures the best cure," or in product liability claims, "safety over profits." This book will help you more fully appreciate the integrating role jury instructions, trial stories, and themes play in a trial.[9] This is not a quick or easy exercise. The Rules of the Road method is an exercise unto itself, and when I seriously do this task, it can take a week or more to complete. But it's worth it.

My Storytelling Checklist

I'm offering my narrated storytelling checklist. It is a modification of the worksheet in chapter 8 of DeCaro and Matheo's *The Lawyer's Winning Edge*.[10]

Checklist

1. What are my best and worst facts?
2. How will I build my framework? Generate a set of proposed jury instructions and a special verdict form. They are the legal framework within which my trial themes and story must flourish.
3. What are my opponent's best facts? How can I either eliminate them with pretrial (using FRE 401 and 403 motions), neutralize them, or own them by turning them to my advantage?[11]

---

9. Rick Friedman and Patrick Malone, *Rules of the Road: A Plaintiff Lawyer's Guide to Proving Liability*, 2nd ed. (Portland, OR: Trial Guides, 2012).

10. Lisa L. DeCaro and Leonard Matheo, *The Lawyer's Winning Edge: Exceptional Courtroom Performance* (Denver, CO: Bradford Pub. Co., 2004).

11. Keith Mitnik, *Don't Eat the Bruises: How to Foil Their Plans to Spoil Your Case* (Portland, OR: Trial Guides, 2015), chapters 13 and 14.

4. How do I own their facts? We go first, and if I can't co-opt or own their best facts (Mitnik, chapter 13), then I need to put them in context (Mitnik, chapter 14).[12]
5. Whom do I want the focus of judgment to be on, and why? Stories need villains and heroes. By their verdict, the jurors write the last chapter to my story and thereby become heroes themselves.
6. What are my themes, that is, the silver bullets that answer every question? Are there any words or phrases from key instructions or from Friedman and Malone's Rules of the Road method I can co-opt as themes?
7. Where do I want to start my trial story? Remember McElhaney's focus on judgment availability bias, confirmation bias, and hindsight bias. Go upstream as early as possible to identify decisions the defendant made that later led to the plaintiff's injuries.
8. From whose perspective am I going to tell the story, and where's the suspense?
9. What is my trial story? Draft five to six sentences (in pencil, with a large eraser) that tell my story. It's an elevator speech. What's the beginning, middle, and end?
10. How am I going to visually *show* the jurors what happened? This doesn't mean telling them.
11. What are my visual aids, including demonstrative exhibits that tell my story?
12. What rhetorical questions can I ask during my closing that will channel the jurors' thinking? The jury's answer on the verdict form is my report card. What are the best facts and arguments favorable jurors can use in deliberations to persuade adverse jurors?
13. How will I keep track of jurors and exhibits? Consider making a jury notebook for each juror. Exhibits don't have to be listed chronologically. The first six exhibits should tell my trial story.
14. What aspect(s) of the case am I most passionate about? Why?

---

12. Mitnik, *Don't Eat the Bruises*.

I encourage you to reread chapter 14, "On Personal Authenticity," for examples of all these points in action.

Exercises

These may seem silly to serious lawyers, but they will dramatically improve your communication skills and presentations.

- *Show* your trial story to an eighth grader. What are the frames of a short comic strip that would tell your story?
- Practice pantomiming your story. Seriously! This will get you thinking about the effective use of your hands and body.
- Whisper your story.

Now you're ready to generate an opening and deliver it to a focus group. What's their feedback, and what are your responsive changes? Remember, you're supposed to lose your initial focus groups while identifying your problem areas and the trial story; then you move on to test your best responses.

Conclusion

As the storyteller, you need to be authentic, that is, real. Be true to yourself at the deepest levels, and let it show. That means you need to be true to your life as lived in order to meaningfully share your trial story. This kind of credibility isn't generated by volume or repetition. In fact, lowering your voice can be intimate, compelling, and powerful. You'll know when it's heart-to-heart, rather than lip to ear.

Persuasive, forensic storytelling appears natural, almost spontaneous. Let's be clear—it's not. It's the result of hours of preparation and practice.

16

The Ubiquitous Presence of Money

Money plays a big role in justice. It's often what determines who gets how much and why. The goal is for money to provide you with choices in work and life. These next four chapters discuss capital in the context of a personal injury contingency fee practice.

- Chapter 17 speaks to a business model based upon my 70/30 rule.
- Chapter 18 involves case evaluations.
- Chapter 19 offers an approach to associating other lawyers that favor you and your client, both short and long term.

Skip these chapters if you are employed by the government, are in-house, or are an associate at a big firm. However, if you're considering going out on your own, then you'll find this material interesting, helpful, and scary.

Money in Your Firm

Capital is neither good nor bad; it's neutral. However, what money can do, not just for us but for our clients, is what makes it so desirable. I couldn't have practiced law and tried cases in the aggressive manner I have without access to capital, what I call credit.

My attitude on money matches studies that confirm it doesn't make us happy; however, at the level of basic necessities, its absence causes unhappiness.[1] Focus on trying to meet your basic fiscal needs. After that, it becomes your choice whether you want to work more or spend time on family, relationships, leisure, hobbies, and so on. Once you make enough money to address the necessities, then you can start giving more time to matters and causes that you deeply value.

Financial Goals

Let's start by talking about the challenges of a monthly overhead. Our ultimate career goal is for you to run your practice, rather than it running you. Easy to say, tough to do. It's concurrently both a state of mind and raw numbers economics.

You'll encounter some early financial challenges. In plaintiffs' personal injury work, the first is your ability to front costs advanced, meaning fund or bankroll about $50,000 to $75,000 in costs to

---

1. Daniel Kahneman and Angus Deaton, "High Income Improves Evaluation of Life But Not Emotional Well-Being," *Proceedings of the National Academy of Sciences* 107, no. 38 (2010), 16489–93. https://doi.org/10.1073/pnas.1011492107. Economist Angus Deaton and psychologist Daniel Kahneman of Princeton examined Gallup poll data from almost 500,000 US households and found that day-to-day happiness increases as income increases, but the positive effects of money had no effect on happiness and moods after an income of $75,000.

adequately prepare and try your cases.[2] Hopefully, sooner than later, you'll get your first case that will demand this kind of money.

Some of my views are pretty straightforward: risk-averse lawyers tend to settle sooner and for less. Settling cases assures prompt payment, no appeals, and they avoid the risk of big losses, which, of course, levels the fiscal peaks and valleys. More aggressive plaintiffs' lawyers seem to tolerate more risk. You see how it's all interrelated and every choice comes with benefits and burdens. Risk-aversion and risk-seeking are both dysfunctional at their extremes; somewhere in the middle is that sweet spot, also known as good judgment.

Costs Advanced

Costs advanced is the money we *front*, or advance, to properly prepare and try our clients' cases. It's necessary to hire quality experts who, in turn, are essential not just to generate maximum legal results but often to create threshold jury questions on questions of liability, causation, and damages.

Make a Business Plan—Start with Fixed Expenses

All the business plans I've seen are designed for practices built on hourly work. This makes for easy number crunching, but it doesn't reflect the realities of a criminal defense or plaintiffs' PI work. Still, you need a starting place, so begin with your fixed expenses, such as rent, telephone, support staff, website, marketing, professional liability

---

2. These costs are in 2024 dollars (the time of publication). Please adjust as needed for inflation.

insurance, office supplies, and so on, and then total them. Expenses are predictable. It's the income side that's uncertain and worrisome.

The best advice is to start with as modest a budget as possible. Maybe you can share office space or secretarial help. Better yet, if you're computer literate, as most young lawyers are, you can be your own secretary and work from your cell phone.

Your business plan will help you visualize success at one-, three-, and five-year increments. This will give you your best shot at building a practice, generating savings, having vacations, doing pro bono work, and eventually helping pay for your student loans, kids' college, and your retirement. Take it from me, you'll be surprised at how fast life sneaks up on you.

As a personal injury lawyer, you need to do the following:

1. **Budget for costs advanced.** They're a necessity that's difficult to plan for, and are a painful and elastic reality. Don't skimp when budgeting these, and that starts with your costs of investigation and expert witnesses' fees. In medical negligence cases, it takes serious up-front money to hire competent experts to initially assess if you even have a case. Remember my earlier comments—we often make more money from the cases we turn down than the ones we accept.
2. **Develop a realistic business plan.** This means a plan that's long on the expenses and short on the income.
3. **Surround yourself with a stable of professional advisors.** They will help plan and then protect your success. You should have your own:
    » certified public accountant (CPA)
    » banker
    » personal and commercial insurance agent
    » financial planner (I recommend a fee-only planner. I don't like planners who have a financial incentive to churn your assets.)

Banking & Credit

Prepare yourself and your spouse or significant other for the reality that you're almost certainly going to have to personally guarantee any business line of credit. This means encumbering your office, house, car, and everything else you may own of value. It's what I had to do. A constant problem was being able to tell the bank loan officer when I could repay my loans. I may have been eloquent in the courtroom, but I stuttered at the bank. Scary? Absolutely. My longest walks have been to the bank. I hated it and felt like a failure.

Don't take a line of credit (LOC) for granted once you get it. Just because at one point you were approved for a certain amount doesn't mean a national bank that buys your local bank won't reduce it.

I discuss alternative litigation finance (ALF) loans or financing versus referring your case in chapter 19, "When and How to Refer Your Cases." ALF is a financing model that wasn't available when I started practicing. Carefully evaluate its benefits and burdens in light of your ethical duties to your client, versus the benefits you can gain from associating your case with an experienced lawyer who will fund your case and invest in you by teaching you.

Steps to Successfully Running Your Practice

Let's review the three steps to running your practice once more:

1. Getting clients.
2. Doing the work.
3. Getting paid.

I know you appreciate that being financially successful isn't that simple. Many of you are living this challenge right now. I could say it's as simple as maximizing income and minimizing expenses, but that's unsympathetic. A good book for guidance is *You Can't Teach Hungry* by John Morgan.[3] He counsels living frugally and within your means. No big shock there! Few of my contemporaries borrowed to the extent I did. They tried to operate within their means and worked to avoid debt. I borrowed often and heavily. This was consistent with my philosophy of spending money to make money, and I still believe it was the right way for me to ethically always put my clients' interests ahead of mine. The loan was mine, not my client's. The key here is, even though early on I couldn't afford to lose, I played as if I could, and have survived myself.

Early in my career, I had a case in which I had $263,000 in costs advanced, and I turned down a $1 million offer. You know what happened. The jury deliberated for six days and returned a defense verdict. I was wiped out. Shortly thereafter, I tried a medical negligence case and turned down a policy limits offer when it was two minutes late. I got a big verdict in that case and later collected a lot more than the policy limits. Was it luck, or talent? No doubt it was both, but my advice is not to do as I did.

Plenty of lawyers, particularly plaintiffs' trial lawyers, are guilty of conspicuous consumption. There are plenty of reasons for this, and a few make some sense. The standard argument is that you have to *look* good in order to impress prospective clients that you *are* good. In other words, spend money to make money, or fake it 'til you make it. It's chicken-and-egg reasoning. However attractive this may be, living within your means remains the smart answer. I view conspicuous consumption as not knowing the difference between want and need. We may want a lot, but, in truth, we actually need very little. I add that there's a certain equanimity and peace that comes with directly confronting the "green monster," meaning money. We spend a lot of

---

3. John Morgan, *You Can't Teach Hungry: Creating the Multimillion-Dollar Law Firm* (Portland, OR: Trial Guides, 2015).

time comparing ourselves with others. The necessity of marketing with its self-promotion can make one blush.

Cash Flow

Contingency work is cyclical and tends to be feast or famine. The peaks can be far apart and the valleys deep and wide. It's nerve-wracking to think of how long it might take to get a case to trial, and that's not even counting the possibility of appeals. The length of time it takes from the date you sign a client up to when you later file and mediate can be a couple of years, and longer if your verdict gets appealed. You can't truly assess a case's value until your client stabilizes medically, meaning reaches maximum medical improvement (MMI). You must know the full extent of your client's injuries and disabilities in order to accurately assess and value their damages.

It doesn't happen very often, but occasionally there can be delays in civil cases from causes of action called *declaratory judgments*, also known as *dec actions*. Getting a judgment against an insolvent defendant isn't much of a win if there's no insurance to pay it. Dec actions resolve whether there's insurance coverage and, if so, in what amount. The more years you practice civil work, the more likely you'll encounter dec actions. They're not common, but they happen and mean more discovery, delays, uncertainty, appeals, and, of course, anxiety as you try to judicially resolve whether there's insurance available. You can appreciate how important these questions are when you're suing a doctor or psychologist and their policies have exclusions for intentional acts, statutory remedies, and sex. I hire knowledgeable coverage lawyers to help me "plead my way into coverage." It's like a legal 3D chess match, pleading facts and law that avoid insurance exclusions.

Setting Up a Professional Corporation

When you're starting out and self-employed, it's easy not to make adequate tax withholding deposits, particularly if you're running on fumes. I remember. If you're a professional corporation (PC), then you must treat yourself the same as any other employee, meaning you must make timely tax withholding. Talk to a business lawyer, but remember, whatever benefits you extend to yourself, you must also give to all other employees. Examples of this are health insurance and retirement contributions. I'm disappointed to say in my early years I wasn't as disciplined as I should have been with my tax withholdings. Setting up a PC solved this, plus I hired help that was both loyal and competent enough that I wanted to treat them well—they were easily worth it.

Sharing Office Space or Partnership

Setting up shop with a friend or sharing office space to help reduce the overhead can be a smart choice. Many solo practitioners suffer from not having anyone to talk to, a friend who'll give them honest feedback about their work habits and case selection. This includes everything from problems with sloppy bookkeeping and trust account management to personal problems with alcohol, drugs, finances, client relations, marriage, parenting, or just plain life. Working with a partner, meaning someone who has a little skin in the game with you, can be a big help. When you're tethered to another, you have the benefit and burden of a second voice asking you the tough questions you're not willing to ask yourself. A trusted partner might also be a lot better than you at managing the firm's finances.

Do You Have What It Takes?

The only barrier to entry for working as a trial lawyer is a license to practice. There are lots of fisherpersons with their lines in the water. It's similar to all the actors waiting tables in Hollywood looking for their big break. Given recent law school employment stats, it follows that those who choose to attend law school in the face of the numbers have got to believe they're an exception. This self-belief will be tested in your practice over and over.

Conclusion

To maximize your courtroom success, identify, develop, and apply your assets, your gifts. My enduring IA message is that citizenship, professionalism, hard work, and caring are more important than experience. Jury trial lawyers are a select group. We share and commiserate with one another because the common law binds us together. We understand that when one of us wins, we all win. We're never alone.[4] I take comfort in that.

---

4. Sarah Parikh, "Plaintiffs' Practitioners Competition and Cohesion in the Personal Injury Bar," *Researching Law* 3, (2003).

17

Running a Law Business

Everyone in private practice faces a monthly bottom line. It never ends. I know how difficult climbing the financial mountain is. I've almost gone broke twice, once in the late eighties and again in the early nineties. Everything I owned was mortgaged, and I was extended beyond the limits of my credit. Looking back, I feel a little like Willie Nelson, the country and western singer, when he described himself as a "twenty-year overnight sensation." How quickly we forget.

My *70/30 rule* is a tool for building a reputation for excellence and maximizes your productivity and profitability. Under this business model (and remember all rules are necessarily generalizations), about 70 percent of your income is produced by 30 percent of cases. Some years it's 80/20 or even 90/10, but it's the big idea that I am emphasizing. When properly understood, 70/30 really stands for the idea and goal of case selectivity. Your case inventory is a process, result, and mindset.

Financial Nuts & Bolts

Let's start basic. The financial side of running a law business has three core steps:

1. Getting clients with paying legal work
2. Doing the work
3. Getting paid

I'll add a fourth rule: managing your money wisely once you've earned it. Conspicuous consumption, foolish investments, and substance abuse are always lurking nearby.

IA is about a lot more than trials, professionalism, and winning. What is money if you don't apply it in the furtherance of a meaningful life? Call it financial responsibility, prudence, or moderation, the labels don't matter; the destructive alternative is that you become the victim of your own success.

Hanging Out Your Shingle

I know if you go out on your own, you've got to do what you've got to do to pay the bills, to keep the lights on. What's this mean? Honestly, it means lots of lean months. Keep your overhead as low as possible, work out of your home, use your cell phone as your office number, and do all your own typing. Do deeds, wills, estates, contracts, bankruptcies, and whatever it takes to pay the bills. Building a practice from scratch is painful—at least it was for me.

There's a lot of good material from the ABA and the young lawyers section of your state bar association for lawyers starting out on their own. Additional help can be found on the AAJ website[1] and at Trial Guides.[2]

At the Big Firms: Grinders & Finders

Let's start with the first step: getting clients with paying work. It doesn't matter how talented you are if you don't have paying work. This may grate on you, but the harsh reality in law firms is—and the bigger they are, the truer this is—that there are two broad classes of lawyers: *finders* and *grinders*. *Finders* are the rainmakers who bring in the work, and *grinders* are the ones who do the work. Finders make more money, and because they're bringing in the business, they get to choose the kind of work they want to do, and then delegate the rest. They enjoy practicing law more and are better at it. Why? Because they get to do what they like, and generally people perform better when they enjoy something. Grinders don't have these choices. They do what they're assigned, and until they excel in a specialized niche, they will remain a fungible economic commodity in a glutted legal market. Finders are partners and grinders end up as associates or staff attorneys who are forever vulnerable to being replaced by next year's class of new hires. A key to financial success is to make yourself indispensable.

A Note about "Beauty Contests"

A beauty contest is a process that clients with bigger cases use to select a lawyer. I started seeing them after I'd been practicing about ten years.

---

1. https://www.justice.org.

2. Trial Guides has a program for new lawyers with specific book and media recommendations, combined with discounts for law students and lawyers in their first five years of practice. For more information, see https://www.trialguides.com/pages/new-lawyer-program.

Beauty contests are when plaintiffs with serious claims (big cases) interview a number of law firms to select one they will hire to represent them. An injured client first approaches their family lawyer who may have done their wills or represented the family business. This lawyer explains they don't do personal injury work, but agrees to generate a list of qualified lawyers for the family to interview. They often help by preparing questions for the plaintiff and their family to ask and help identify desirable qualities in the lawyer they choose to hire. Typical specialty areas are products liability, medical negligence, or sexual abuse. The family and/or family lawyer reviews the potential candidates' websites and narrows the field down to three to five firms. The family lawyer may sit in on the interviews. During the interviews, the clients can compare fee agreements, experience in the field, and the lawyers' personalities and philosophies. This can include multiple interviews with the family.

I believe the attorney–client relationship is the second-most intimate of all professions, behind only the psychiatrist–patient relationship. In the nonprofessional world, an exchange of love between two people says, "I'll always be honest with you, and I'll never put anyone before you." At the deepest levels, this is close to what vulnerable clients want to hear from their lawyer. They're vulnerable, frightened, and angry. They want to know you're going to be there to legally protect them, that you'll always be faithful to them, that you've "got their backs," and will put no one before them, including yourself. All the lawyers who compete in a beauty contest are competent or they wouldn't be there, so what distinguishes the ones that get hired? Remember chapter 1, "What Integrated Advocacy Offers You." It's obviously not just acquiring competence or capital; all the candidates have that. It's often for the level of caring and concern that distinguishes the firms that get hired. It's what you'd want if you were in the injured person's shoes. That's why I think of myself as a shepherd, seriously.

If you expect to get hired, you've got to sell yourself as the lawyer who'll be there for them, care for them, and champion their case. Not everyone's good at self-promotion. However, if you can't sell yourself and the legal services you're offering, then you're probably not going to get hired no matter how competent you are. Think about it. If you can't sell yourself to the client, then the client is entitled to question whether you're able to sell them and their case to a jury of strangers. Seems fair to me.

You don't need to crow or beat your chest, please don't. Instead prepare. Educate yourself about the injured person, their family, and the prospective case. Visit the injury scene, read everything in the public domain, particularly any prior lawsuits or complaints, and the latest decisions in the area of law. This shows you're concerned, serious about their case, and are competent. You know your business. Clients are interested in your thoughts and impressions.

My next piece of advice is counterintuitive. Not only do I never bad-mouth my competition, but in keeping with IA and the best of myself, I go a step further and volunteer good things about each of them. They're all good or they wouldn't have made it to the final cut, so it isn't hard to find good things to say. Of course, I'm flattered to be considered; however, the prospective clients will be well served by any of the highly qualified lawyers that they're considering. This approach is graceful, true, and the mark of a real professional; plus, it's a real statement of personal confidence and professionalism. Odds are that none of your competition will be so gracious. Persuasively presenting yourself is as much about preparation and caring as it is competence.

Even if you're just starting, forcing yourself to answer the questions an imaginary client might ask will prepare you for a real interview. Think of yourself through the lens of product differentiation. What distinguishes you? You're always hardworking and well prepared; you enjoy your work and love helping people. You believe in accountability and wrongdoers being held responsible. All this, you can offer right now. If I could simplify this exercise, it would be this: Get to a place where you appear confident and competent. Prepare yourself for the interview. Finally, remember caring is also fully available to you right now.

Doing the Work: IA's 70/30 Rule

There are no easy answers when it comes to the second step—doing the work. However, there is a map. Start a strategic business plan with IA's 70/30 rule at its center. The 70/30 model provides the principles and markers to guide you.[3] This maximizes the value of your case inventory by emphasizing quality, excellent client service, and maximum legal results.[4]

Invest in Your Better Cases

Consistently applying the 70/30 rule redirects the resources (your time, money, and talent) that you were investing in your worst cases into your better ones. Your better cases aren't just larger potential recoveries; they're the foundation of your future reputation. In a reverse way, you are also building your reputation with your less productive cases, only it's not so impressive.

OK, maybe in your situation it's 80/20, 75/25, or 60/40. It's not the numbers, per se, but the principle that matters. The opposite is where you're paid by the hour and your composite productivity is expressed in your fixed hourly or monthly salary.

Here's an IA work-life insight: make it a career goal to target a caseload in which you operate *slightly under capacity*. Why? It affords you the ability to jump on a great case when it walks through your door. Plus, it makes your practice less stressful and more enjoyable. I know how starting out works. You're constantly working at 110 percent capacity, and when you get a new case, you simply work more nights and

---

3. Susan A. Berson, "Starting Up: If You're Hanging a Shingle in 2011, Financial Strategy Begins Now," *ABA Journal* 97, no. 1 (2011), 40–43, http://www.jstor.org/stable/25798985. A separate but deserving topic.

4. So, you're interested in advertising? Whether you know it or not, you already are, at least in an old-fashioned sense; it's the present level of your service, results, and client satisfaction.

weekends. There's nothing wrong with that; however, after a few years, IA invites you to work differently.

Under my 70/30 model, once you're (profitably) investing the time you used to sink into your worst cases into your better ones, you can invest the leftover time in your family, friends, community, pro bono work, or self. Your aspirations should be more than vocational; it's the challenge of a balanced life, and that's what IA can help you achieve.

Limited Case Inventory Example

Here's an oversimplified, hypothetical example to make my points. Suppose you have ten cases: two worth $100,000 and eight worth $10,000. Under a literal interpretation of my approach, you will expeditiously and ethically process the eight $10,000 cases. This will allow you more time and energy to focus on your two remaining bigger cases. You'll make more money in the long run because you'll have more time to do better work on the cases. Focusing on the two bigger cases is economically justified because there's a better return on the investment of your time and costs advanced. This doesn't even include the additional benefits of not having to spend a disproportionate amount of time managing the unrealistic expectations of your clients in the eight lesser cases or defending their bar complaints.

You'll soon have a reputation as an excellent lawyer with a select practice consisting of $100,000 cases. By the way, it'll be true, even though you have only two of them! You'll do better legal work, make more money, enjoy your job more, and, maybe most importantly, have extra time for nonwork matters. Of course, my hypothetical assumes you have two cases of sufficient quality that allow you to pursue this approach. However, no matter where you are along the financial continuum, and even if you don't have cases this large, the basic IA principles remain the same.

Productivity and fiscal efficiency create the space and place in our lives that allow us the freedom to make nonwork choices that reflect our values. It's easier to achieve work-life balance when you're fiscally productive at work. IA is about you, the whole you, and you're more than just a lawyer. You're also a spouse, parent, partner, sibling, daughter or son, and yes, a person. The 70/30 rule is an IA foundation that helps you author a satisfying personal and professional life.

Deal with the Cases You Hate

Productivity demands you ethically and efficiently process the worst cases in your inventory. These cases demand a disproportionate amount of your time and energy, but you signed up the clients, so now you've got to deal with them. Yet, we often do just the opposite. These "bad cases" are the last ones we work on. It's all so foreseeable. Most have problems you should have seen before you accepted the case.

You know the files I'm talking about; they're sitting on the corner of your desk, gathering dust. You knew you shouldn't have taken them when you signed them up, and it's only gotten worse. So, what happens? The files continue to languish.

For understandable reasons, these clients are difficult to satisfy and will end up criticizing you regardless of the outcome. This is apart from the fact that you probably haven't treated these files with the same level of enthusiasm as your better cases.

There's often a big disconnect between the clients' expectations and the true value of their case—and that's generally on us. Clients aren't entitled to have you agree with them; however, they are entitled to straight talk and your best advice. Often they think they've got a big case and you're going to get them a lot of money, it's no wonder they're disappointed even if you deliver them a decent result. It's your ongoing responsibility to correct clients' misguided expectations, and sooner is always better than later.

Remember the first interview? You signed the clients up in order to get the case. Then after finalizing your investigation and research, and receiving all the health-care records, you realized things weren't as rosy as you'd thought. This happens to all of us. Promptly have them in for a "come to Jesus" meeting where you explain the legal realities. If one of you elects to terminate the attorney–client relationship after this talk, then once again, sooner is better. If they want to take their case to another lawyer, then let it go and don't put a lien on the file. The case probably isn't big enough to justify a second lawyer taking it when it comes burdened with your prior lien. Do the right thing, and in the process, you'll be doing yourself a big favor.

Is there a moral downside to the 70/30 model? It certainly emphasizes raw economics. Is there more to practicing law? Of course, and there should be. Is every case and client equally profitable, special, interesting, or irritating? No, so strike a balance: strike *your* balance. But keep a close eye on the economics, and in the process you'll be inching closer to the kind of financial freedom that allows you to practice law the way you want.

Lest we overlook the obvious, following IA's 70/30 rule will allow you more time to live as you aspire to live, and do what you want to do. The 70/30 rule says nothing about what you should do with your extra time. Take some smaller cases, or do pro bono work. The point is, because of your profitability, you have real choices, *your* choices.

Self-Promotion versus Courtroom Results

Good marketing may get you hired, but it's not the same skill set as being effective in court. In court, it shouldn't be about you. The accent shifts to the effective delivery of your services. The reality is some lawyers are better at self-promotion and marketing than they are at courtroom advocacy. They get decent settlements because their promotional skills got them hired in good cases, but it doesn't mean they're getting top value.

Building a Practice

Start by establishing your reputation with bigger verdicts in smaller cases. This means consistently getting more money than your opponents offered. You will get bigger and better cases as your competence and reputation grow. The good cases usually settle because of their quality and the reputation of the lawyers handling them. Chapter 12, "Framing Your Damages," will help you maximize the value of objectively smaller cases. This is where your legal creativity will shine.

Building a Personal Injury Practice

It can easily take five to ten years to build a decent personal injury practice. Some lawyers are more competent and comfortable in the promotion of their own practice. Call it what you want, be it community outreach (bottom up) or marketing (top down), you've got to educate prospective clients about why they should hire you rather than your competition. "I'm the greatest!" (There's not much tasteful or professional about that.) Find your comfort zone. You're selling a service, and you must accept responsibility for tastefully promoting your product, meaning you. If you love your job and care about people, then we're really talking about how you're going to show it. It takes time to build a personal injury (PI) practice. You'll start with a couple of smaller claims, then it will grow to half a dozen, and so on. After a while, a few of them will have six-figure values.

However, here's a problem: you need to make sure the defendant has an insurance policy with coverage to pay any possible verdict. It doesn't do you or your clients much good to have a case worth $1 million if there's an insolvent defendant and/or a nominal policy. So, what's the case worth? The blunt answer is this: no case is worth more than you can collect for it. These are the times when you need to be thinking about generating a potential first-party and third-party bad faith claim. I discuss how to do this in chapter 18, "Evaluating Cases," where I cover bad faith claims and how to properly make a demand upon the defendant.

High-Volume Settlement Practices

Many highly successful personal injury lawyers and firms use business models designed to process a high volume of smaller- and medium-sized cases. They tend to advertise heavily, employ many paralegals, and can be highly profitable practices. These firms provide important legal services to many injured people with smaller cases. Most cases can and should settle. It's no different in the criminal justice arena where most cases are resolved by plea bargaining. The system can't function any other way. Once again, where you're comfortable along the volume continuum is a personal choice. Either model can and should be profitable when competence, caring, and capital are present.

It's important to not paint with too broad a brush. There are some medium-sized plaintiffs' firms (three to six lawyers) that manage to combine advertising and volume, and, yes, the partners try cases, and try them well. They are well capitalized, know when to settle and when to fight, and have seriously talented lawyers at the top. When this combination exists, it's a beautiful thing. A perennial problem is stabilizing with young talent coming up and the old ones hanging on too long.

Choosing Quality or Quantity

Variations on my 70/30 IA model are matters of emphasis rather than substance. You can begin to apply the rule once you gain an improving case inventory. You might choose to expand your practice by hiring additional lawyers and paralegals to process the volume. Where a firm lands in the quality-quantity continuum is a policy decision. Accepting additional smaller cases shifts the firm toward advertising and a volume practice with its economies of scale. Everybody is temperamentally different; I don't like administration, so I naturally favor quality over quantity. There are no right or wrong answers—it's all a choice with mixed advantages and disadvantages to each.

While a volume practice certainly increases overhead, there are also obvious benefits. It stabilizes revenue, expands the client base, and provides competent representation to many deserving clients with smaller cases. The question becomes: how big do you want to be? At some point, you can either continue growth and staffing (alternatives are increasing the minimum value of the cases you'll accept) or trend toward a specialty area. When PI firms grow, they add departments and expand into allied specialty areas: workers' comp, criminal defense, employment law, and Social Security are examples. It's no different when a solo practice has a mix of divorces, criminal defense, wills, real estate, and some PI. As the volume grows, you will make choices; however, the 70/30 principles are generic.

When Law Firms Split Up

Plaintiffs' firms often divide when they become populated with impatient, talented young lawyers who don't want to stand in line waiting for their chance to try bigger cases. They're often willing to strike out on their own once they've gained some confidence and trial experience. They want to go to court. Here's where loyalty and ambition collide. It can get messy when they try to take a few of the firm's bigger cases with them when leaving.

It's easier for plaintiffs' firms to stay together when they aren't making much money. Why? Because there's nothing to fight over. When cash flow is down, it can be difficult to agree on how much costs to advance to a particular case. Building consensus among plaintiffs' lawyers can be like herding cats. We're mavericks and often don't play well with others. It's when a big contingency fee rolls in that plaintiffs' firms often disintegrate. This is another application of the difficulties in surviving success.

Law firms are totem cultures. As with teams of sled dogs, there are acknowledged leaders who are partners because of tenure, talent, and/or rainmaking abilities. Successful trial firms need lawyers with energy and talent involving a blend of ego, risk, tolerance, and solid judgment.

Making Law Firms Tick

The best way to understand a law firm as a business entity is to study how it makes money. Big firms and insurance defense firms are built on hourly billings. This promotes stability and allows them to become big, sometimes very big, even into the hundreds and thousands with offices across the nation and the world. Plaintiffs' firms tend to be much smaller with two to four lawyers. This is because of cyclic contingency fees with their economic instability and the sometimes difficult personalities of the participants. Some high-end plaintiffs' lawyers don't play well with others, or as they like to say, "eagles don't flock!"

Conclusion

Grow by applying IA's 70/30 rule. Success in the cases you accept will attract more and better quality work. Success begets success.

18

Evaluating Cases

You learn from your mistakes in evaluating cases. This is especially true when you're starting out and unmentored. You've got to keep the lights on and you don't have the luxury of being very choosy. I get it. I remember settling many small claims for a few hundred dollars. The fees were small, but I needed them. This chapter and chapter 3, "Thoughts on Losing and Best Practices after a Loss," were the most painful for me to write. So many younger lawyers are burdened by huge school loans, and here I sit, looking over my shoulder, writing books. I promise you, I do remember.

Learning to Analyze Cases

The decision of whether to accept a new case always occurs in the context of your existing caseload. During the first interview, listen carefully to the potential client and then follow up with any necessary investigation and legal research. Later, you can have a second meeting with the potential client, where you can have a knowledgeable discussion of their case's strengths and weaknesses. Don't sugarcoat anything, even if you want the case. Yes, you need to win the potential client's trust, but this is similar to a doctor obtaining informed consent before surgery. Managing client expectations is a big part of your job. Failure to communicate the realities of their case just makes your job tougher in the long run. Even if you get a great result, you'll be a failure in your client's eyes if they expected more.

In an ideal situation, you'll meet with the potential client long before the statute of limitations runs out, so you'll have plenty of time to properly evaluate their case's merit. Have the client sign the releases for your office to obtain all the necessary records. If you think the case has serious potential, consider vetting it with an experienced lawyer. However, brace yourself: all that glitters is not gold. There's a real chance you'll be disappointed in what you hear.

Factors to Consider when Evaluating a Case

Here are some of the factors that you must consider in evaluating a prospective case:

- How strong (good) is the liability?
- Are there any questions of comparative fault or assumption of risk?
- How serious are the plaintiff's damages in terms of disability and permanency?
- How old is the plaintiff and generally what was their pre-liability-event state of health?
- How likable and presentable is the plaintiff?
- How likable and presentable is the defendant?
- Did the plaintiff have any preexisting medical conditions that might cloud the question of damages causation? Remember the

strategic benefits of the *as is* rule and the qualitative measure of damages arguments.
- What's the probable verdict range? Think of a bell-shaped curve.
- What are the applicable insurance policy limits? Are there any umbrella or excess policies? Is there enough to pay for all the potential damages?
- If it's a car wreck, does your client have uninsured or underinsured motorist protection?
- Are there any insurance coverage questions? If so, can you "plead your way into coverage," meaning pleading negligent acts the defendant's insurance policy will cover? Are there any policy exclusions, such as sex acts, intentional acts, statutory remedies, or punitive damages that you need to "plead your way around"?
- In a medical negligence case, how easy is the case to defend? Even if the case "has color," meaning there appears to be decent proof of fault or the breach of a duty, damages, and causation, as an entirely separate matter, how easy to defend will the claim be? Even if the doctor was negligent, the jury will probably forgive them if it involved, or even appeared to involve, matters of medical judgment.
- Are there any obvious appeal issues? Can you avoid them (plead your way around them) and still win?
- Are there any nonfiscal reasons to take the case or not to take the case? Examples might be to change unfavorable law, or to confront a compelling moral problem, or to show the defendant's conduct is part of a larger threat to the community.
- What would an experienced lawyer say about the case? Write out your evaluation and ask a senior lawyer to review it. No matter what happens, you will be pleased. If they agree with you, then it's a pleasant experience. If they identify additional factors or weight features differently, then you've learned something the "soft" way, rather than the hard way later in trial.
- How much time and money will it take to prepare and try the case? Do you have the time and money? If not, can you borrow it? Do

you want to? Alternatively, consider associating a senior lawyer to mentor you and bankroll the case.
- If you try the case, can you afford to lose? This is a serious question with profound, ethical implications.
- Is the case ripe enough to consider a focus group, maybe just for parts of it?

Work to maintain objectivity in the face of a client's compelling circumstances. The nature of the damages in sex abuse, birth trauma, burn, and other serious injury claims evokes sympathy, lots of it. Learn to watch and assess your own emotional reactions. Psychologists call this *countertransference*. This will provide insights into how jurors might later react. You need to get outside of yourself and see the client, case, and yourself with objectivity.

Of course, it's hard to say no to a potential (case) client. You naturally feel bad for anyone who's suffering. Maybe the prospective client is a friend or your high school English teacher. While you might want to help them, if their case doesn't pass muster, then turn it down. If you do accept a questionable case, at least do it after carefully computing how much it'll cost you in both time and money. In other words, if you want to charge ahead, fine, just do it with your eyes open. Think of yourself like a contractor making a bid.

The Truth about Bad Cases

Even when you're just starting out, the reality is you never can afford to take bad cases, even though you don't have much paying work. Bad cases are legal sinkholes in terms of your time, money, enthusiasm, and reputation. They can cost you a lot more than uncompensated time and lost advanced costs. You could end up with a bar complaint, a legal malpractice claim, and more likely, ex-clients bad-mouthing you. I've heard it takes five compliments to offset the damage of one complaint. Most of the time, you knew from the start you shouldn't have taken the case. It's the file that just sits at the back of your desk, glowing in the dark. It's the last one you'll want to pick up; meanwhile, it's the same upset client who is constantly calling you.

Everyone has taken cases they regret. Make the best of it and learn from those cases. Every time you take a lousy case and suffer the consequences, you will be improving your ability to spot bad cases or clients in the future. If you don't learn, you're not going to get very far in this business.

Paradoxically, when you reject marginal cases, you're transmitting favorable messages of competence and confidence, and are actually enhancing your desirability as a legal commodity. Scarcity creates value. I stumbled upon this insight early, when I was doing criminal defense. After much thought, I chose to double my fees, and just as I'd suspected, hiring me became more desirable. I advised prospective clients that I was expensive, and I would be glad to give them a list of names if they wanted a cheaper lawyer.

Sure, some of the prospective clients couldn't afford me, but most, maybe 75 percent, could, and more to the point, 100 percent of that 75 percent hired me. This gave me 25 percent more time to prepare for the 75 percent of the clients who hired me. The result? I had more time to do a better job for fewer clients. Because the clients who hired me could afford to pay, my accounts receivable dropped and unpaid accounts dwindled—not to mention, they always showed up on time for their appointments. Most clients value their lawyer in direct proportion to the size of the fee. I did better quality work, won more cases, made more money, improved my reputation, and enjoyed the practice of law even more. It follows that you've got to produce results worth your increased fee, and I did. It's an ever-ascending positive cycle fueled by better client service, better results, increased profit, an improving reputation, more case selectivity, and maybe best of all, I loved my work even more!

Is increasing your fee the right thing to do? Analytically, it's a financial decision, not a moral one. The market is blind and won't support an increased fee if you don't deliver results worth the fee. Maybe your level of competence and the market will only support a fee increase of 20 or 30 percent, or perhaps none at all. Just think about the ideas and don't sell yourself short. Buried in this equation are increased efficiencies, profitability, and more discretionary time. Yes, Newport, Oregon, where I practice, is a small, geographically isolated market with limited competition. However, the principles are generic. Taking fewer cases frees up time for yourself and your family and, yes, increases your ability to afford to do more pro bono. It's interesting. The extra time I now had I put into doing an even better job for the cases I had accepted. I wanted to be a really good lawyer and this approach allowed me to focus on quality over quantity. The better I got, the more I liked my work. I found that creating time for non-work (family and self) matters came more from delegating than taking fewer but better cases. The bigger the cases, the harder I worked.

Prepare a Case Budget

Focus on economics when deciding whether or not to take a case. Generate a case budget. The following is a generic example of a personal injury contingency fee case. The probable verdict range is a bell-shaped curve of likely results. Be realistic, meaning cautious. Generate a probable value if the case is settled or tried. Remember, clients are interested in the bottom line. You're the professional; they come to you for advice. To prepare a case budget, follow these steps:

1. Make an educated guess of the percentage or odds of winning.
   » For this case, let's say it's 60 percent. For simplicity, I haven't included a discount for comparative fault. This is a guesstimate or a prediction, not a calculation.

2. Then multiply that percentage (60 percent) by the middle of the probable verdict range.

» Let's say the probable verdict range is $50,000 to $70,000, with an average of $60,000. Our example then would look like this:

0.6 x $60,000 = $36,000

So, the case has a present (actuarial) value of $36,000.

3. Next, subtract your costs advanced per your fee agreement, either from the total before you deduct your fee or after.
   » For example: you spent $3,000 pretrial preparing the case:

   $36,000 − $3,000 = $33,000

A Digression on Attorney's Fees

Consider what happens if you go to trial:

- How much does your attorney's fee increase if there's a trial or an appeal? Is it 33 percent of $36,000, meaning $11,880?
- Does your fee percent increase if you start trial? It should: 40 percent is typical.
- How much will the costs advanced be? In our example, there's a 40 percent chance of losing and receiving nothing, and that's in addition to losing the hard-earned money you fronted as costs advanced. I usually apply the attorney's fee percentage to the total, subtract my fee, and then deduct the costs from the client's share.
- Why do you calculate like this? Because technically the client is responsible for paying the costs advanced, yet everyone knows they're injured and can't afford it. You front, or loan, the client the costs advanced interest-free; it's what a competitive market demands. It's the client who ultimately

pays for the costs advanced from their share of the recovery. When the client's recovery isn't much, or if we lose, I bear the entire loss of any costs advanced, because the client's recovered little or nothing from which they can repay me. You absorb the losses as a cost of doing business.
- Estimate the number of hours necessary to work the case up to mediation, and then for a trial.
- What if there's an appeal? (And yes, your fee should again increase.)
  » *These will be guesstimates, but it forces you to at least walk through the process.*

4. Now, estimate how much money you'll need to prepare the case, including:
   » mediation
   » trial
   » a possible appeal

I assume all my cases will be tried. I don't take cases with the hope that the insurance adjuster will just roll over and I'm going to take the best number I can get. This may be what happens, but you shouldn't start that way. This is as much an attitude as a fact. There's a good reason why some people say trial lawyers are the most effective settlement negotiators. You needn't raise your voice; please don't. Neither volume nor repetition improves the quality of what you say.

You've got about 1,800 to 2,600 billable hours in a year. How much is your monthly overhead? How much are you currently out in costs advanced for your other cases? In other words, what's your present capacity to front the predicted future costs in this case (and all the others you've accepted)? Ask yourself: Would I bid on this project if I were a (legal) contractor (which you are)? Have experienced lawyers critique your analysis and math. Show them my criteria. They'll add or subtract a few things. Good. Everybody views things a bit differently, and getting a second opinion never hurts.

Let's suppose you've accepted a smaller case, assuming you'll settle it, but the adjustor is low-balling you and now it's set for trial. You filed it and you've put yourself where you're at—so whether you like the client, the case, or the odds, it doesn't much matter now. You've got to bring your A game. Call it pride, ego, professional responsibility, reputation, consequences for stupidity, or all of the above, it doesn't matter. It's your client and your case. Let me offer you a helpful way to reframe the situation. The reason for doing your best isn't because of money. It can't be because, even if you win, it's probably not going to be much, and you may financially end up in the hole. Doing your best furthers your reputation as an up-and-coming trial lawyer who always does their best and therefore must always be taken seriously. It's the kind of reputation you want, but you can't give it to yourself; you've got to earn it. You filed the lawsuit, and now you're accountable for your lousy decision. It's all part of your learning curve.

This takes a long view of your career and speaks volumes about who you are, and who you're becoming when you consistently generate verdicts that are at least 30 percent bigger than the last offer. You're then on a professional trajectory that will result in future referrals. I discuss writing your professional obituary in chapter 5, "Constructing Your Life Story." By your daily decisions, you're doing it right now.

Caring versus Capital (Money)

Every client wants their lawyer to care about them and be enthusiastic about their case. They assume you're competent; otherwise, they wouldn't have hired you. When they ask, "Do you think I have a good case?" they're asking you for a lot more than a sterile analysis. They want you to be excited about the possibility of representing them, maybe even indignant and angry at what's happened to them. Clients usually have at least these large questions:

- Do I have a case?
- What do you think it's worth?
- Will we have to go to court?
- How long will it take?

But how about we add these tough business questions:

- How much time and money can you afford to invest in this particular case and client or, more accurately, invest and possibly lose?
- What if a client and case you really care about might financially drown you? And by this I literally mean "take you under."[1]
- Do your spouse, banker, or nonrecourse alternative litigation finance (ALF) lenders share your client-centered enthusiasm?

It's accurate to call your costs advanced an investment. The question is whether it's a good one.

It feels cynical to think about cases as financial investments, but the economic reality is they are. We're psychologically wired to fix wrongs; it's what we do. But at the end of the day, we're also running a business. So, when should your finances be a factor in deciding which cases you accept and how you're going to capitalize or fund the ones you've accepted? The obvious ethical answer is you should consider your fiscal circumstances *before* you accept the case. Once you've invited them to sign your fee agreement, then your new client's interests legally trump yours. You're entitled to think about self-interest and your finances all you want when deciding whether to accept a case; however, once you do, then you can't ethically or legally put your financial interests ahead of your client's interests.

---

1. The movie *A Civil Action* with its portrayal of the financial hard times plaintiffs' lawyers can face is accurate. *A Civil Action*, directed and written by Steven Zaillian (Burbank, CA: Touchstone Home Video, 1999), DVD.

Learn When to Say No

I'm proud to say our profession has a long tradition of lawyers taking pro bono cases; however, when they do, they usually know why they're doing it and have the capacity to handle the outer limits of uncertainty. Think about the composite cost, not just in terms of your time and money, but also your emotions. And by the way, your time is actually an asset, a stock in trade, that you're now attempting to capitalize.

A good example of this selectivity is how a legal amicus committee for a state trial lawyer association will wait until just the right case comes along to challenge a legal rule. For example, if you want to challenge the constitutionality of a damages cap, the bigger the damages and verdict, the more unfair a legal cap is. All I'm saying is for you to try and make good legal bids.

Be leery of your emotions and patriotism. This is when you most need the counsel of others. Talk to someone who's been there, who has actually tried this kind of case before. Veteran plaintiffs' lawyers excel at cases with big damages and skinny liability. What may look to many attorneys like a poor investment or bid, might well be a profitable investment to an experienced lawyer with the money and direct access to the best experts. Much of being a winner relies on being well capitalized and carefully picking your fights.

Be Choosy in the Cases You Accept

Sure, it helps if the jury likes the plaintiff, but on a forced choice, it's a lot better to have a "bad" defendant than a "good" plaintiff. Jury consultants all urge you to keep the jury's focus on the wrongdoers and their choices that lead to the negligent conduct. Then, later in the trial, when the defendant predictably attacks your client, you can argue that now the defendant's showing their true colors; they're trying to defend themselves based on the shortcomings of *their* victim—the one, in effect, they picked.

Using the previous infirm condition, also known as the *as is* instruction, and qualitative damages arguments can turn your client's shortcomings into strengths. Jury trials are partial referendums on the citizenship of the lawyers and their clients. Many of my wins are more "self-inflicted" losses by aggressive opponents. That said, you're not going to win medical negligence cases without both a presentable plaintiff and some pretty egregious fault.

Early investigation is important in nailing the liability down. Locate all the witnesses and secure the scene or product. Just as important, an early investigation allows you to reject cases that initially might look good. The quicker you eliminate bad cases from your inventory, the more profitable your practice will be. We often make more money from the cases we turn down than the ones we accept.

Be wary of cases that walk in your door just before the statute of limitations runs. If you file just before the statute of limitations runs, you must complete service on the defendants within a limited number of days after filing. Sixty is typical, but check your state's rule. Determine when the clients legally knew, or should have known, about facts giving rise to their potential claim. A fast-approaching deadline may force you to file the case simply to CYA (cover your ass) or protect you and the client. When you reject a case, promptly deliver the client a clear decline letter that cautions them about any statutes of limitation. This is defensive lawyering, but it's necessary.

Types of Liability: Simple & Complex

At the risk of further oversimplification, there are two classes of liability: simple and complex. Obviously, there's always a range or continuum in each. Car wrecks are usually simple because normally they only require testimony from the plaintiff, an investigating police officer if there was one, and any incident witnesses. Complex is any case more difficult, including all medical negligence, products liability, and car wrecks requiring accident reconstruction experts. You shouldn't need much help with simple cases.

Small complex cases are a bad investment when the cost of properly preparing and trying them exceeds the reasonable value of their damages. Think about the dollar value of a case from the bottom line or net to both you and your client. No matter the result, clients aren't going to be happy if you recover as much as they do. After all, they're the ones who got hurt. You knew this could happen, so stop early and think about it.

Always pay your experts before they testify; otherwise, the witness faces an impeaching cross suggesting your side must win in order to assure the expert will get paid.

Fee Agreements & Appeals

Most personal injury fee agreements include an increased percentage if the case is appealed. That's fine when the defendant appeals from a good-sized plaintiffs' verdict that will probably be affirmed, because then the result is big enough for you to contract out the appeal.

You may think doing your own appeal is easy, but there are serious procedural hurdles that the uninitiated can miss. For example:

- Was a proper, legally sufficient exception properly taken?
- Was an adequate record made in support of the assignment of error?

Have an experienced appellate lawyer review any potential assignments of error to make sure both you and your opponent have adequately preserved or perfected them.

The skills required to successfully argue to a jury versus to appellate judges are different and, in some respects, inconsistent. Maybe the biggest difference is emphasis. Jury trial lawyers are intent on presenting facts and arguing their significance to lay people. Appellate lawyers emphasize precedence and how their case legally compares with previous appellate decisions. I think of this as *case matching*. Trial lawyers work to persuade legally untrained jurors from diverse backgrounds to return a favorable verdict with a mix of emotions, morality, and competing trial stories. Appeal lawyers argue to busy appellate judges with overworked law clerks who are concerned with perfected assignments of error, precedence, and legal consistency. In appellate work, analytical legal and writing skills are preeminent.

Yet, in some ways, trials and appeals are similar. At the appellate level, a compelling statement of facts tells the court why it's morally right that you should win, while legal authorities show why you should prevail. On appeal, you must distill your arguments down to the key facts. Remember the importance of facts? Sanitize out the adjectives and adverbs and let the essential facts tell your story.[2]

Building a Practice

Building a personal injury or criminal defense practice starts with joining great trial organizations like AAJ and its state affiliate, or the National Association of Criminal Defense Lawyers and its state chapter. Low-key marketing includes participating in potential nonlegal referral sources, such as athletic clubs, health clubs, social and civic groups, charitable services, your church, and so on. Most important,

---

2. David Ball, *David Ball on Damages*, 3rd ed. (Portland, OR: Trial Guides, 2013), and James W. McElhaney, *McElhaney's Trial Notebook* (Chicago, IL: ABA Press, 2006.)

past successful verdicts and settlements are the foundation for your future when supported with great client service. A solid reputation results in better and better referrals and cases. I live in a small town with eight stoplights. I developed a reputation by trying my best to provide great client service, and by maximizing recoveries in what were smaller cases using my qualitative approach. Smaller cases are where we all start and, when handled to full value, are your vocational elevator.

Bad Faith Claims

First-party bad faith claims are direct actions by an insurance policyholder against the company that issued the policy, such as life, health, and general liability policies. This is a tort action, not a breach of contract, although a traditional breach of contract action may be an additional theory of liability, which also provides for an award of attorney's fees. This means you can claim emotional damages and possibly even punitive damages. This often is a negligence per se action for the violation of the state's insurance laws. "Bad faith" is a misnomer; the applicable legal term is merely negligence, or a failure to act reasonably.

A third-party bad faith claim occurs under the following circumstances:

- A legally responsible party has clear exposure for an adverse judgment that exceeds the limits of the insurance protection they've bought.
- You make a time-limited offer on behalf of your injured client to the defendant and their insurance company to settle the case for the limits of the defendant's insurance policy.
- The insurance company then either fails to respond or refuses to accept your time-limited offer to settle the case for the limits of the policy it sold the defendant.
- You then proceed to trial and obtain a verdict and judgment against the defendant that's larger than, or in excess of, the defendant's insurance protection. Henceforth this is known as the underlying

judgment. An alternative to trial is the possibility of a stipulated judgment (with an agreement you will not attempt to collect on the judgment pending resolution of your bad faith claim). In some situations, the insurance company may both deny coverage and also refuse to provide a defense.

- The defendant policyholder (the one who bought the insurance policy) then has a bad faith negligence claim back against their own insurance company for the amount of the entire verdict, plus possible attorney's fees (under a contract remedy), emotional damages, and maybe even punitive damages.
- The defendant policyholder (the defendant against whom the original judgment was entered) will often be willing to assign their personal cause of action or its proceeds against their insurance company over to the plaintiff who won the underlying judgment.
- The defendant policyholder or their assignee then files a second lawsuit back against their original insurance carrier for refusing to accept the plaintiff's earlier time-limited offer to settle for the applicable policy limits. The theory of liability can be either tort (which includes emotional damages and possibly punitive damages) or a breach of contract (which includes the attorney's fees and the amount of the judgment). Each state is a little different, but that's the general idea.

This is what's called *third-party bad faith*, meaning there are three parties: the plaintiff, the original defendant, and the defendant's insurance carrier. Some states have *first-party bad faith* where purchasers of an insurance policy, such as for life, health, or fire, have a direct action back against their own insurance company. Lawsuits of this nature are often grounded in their state's insurance regulations, also known as Unfair Claims Practices Acts (UCPA). There also may be a negligence per se claim predicated upon administrative rules promulgated by the insurance commissioner or terms of the UCPA. First-party claims are simply breach of contract claims that don't allow for emotional injuries or punitive damages; however, first-party tort claims are now common.

It's important you correctly draft a demand letter to the insurer that contains a clear offer to settle for the policy limits that is time-limited.

Medical Negligence Claims

Medical negligence claims are a species unto themselves and demand screening by expensive, high-quality medical experts. The breach or violation of the standard of care should be more than just negligence, even though that's the legal standard. To accept a medical negligence case, the liability should be what I call "jaw dropping." Even though the burden of proof is by a mere preponderance of the evidence, as a practical matter, I think of it as being equal to a criminal case, that is, "beyond a reasonable doubt." Why? Because jurors like doctors and, deep down, don't want to believe they make mistakes. It scares them.

A doctor who has a bad bedside manner or a rude demeanor isn't the same thing as medical negligence, and neither are bad results. Here is a standard jury instruction:

> Physicians are not negligent merely because their efforts were unsuccessful. A physician does not guarantee a good result by undertaking to perform a service.

We probably decline forty-nine out of fifty medical negligence claims. Even if the negligence is obvious, an economically viable medical negligence verdict requires serious permanent damages, and a likable plaintiff. The jurors must be able to see themselves in the plaintiff's shoes.

Look for hospital (institutional) or personal failures in communication, that is, where "the left hand didn't know what the right hand was doing" or where somebody clearly "dropped the ball." Jurors are much more willing to second-guess this type of breach than a personalized medical judgment call by the good doctor. Insurance companies have deep rosters of talented defense lawyers, unlimited budgets, and plenty of excellent doctor experts from the nation's best medical schools eagerly waiting to protect their brethren. Even if you have a good case on the facts, medicine, and law, you may still have trouble finding quality doctors to testify for you. This means you end up hiring a 1-800-call-an-expert from out of state. This is usually a recipe for a quick defense verdict. The opposing lawyer will smugly ask your expert, "Doctor, how many board-certified experts did you fly over last night on your way out here to tell this jury that Dr. Jones was negligent?" I don't mind out-of-state experts on causation or damages, but I definitely want in-state experts on the standard of care—if I can get them.

Not only must you as a plaintiffs' lawyer have the competence to effectively present the case, but you must also have the money to evaluate, prepare, try, and then appeal the case. It's easy to justify spending big bucks if you're sure you'll win the case or it will settle. It's quite another when you're facing the reality of a hotly contested trial and there's a real chance you'll lose. When it comes to medical negligence, be careful. Just take the really good cases, and I can tell you they are few and far between. A dubious or defensible case is going to get tried, and in medical negligence cases, you're almost always going to lose. That's just the way it is.

You've also got to learn the medicine. This is hard. I find it best to start learning the medicine by doing your own research on the particular medical topic. Use PubMed and other internet research tools. An overview of the medicine is a good start. After reading up on the subject, it helps to have an expert review the records and explain the standard of care, and how the defendant did or did not deviate. Medical journal articles specifically addressing the issues involved in the liability and causation analyses are essential.

Read David Wenner, David Bossart, Gregory Cusimano, and Edward Lazarus's *Winning Case Preparation*.[3] It's included in my rec-

---

3. David R. Bossart, Gregory Cusimano, Edward H. Lazarus, and David A. Wenner, *Winning Case Preparation: Understanding Jury Bias* (Portland, OR: Trial Guides, 2018).

ommended reading list. Their big idea is that people are risk-averse to losing something they already have. In other words, "a bird in hand is worth two in the bush." Therefore, don't frame your case as an opportunity to improve the quality of our community's health-care services. Instead, argue that a verdict for the plaintiff simply preserves what the jurors already have: an existing level of care that presently protects each of us. It's not the plaintiff who wants to elevate the standard of care; it's the doctor who wants to lower it.

Defendants win five out of six malpractice cases that go to trial. Why? Because the insurance companies settle the cases that the plaintiffs will probably win, thus, leaving only the weaker ones to go to trial. That's one of the reasons why trial judges often aren't good mediators in malpractice cases. During their years on the bench, all they saw were the many cases the defense won. Insurance companies decide which cases get tried by deciding how much they're willing to pay to settle.

Settling Malpractice Cases: NPDB & Consent

Two interrelated considerations affect the chances of settling malpractice cases. They're the National Practitioner Data Bank (NPDB) and the consent clauses found in almost every doctor's insurance policy.

The NPDB was created by the Health Care Quality Improvement Act of 1986, as amended 42 USC § 11101, 01/26/98.[4] It's an information clearinghouse that collects and releases information on the competence of physicians, dentists, and other health-care practitioners. Any insurance company, self-insured hospital, or HMO that makes a payment to settle a claim against a doctor, dentist, or other health-care practitioner must report it to the NPDB. Adverse actions against a physician's privileges or license must also be reported. Plaintiffs' lawyers can't get this information except in very rare circumstances.[5] NPDB

---

4. The NPDB regulations are codified at 45 C.F.R. Part 60.

5. A plaintiffs' attorney in a medical malpractice action may obtain NPDB information on a physician only after evidence is submitted to the Department of Health and

information impacts a doctor's ability to obtain privileges at hospitals, clinics, and surgical centers, and also whether they're included as a preferred provider in health-care plans. State medical boards review NPDB information when physicians apply for a license. Understanding that settling doctors are reported to the NPDB is important, because it obviously drives the doctor's decision about whether to settle your claim. There's no minimum amount required for reporting, so doctors won't settle just to avoid the costs of litigation. Physicians can prevent their carrier from settling a claim because their consent is required. Even if an insurer is willing to settle your case for $5,000, the insured doctor can withhold consent, forcing the insurer to defend the case through trial and appeal, even though it may cost the carrier $200,000. This isn't true in most other insurance policies, such as in your typical auto or homeowner's policies.

So, now you know another reason doctors take malpractice claims so personally. Think about it—how would you feel if you were sued? It's personal, and I get it. It's an additional reason I'm so careful in reviewing these claims. It's how I'd want my professional license respected.

Conclusion

Building a practice, whether plaintiffs' personal injury or criminal defense, demands not just the competent delivery of services, but also smart business decision-making. You can't, nor should you, take every case that walks through your door. Keep in mind you're running a business when deciding which cases to take and how to turn down the ones you reject.

Human Services demonstrating that the hospital or other credentialing entity failed to submit a mandatory query to the NPDB regarding the subject named by the plaintiff in the action. This evidence is not available to the plaintiff through the NPDB. 45 C.F.R. § 60.13(a)(1)(v). In practical terms, this evidence is legally privileged and not available to the plaintiffs' bar.

The next chapter provides a win-win model for cases in which you may not have either the money or experience. I suggest you sign up the client and then associate with an experienced lawyer who will teach you along the way.

19

When & How to Refer Your Cases

Self-interest and serious ethical questions lurk within and behind the large subjects of referring, mediating, and settling cases. I'm going to recommend a way to be ethical and grow professionally while making money for both you and your clients; however, my advice requires a longer view of your self-interest.

Financing Cases

The private practice of law is a business. You must finance your inventory of PI cases. A threshold capacity question is, "Can I feed my family, pay my personal and law firm bills, and still fully bankroll all of the costs necessary to both prepare and try the case through a lengthy appeal?" Serious litigation isn't cheap. My view is, if you want a million-dollar verdict, you have to try a million-dollar case; in other words, you've got to spend money to make money. So much for the romanticism of law school. Our intensely competitive legal market is Darwinian, and demands that in contingency fee cases, if you don't win, then you don't get paid. Further, you must be willing to fully finance any case you accept

If you're competent and the problem is a lack of money, then you have three choices.

1. Refer your case to a more experienced lawyer who will front all the costs while bringing expertise to you and the case.
2. Convert your present credit line into capital by taking out a loan from a traditional bank.
3. Explore alternative litigation finance (ALF) options.

Getting a loan from your local bank is harder than it used to be. The commercial banking industry has tightened up, and many local banks have been bought up by bigger regional ones. I embrace the older view that financial success means not just that you can bankroll your own cases but that you also can afford to try them and lose. Like gambling, if you can't afford to lose, then you can't afford to play. Why? Because instead of playing to win, you end up playing not to lose, and that's a big difference—a difference that defense attorneys smell in a heartbeat.

Insurance companies are holding companies for capital and are professionals at managing risk. They only hire good to great lawyers.

What about ALF Loans?

The third alternative is what I call nontraditional or ALF (alternative litigation finance) loans. The biggest gripe young lawyers have about older lawyers (like me) is this: "All they want from me is for me to refer them my big cases." In AAJ's *Trial* magazine, you'll find ALF ads making statements like these:

- "Avoid co-counsel and case referrals."
- "No need to ever share your fee."
- "Stay in charge and receive the entire fee."

There's another ALF advertisement showing two lawyers chatting over coffee. One says, "My firm has $200,000 in costs advanced."

The second lawyer says, "Mine has over a million."

At the bottom of the page, a caption reads, "What's wrong with this picture?"

This ad highlights the ethical issues ALF ads don't mention. It's not that simple. A competitive market demands that retained attorneys front the costs in personal repay claims. This is both necessary and proper because injured people don't have the money to bankroll lawsuits. The system is structurally asymmetrical (also known as rigged) because well-funded insurance companies bankroll the defense and have a waiting inventory of talented lawyers and eager experts.

Go ahead and apply for *working capital* loans. One ALF company advertises loans up to $5 million, depending on the total value of your contingent fee cases. It further says that you can use the borrowed money for any law firm expenses, including advertising and payroll. A closer reading of the advertisement reveals a small print clause at the bottom saying it's for *successful* trial firms. As a new lawyer, you'll want to find out exactly what *successful* means.

If you've got the money, or access to it, then you assume responsibility for everything that's necessary to maximize the case's value. We can actuarially predict the odds of a loss; however, the fiscal effects of a loss depend upon your capacity to absorb that loss, and implicates your ability to properly fund your future cases after this loss. Everything's connected. If this discussion is scary (and it is), then imagine how it feels for your client. They get only one chance. The outcome will almost certainly be life altering, and a loss would be devastating. Compare this with insurance companies that never die, amortize any losses over thousands of claims, and at worst, pay disappointing quarterly returns to their stockholders.

If you can use ALF, make sure you've got access to all the money you will need, and that it's without recourse, meaning it truly is a loan without consequences if you ultimately lose.

Associating with Other Lawyers

I've associated other lawyers. I do it if I don't have the background or expertise, such as in employment cases. I need their help, and so do my clients.

If you're a new lawyer, you're probably struggling to build a practice. That situation favors associating an experienced lawyer who is willing to teach and mentor you. Let me explain. Your client is entitled to competence and capital. Apart from ethics, associating now will help you in all your future cases. When done properly, associating is the shortest path for you to gain serious experience. In other words, you will grow better, faster.

Defense lawyers and insurance carriers are trained to assess the risk of a significant jury verdict in your case and thus its present value. The less the risk, the less financial exposure, the less the case value. Risk, and thus value, isn't some immutable or fixed sum. There's a fluid and evolving context to the case's value, and you, your skills, and your reputation are at the center of the analysis. If the lawyer you refer to increases that risk, then your opponent's assessment of your case's value will correspondingly increase.

Newer lawyers understandably want to hold on to a big case in hopes of settling it and thereby avoiding a fee split. That's why ALF loan ads trumpet, "You won't have to share or split your fee." I also smile at the one that begins, "As a trial lawyer, you want the best for your clients. You deserve the best way to finance." Then two lines later, the ad closes by saying, "It's more cost-effective financing than co-counsel." It's a seductive syllogism that starts with you wanting the best for your clients, yet ends up being about you. Apart from the obvious ethical question about whose interests are primary, a separate threshold problem is the earlier you investigate a case and retain the best experts, the better. Medical negligence and products liability cases can be races to retain or tie-up the best experts, who are expensive. Why can they charge so much? Because they're worth it. Not promptly associating an experienced lawyer who knows the best experts and can afford them isn't just penny-wise and dollar-poor; it's actually putting your interests ahead of your client.

As an aside, don't refer me your cases. I'm offering this advice out of my concern for you as my professional heirs. I want you to get better, faster. Go find yourself an experienced lawyer who's also a great teacher and will invest in you. That's good advice for both your client and you.

An early referral offers serious advantages. To start, a seasoned lawyer will properly evaluate your case, and have quality experts investigate the scene and evaluate the product. Many times, I have explained to an inexperienced lawyer there are serious problems with their case. Even if you're competent, a second seasoned opinion is always an advantage, and sooner is always better.

Include Mentoring in Your Association Agreements

Negotiate your referral fee. If the case is good enough, you might get up to a third back. Explain that you want to learn and be actively involved. Include being mentored and participating in the case as written conditions of the association. You will gain in ways that are more valuable than any additional money you might keep if you don't associate. Negotiate for a real learning opportunity in the preparation and trial of *your* case. The knowledge you gain is a present investment in you and all your future cases.

Here's a sample clause for an association agreement that you can include:

> Associating lawyer agrees to mentor the referring lawyer in all aspects of the litigation to the edges of their competence. Referring lawyer will be copied on all internal and external correspondence, research, and memos. If the matter is tried, referring lawyer will be second chair and will participate subject to the associated lawyer's judgment. Associated lawyer agrees to teach and mentor referring lawyer to the maximum of their abilities.

When considering whom to associate, consider whether the senior lawyer is a good mentor and teacher. Check out their reputation with prior associates. Do they respect women and minorities? Do they have an alcohol or temper problem? Being a successful trial lawyer has little to do with being a good teacher. This means you're not just evaluating your case, but also a perspective mentor.

How to Associate Cases & Win

Maybe I shouldn't say *refer* cases, but instead say *associate* cases. I prefer *associate* because it places the accent on your involvement. The client signed a fee agreement with *you*, not with the lawyer you associate.

Maybe you already know an experienced trial lawyer. Great. Then talk plainly with them. Look for someone you can trust, work with, and will invest in you in every sense of the word. Shop for a friend and teacher, and not just for help on this particular case. You should want them to care about you as much as you care for your client. You're this lawyer's professional heir, and they should want you to grow as much as you do.

Let's say you've got a bigger case and want to associate, then you need answers to these questions:

- What does the senior lawyer assess the verdict range to be and why? Compare this with your earlier analysis.
- What percentage of the total attorney's fees will your association or referral fee be? In other words, what's your cut of the fee going to be?
- Will the senior lawyer front all the costs without interest to the client? The answer must be *yes*.
- Subject to your state's rules of ethics, does the client have any financial obligations in case of a loss? The answer should be *no*.
- What involvement will you have in the case? More specifically, what learning opportunities will be available to you? The answer should be everything you're capable of doing—with guidance. As an example, if you're going to take some depositions, will the supervising lawyer review your pre-depo questions and later critique your performance with constructive suggestions? It's up to you to ask for these opportunities, and then to prepare and thereby take full advantage of them. Don't be shy or lazy. You should also be copied on all correspondence. Your enthusiasm and work ethic should be obvious.
- If you haven't signed up the client yet, whose fee agreement should you use and why? What if there's an appeal or a declaratory judgment action? Does your fee agreement anticipate these questions? If you haven't signed up the client, have the senior lawyer review your contingency fee agreement and consider modifying yours to match the terms of theirs. If you don't have a contingency fee agreement, then copy the associated lawyer's. Have the client sign your fee agreement and then confirm in writing the client's consent for you to associate the second lawyer.

Issues to consider when drafting your fee agreement:

- Does the fee agreement specify that the attorney's fees are taken "off the top," meaning subtracted from the total recovery before any costs advanced are deducted? The alternative is to first subtract the costs advanced from the total and then apply the contingency fee to the balance. Your choice.

- What's included in the definition of costs advanced? It should include all case-specific expenses, such as investigation costs, travel, depositions, experts, court costs, and so on.
- What events trigger an increase in the contingency fee? For example, what's the percentage if the case is resolved before or after filing, mediation, trial, or appeal? What if mediation happens before it's filed?

You can always shop around for money, but you can't sell competence you don't have. You gain that by doing. An experienced lawyer who cares about you, invests in you, and is a good teacher will be more than value added to your case; just as important, they will accelerate your professional training.

Fees to the Associating Lawyer

The referral fee that you can expect back from an experienced lawyer is, unfortunately, dropping. It's often between 10 and 20 percent; the rare upper end of the market is between a fourth and a third of the net attorney's fees. In medical malpractice and products liability cases, it's on the low end because of the risks and large costs advanced. Of course, the primary driver is the value of the case. If the case isn't that great, then it's not going to be that desirable; therefore, you don't have as much leverage when negotiating your percentage. Obviously, the bigger the case value, the more you can ask for.

Mentoring takes serious time, experience, and patience. It's always easier for the senior lawyer to just pay a referral fee without the added responsibility of teaching you. Your desire to be involved isn't convenient for the senior lawyer. Be a good partner on your responsibilities.

What does being a good partner mean? It means all the basics that you would expect if you hired an associate. Be on time, be prepared, ask thoughtful questions, watch, and listen. I am willing to let the associated lawyer work up to the edge of their competence. I include them in all the strategy sessions, focus groups, generation of trial themes and story, witness and exhibit preparations, pretrial motions, and the instructions. They are always surprised at how many times we videotape and practice our openings and closing. That's what excellence looks like.

What if the case goes to trial and results in a defense verdict? Then both you and your client have won because you didn't lose any of your own money, your client received excellent representation, and you gained valuable experience—all at no cost (other than your time) to you. That's better, faster.

Your state's ethical rules require disclosure and client consent regarding any referral or association agreements. Everything must be in writing with copies around. Client consent is never a problem. It's a good deal for them; after all, they're getting more lawyers for the same fee.

Do the Math: A Story Problem

Let's do the math; meaning, let's follow the money. To simplify, I'll ignore the matter of costs advanced, which, again, depending on the fee agreement, are either subtracted off the top of the total recovery or from the client's share after the attorney's fees are deducted. You'll easily see how it goes.

Scenario 1: Don't Refer the Case

Let's assume that you don't refer the case, and:

- You settle the case for $500,000.
- You receive one-third, or $166,666.66, as your attorney's fee.
- Your client receives $333,333.33.[1]

---

[1]. Most personal injury awards are not taxable; however, in some situations, you may benefit from getting the advice of a tax lawyer.

- Further, assume that the settlement is entirely defensible and ethical, such that if your client was a juvenile and the settlement required court approval, you would be able to sign an affidavit of reasonableness, which any judge would rely on, and thereafter approve the proposed settlement.

Scenario 2: Associate with an Experienced Lawyer

Assume that it's a quality case with serious damages, and therefore you will want a referral fee back of one-third of the total attorney's fees. Remember this is on the high side, and the market is less, but we'll use a third in our example.

- The case then settles or there's a verdict for more than you could have gotten on your own. Let's say it's $1 million.
- You and the senior lawyer together now will receive one-third of $1 million, or $333,333.33.
- The client gets $666,666.66.
- The senior lawyer's share of the $333,333.33 is $222,222.22.
- Your share of the $333,333.33 is $111,111.11.

Your client obviously gains, as does the senior lawyer, and, yes, you make $55,555.55 less than you would have if you'd settled the case and not associated a senior lawyer. If the case went to trial, and the attorney's fees increased to say 40 percent, then you get one-third of 40 percent or $133,333.33. And as I explained, if there's a defense verdict, you still win. Of course, everything gets rosier if the result is more; not to mention, any delays caused by appeals aren't as stressful because you're not bankrolling everything in the meantime.

My advice acknowledges all the tensions and ethical conflicts; but even more important, everyone gains. This is all assuming the case is good enough to interest an experienced lawyer. Your job is to get the best lawyer you can for your client, and also the best teacher for you. Nobody can negotiate for you. Take this seriously and make your choice an ethical one in which everybody wins, starting with your client and you.

Settle or Go to Trial?

How do you know whether you should settle or go to trial? It can be a tough call. Questions of ethics and judgment are front and center. Many defense friends and some judges say working at the "edge of reasonableness" is why they couldn't do plaintiffs' work. It's also the domain where you can hear others accuse you of being reckless or a cowboy. I admit to having a *strong* ego; it's necessary to do this job. However, I don't agree to a *big* ego. That's different. Once in a while, your opponents, and maybe even a mediator, may suggest that your ego is getting in the way of your responsibilities to your client, or that your client is motivated by greed, not need. While I'm talking to the defense about paying money consistent to their risk, they want to reframe the negotiations to be about them helping my client while assisting me in honoring my ethical responsibilities. Strange, here I thought that representing my client was my job.

So, what happens when their low-ball offer is much less than their exposure? Defendants may try to get in your head by making you and your client feel ashamed, greedy, or even unethical for demanding more money than they believe your client needs or deserves. Don't allow them to reframe their legal responsibility by focusing on your client's needs rather than the defendant's exposure. The defendants are the ones who caused this problem.

Getting Value for Your Claims

Assuming hard work, preparation, organization, learning the magic legal words, and consistently applying IA, you are competent for smaller cases now. As your competence and financial capacity grow, you will discover your bigger cases generate an increasing percentage of your income. This is the 70/30 rule.

Money & Ethics about Settlement

Of course, you know the answers on a law school ethics exam, but this is the real world with personal and professional debts, fears, and, yes, egos. So, when it comes to settlements, what's your advice to your client going to be? Should your client take an offer that's in the lower range of reasonable? And why or why not? Are your motives mixed? If so, how so? I'm sure I'm not the only one who has these troublesome inner dialogues.

There's an understandable affront in the suggestion that any of us would ever place our personal interests ahead of our clients. Self-interest has a myriad of faces, ranging from ego to finances, and yes, it's always difficult to "grade our own papers."

Here's a brief review of some of the essential questions you'll need to answer:

1. What is the case value? Assess the case value by determining the actuarial odds of a win multiplied by the probable recovery. Remember to factor in any pled or unpled comparative fault. Get a second opinion, or even a third one.
2. How well can my client emotionally and financially absorb a loss? We know the answer is almost always "very poorly."
3. How will my client perform as a witness at trial (with best practices preparation)?

4. How can I present my client to their maximum advantage? This often means less is more, that is, emphasizing lay witnesses and effective experts who can teach and communicate, thereby leaving less heavy lifting for the plaintiff.
5. How will my client handle the stresses of a trial (with your competent support)?

Carefully separate questions 1 and 2 from 3 and 4 and 5; lawyers often lump these together. I've already suggested that risk-averse lawyers can express this personal attribute by unconsciously elevating their ethical duty to their clients. I admit lawyers (like me), who are more comfortable with risk, might also unconsciously be doing just the opposite.

We know our clients almost always follow our advice. But we also know it's not us who makes the final decision; it's the client. So, what's the big deal? Where's the ethical problem? Once you creep into the lower range of a case's reasonable value, arguably there isn't an ethical problem. This entire matter's something I try to carefully think my way through. My informed consent letters are honest and thorough, and probably over-emphasize the risks. When I recommend my client turn down a significant offer, I often hire an ethics lawyer to critique and proof my informed consent letters. In bigger cases, I'll occasionally hire, at my expense (without billing the fee back to the client), a second competent lawyer to write my client an analysis letter that I know will disagree with me. Now, that's real informed consent! I select a respected lawyer who I'm sure will recommend my clients accept the present offer. And, no, I don't recruit someone who agrees with me—that's not true informed consent. I'm not defensive; I have my opinions and they have theirs. Remember, most states' professional rules of responsibility now permit the following: "In rendering advice, a lawyer may refer not only to law but to other considerations, such as moral, economic, social, and political factors that may be relevant to the client's situation."[2]

---

2. American Bar Association, *Model Rules of Professional Conduct*, "Rule 2.1: Advisor" (Chicago, IL: ABA Press, 2024).

A Different Way to Look at Settlement

Good or bad, every future client is the beneficiary of your present reputation. While reputations are difficult to measure, they're an important factor the opposing counsel and the insurance carriers are going to consider in assessing their risk and, thus, your case's value.

The ethical way to handle all of this is to be up front with your clients during the first interview. Explain your aggressive negotiating philosophy, if that's what you have or, at least, think you do. Use an informed consent model. Next, tell them that they're always the boss with the last word, and you're merely an agent who can't and won't do anything of substance without their permission. If they aren't comfortable with your aggressive advocacy, assure them that's okay. It's their choice and you respect it, however, it's probably best they hire a different lawyer. I say this well knowing almost every client wants an aggressive lawyer; therefore, you're not going to be at a disadvantage with this honest disclosure.

Conclusion

Competence isn't enough to win cases to their full value, you also need the money for the experts. Smart associating gives you the tools to ethically meet your financial needs, gain experience, and win cases. It's better, faster.

RECOMMENDED READING

- *Becoming a Trial Lawyer: A Guide for the Lifelong Advocate*, 2nd edition (Trial Guides, 2015), by Rick Friedman: This is a great read if you're wondering whether the courtroom's for you.

- *Rules of the Road: A Plaintiff Lawyer's Guide to Proving Liability*, 2nd edition (Trial Guides, 2010), by Rick Friedman and Patrick Malone: So, the defense is suggesting your client's a liar? Here's what you do.

- *Win Your Case: How to Present, Persuade, and Prevail—Every Place, Every Time* (St. Martin's Griffin, 2006) by Gerry Spence: Chapter 6 on harnessing your anger is a must read.

- *You Can't Teach Hungry* (2015) by John Morgan: It's great on the business side.

- *The 80/20 Principle: The Secret of Achieving More with Less*, 3rd edition (Penguin Random House, 1999), by Richard Koch.

For advocacy tips on how to prepare and present your case to a jury, I recommend:

- *Deposition Techniques: Strategies, Tactics, and Skills*, video available on DVD and on demand (Trial Guides, 2010), by David B. Markowitz.

- *David Ball on Damages*, 3rd edition, (Trial Guides, 2012) by David Ball: This is a must read for every aspiring plaintiffs' lawyer.

- *McElhaney's Trial Notebook*, 4th edition (Chicago, IL: ABA Press, 2005), by Jim McElhaney: Jim's deceased, but his book's still fresh.

- *Recovering for Psychological Injuries*, 3rd edition, (Trial Guides, 2010) by yours truly: Don't let the title of my book fool you. Rick Friedman says: "Great trial insight and wisdom jump off almost every page of this book, insight and wisdom applicable to any plaintiff's case."

- **"Trial Strategies Part 1"** (Fall 2009) and **"Trial Strategies Part 2"** (Winter 2010) from the Oregon State Bar *Litigation Journal*, also by yours truly.

- **"Trial Strategies and Evidence Part II"** (*Litigation Journal*, 2010 by William Barton, available at http://bartontrialattorneys.com/uploads/pdf/Trial-Strategies-and-Evidence-Part-II.pdf.

- *The Creative Lawyer: A Practical Guide to Authentic Career Satisfaction* (Chicago, IL: ABA Press, 2014) by Michael Melcher.

- *The Lawyer's Winning Edge: Exceptional Courtroom Performance* (Bradford Publishing Company, 2004) by Lisa L. DeCaro and Leonard Matheo.

- *The Happy Lawyer: Making a Good Life in the Law* (Oxford University Press, 2010) by Nancy Levit and Douglas O. Linder.

- *Winning Case Preparation: Understanding Jury Bias* (Trial Guides, 2018) by David R. Bossart, Gregory Cusimano, Edward H. Lazarus, and David A. Wenner.

- *Focus Groups: How to Do Your Own Jury Research*, video available on DVD and on demand (Trial Guides, 2008), by David Ball with Debra Miller and Artemis H. Malekpour.

- *Polarizing the Case: Exposing and Defeating the Malingering Myth* (Trial Guides, 2007), by Rick Friedman.

- *Trial in Action: The Persuasive Power of Psychodrama* (Trial Guides, 2010) by Joane Garcia-Colson, Fredilyn Sison, and Mary Peckham.

I've kept this list short. If you can't find the time for all these books, I suggest you read Ball, McElhaney, and Markowitz's work on depositions. If you understand and incorporate their advice, you'll be in the 90th percentile.

ABOUT THE AUTHOR

As a plaintiffs' jury trial lawyer, William "Bill" A. Barton considers himself a social engineer and architect, a legal artist who works in the medium of the law. One of his successful insurance bad faith claims took seven appeals and twenty-one years. He's tried over 500 jury trials, delivered 550 lectures on trial advocacy, and has practiced law with passion and gratitude for over half a century.

Bill is a pioneer in holding institutions accountable on behalf of victims of sexual abuse. In the mid-80s he tried the first case against the Boy Scouts; now there are 82,000 pending claims. His 2004 case against the Portland, Oregon Archdiocese resulted in the defendant filing for bankruptcy, a first. His book, *Recovering for Psychological Injuries*, is a legal cookbook for the "Me Too" movement.

As a "transgenerational keeper of the meaning," Bill believes in paying it forward. Since 2005, he's conducted a legal boot camp in Portland, mentoring ten young lawyers each year. He teaches Integrated Advocacy, emphasizing the clinical application of professionalism and personal growth. If you want to become a better lawyer, strive to become a better person.

Bill agrees a strong ego is essential to being a successful trial lawyer, however, he differentiates between a strong ego and a big ego. He aspires to the wisdom of Lewis Carroll: "Humility isn't thinking less of yourself, but thinking of yourself less."

His latest book, *Integrated Advocacy*, focuses on the challenges of work/life balance and reflects his emphasis on family. He's a proud father, and his son Brent has been his law partner since 2010.

Bill has had a diverse career. He's served as a trial judge *pro tem* and been on the board of directors and served as chairman of the board of an insurance company, the Professional Liability Fund. It's a capital mutual trust that provides insurance coverage to attorneys in the private practice of law in Oregon.

He is a member of the American College of Trial Lawyers, a fellow of the International Society of Barristers, a fellow of the International Academy of Trial Lawyers, and is listed in the *Best Lawyers in America* in four categories. In 2024, he was inducted into the Trial Lawyers Hall of Fame located at Temple University in Philadelphia.

His influence extends far beyond courtrooms. He and his wife JoAnn generously support children, the environment, and the arts. Their shared vision includes the creation of the Yakona Nature Preserve (yakonaoregon.org), a 400-acre sanctuary near their home in Newport, Oregon. The preserve is dedicated to educating children and the public about the value of nature and cultural history. The coastal spruce preserve is home to bears, cougars, elk, deer, bobcats, and river otters, and it has an active bald eagle nest.

In his free time, Bill channels the Hon. Oliver Wendell Holmes, Jr., Associate Justice of the US Supreme Court (1902-1932). He has even performed in character for members of the US Supreme Court. Since 2010, he has been life coach for the Portland State University men's basketball team.